The Little Book

Big Bucks

FROM THE PUBLISHERS OF DEER & DEER HUNTING MAGAZINE

—— Third Edition ——

**Published by
F+W Publications**
700 E. State St. • Iola, WI 54990-0001
Telephone: (715) 445-2214   Fax: (715) 445-4087
World Wide Web: www.deeranddeerhunting.com

Please call or write for our free catalog of outdoor publications.
Our toll-free number to place an order or obtain a free catalog is (800) 258-0929.

Library of Congress Catalog Number: 2003106645

ISBN: 0-89689-282-4
Printed in the United States of America

Cover photo by Charles J. Alsheimer

Contents

Special Big-Buck Hunting Section

Editor's Note

By Joe Shead

Story Contributors Spin Tales Worthy of Special Merit

Some of my earliest hunting memories weren't really hunting memories at all. At least not mine, anyway. Rather, they were memories of men in sports shops reciting tales of their grandest and most extraordinary hunts. Many were the tales I heard of giant bucks — that seemed to grow just a bit larger with each telling of the story — that escaped hunters to live another day. Usually these stories involved severe cases of buck fever on the part of the hunter, which bought the buck another day in the woods and the hunter a permanent reputation as a weak-nerved nimrod.

Even at a young age, I was swept up in these stories, and when my brothers grew restless and began wandering the aisles of the shop to play with the colorful assortment of soft-plastic fishing lures, I stayed on my bar stool, struggling to peer over the counter at the grand old storyteller as he spun his next tale.

Well, I'd like to think that after listening to all those yarns, I picked up at least a little of the old master's storytelling flair. Maybe I just sound like a fool when I start rattling off my own stories these days, especially when I find myself down on one knee, drawing an imaginary bow in the middle of a grocery store as my audience listens ... or at least pretends to. Maybe story-telling hunters can get a little overzealous when talk-ing about a big 10-pointer, but when a body gets wrapped up in such an emotional sport as hunt-ing, well, sometimes you've just got to get those words out of your heart and into the ears of anyone who'll listen.

That's what the folks in this edition of the *Little Book of Big Bucks* did, and they sure have some amazing stories. In fact, I enjoyed some so much that I thought they needed special recognition. That's why this year, five stories have received the newly created *Little Book of Big Bucks* Editor's Choice Award. These stories have that little something extra that make them stand out from the rest. Some are heart-warming, some are inspi-rational and some are just plain outrageous!

Picking the winners for this year wasn't easy, and several other stories could have earned the Editor's Choice badge, but here are the winning authors: Neil Callahan of Merrill, Wis.; Kelly Raab of Hammondsport, N.Y.; Doug May of Massillon, Ohio; Robert Law of Royal Oak, Mich.; and Deacon J. Crocker of Massachusetts.

I hope you enjoy reading their stories, and all the other stories that make up this book.

Good luck this hunting season, and when you shoot your buck of a lifetime this year, keep us in mind. Who knows, you may be reading the story of your own hunt in the *2007 Little Book of Big Bucks*.

Wisconsin Bow-Hunter Arrows Huge 8-Pointer

John Albert, of Sun Prairie, Wis., hit the big buck jackpot on Nov. 3, 2004, while hunting near Bear Valley, Wis.

Albert hunts a beautiful 751-acre parcel in southern Wisconsin's bluff country, consisting of high ridges, open areas and thick cover, all topped off with a creek running through the property. It is not only a beautiful place, but a big-buck haven. Trail-camera photos of spectacular bucks prove it, and a pair of sheds a local taxidermist found two years earlier indicated a huge 8-pointer frequented the area.

But Albert probably wasn't thinking about any buck in particular that Wednesday morning when he climbed into his stand, which was positioned 35 yards inside a wooded area that bordered a CRP field. More likely, he was thinking about the 25 deer he'd seen the morning before. Early November is prime rutting time in Albert's area, and he always takes vacation the first week of November to capitalize on some of the best bow-hunting of the year. However, this particular morning, deer activity was seemingly absent, and after 3½ hours, Albert hadn't seen a deer. The night had been clear, and Albert theorized bucks may have chased does all night. With a lack of activity, Albert was getting frustrated. In fact, at one point he even thought about shooting a squirrel with a judo point-tipped arrow in his quiver, but decided if he did so, he might scare a buck, so he refrained. We'll never know for sure, but it may have been a good thing he held off.

Finally, Albert saw his first deer of the day. The first thing he noticed was the deer's incredible body — the largest deer he'd ever seen. The deer was about 50 yards away when Albert first saw it, and it was coming his way.

As soon as Albert saw the giant deer, he looked away from the buck's headgear and focused on where he wanted to shoot. There would be no shooting lane until the deer reached a trail heading into the CRP field. If the buck kept coming, Albert would have a shot. If it turned to go into the field, he would have to try to call it back to him.

A scouting camera caught John Albert's incredible 8-pointer on film earlier in the 2004 season.

Luckily, the buck continued coming, and presented Albert with a 30-yard broadside shot. Before shooting, Albert glanced once at the antlers. The property Albert hunts is enrolled in a QDM program, which Albert credits for the number of large bucks in the area. Albert was concentrating on looking away from the antlers, so he didn't get his nerves up, but glanced at the rack before he shot. Although he couldn't tell how many points the buck had, he knew it was the largest deer he'd ever seen, and the spread was outside the ears, so he shot. Albert's aim was true, and the mortally wounded deer trotted off.

Albert immediately climbed out of his stand, not because he wanted to quickly take up the trail, but to prevent himself from falling out of his stand in his excitement. Albert found a good blood trail and knew the deer couldn't have gone far. He found the buck just 40 yards from where he'd arrowed it.

Although Albert knew the 8-pointer was huge, it didn't sink in how large his buck was until after he took it to the registration station. Albert first noticed the buck's huge body, which had a field dressed weight of 225 pounds. The rack had an inside spread of 24 inches, and 5-inch bases. The rack's heavy mass helped drive the green score to $167^{7}/_{8}$ inches — not bad for an 8-pointer. Although one G-2 measured 13 inches, the other was only 8 inches long. This trait was also evident in the sheds the taxidermist had found two years earlier. All the tines had grown since then, except for some reason, the one G-2 had remained at only 8 inches long.

— *Joe Shead*

Trophy-Class Whitetail Was Years in the Making

Russ Nitchman had waited more than 25 years to kill a trophy buck. He finally got his chance when he traveled out-of-state to hook up with an old friend who had cracked the big-buck code. The result was Nitchman's 192-pound 16-pointer.

My friend, Al, lives in the Midwest in a state that consistently grows big deer. Al has been deer hunting his whole life, and has downed many deer. Until two years ago, he had yet to tag a trophy buck. Then he took a magnificent 160-class 8-pointer with long tines. The next year he tagged an enormous 11-pointer with lots of character. During the past several years he has been figuring out how big bucks move in the area he hunts, and it has paid off for him.

Although I've killed more than 70 deer, mostly does, my wall was still bare, waiting for a trophy to grace it. Last year my wife said, "You should go visit Al and hunt with him. You may finally get your trophy." So Al and I made plans. Upon my arrival, we went out to set up our stands the day before season. We chose a spot just off the logging road that we walked in on, along a ridge top.

The terrain is open hardwoods with flats and steep ravines in between. Some ravines are quite deep (30 to 60 or more feet down, and many at greater than 45-degree angles).

We were at the tree where I chose to hang my stand, just a few yards off the logging road, when I clanged the metal climber against the tree. Moments later, I noticed some deer moving across the flat on the other side of the ravine, 120 yards away. There was a doe and two bucks. One buck was a nice one — maybe a 10-pointer or so with a high rack.

As the deer slowly worked up the hill across the flat, I noticed two more deer behind them. The first was a doe and the second was a large buck. No, make that a huge buck!

The doe meandered our way, then veered off. The huge buck hung up in a thick group of trees. Although we could not get a good look at it, there was no mistaking the rack.

After five minutes, the big guy bedded down. We could see his rack from the side now, and it was big.

But now we had a problem. We were pinned by the very deer we wanted to shoot the next day when the season opened. Al said, "That is a mature buck. They are never quick about moving. They take their time and are last to leave an area."

We made a plan to quietly step back onto the logging road and head up it like people often do. When the buck spotted Al, we hoped he would slip away without being too frightened. The plan worked beautifully, and I was able to see his escape route.

As I pondered this event the rest of the day, I wondered whether this might be some terrible joke of God's in which I would get to see a giant deer the day before season, never to see it again. I want a large trophy, but my life is not centered on that. Time would tell.

On opening morning, the deer began to move an hour after sunup. A doe passed along the logging trail within a few yards of the stand. Then a small 6-pointer crossed her path. As I looked him over, a larger deer came into view. He was high-racked, with antlers out to the edge of his ears. I counted 10 points, but was he big enough? It was a tough question, especially after seeing the huge buck yesterday. He was very nice, and I would guess a $3^1/_2$-year-old deer. But his brow tines were not impressively tall nor heavy. As he walked onto the logging trail and stood broadside at 3 to 4 yards, staring intently at the doe 60 yards ahead, I decided to pass on him.

By 11 a.m., I was beginning to question my passing of that 10-pointer. If I didn't return home with a wall-hanger I would be kicking myself. Plus, with all the shots around me, who knows whether any big ones were still around.

I saw a couple of other does as mid-morning came, each with a buck on her backside. But none of those bucks were big enough. I even had a 4-pointer bed down for an hour or so 130 yards away. I watched him as he groomed himself. Then he left to chase a doe.

Later, a large doe appeared, coming down the hill on the flat, heading in my direction. The sunlight glistened off her brown coat. It was 11:25. I could see another deer behind her, but there were too many branches in the way to see what it was. Then I saw a flash of white and knew it was a

8

buck. But how big? In the next few moments, I knew he was a shooter. He was behind me and to my right, so I adjusted myself in the stand so I could get a good rest for a shot.

The doe meandered within 100 yards, and the buck walked across the flat 130 yards from me. I got him in the scope, but twigs prevented me from taking a shot. Another doe entered the flat and headed toward the area from where the buck had come. The buck trudged back up the hill to check her out. Now I could see how large this deer really was. I was glad I had passed up the 10-pointer, but this buck was now walking away. I kept trying to get an opening, but there were none. Even when he was 200 yards away, I could not find any gaps.

I could not believe this! Here was the big buck I had hoped for, and I could not get a shot. I prayed, "God, bring him back. Please!"

In a few moments the big boy lost interest in the other doe and headed back toward me. He crossed the flat as before and stood 130 yards off, broadside. But there was so much debris in the way. I decided to try to slip a slug into a hole only a few inches large. As the shot cracked off, he trotted forward a few steps. The doe ran off 30 to 40 yards. His body language told me that I had missed.

He stood like a statue, just looking around. I thought he would never move again. Finally, he headed back across the flat, stopping as he went. At about 120 yards, I found a small window to shoot through, smaller than a pie plate. The shot rang out and he ran

forward, crossed an 8-foot ravine, then stopped in the same thick group of trees where we had seen the buck yesterday. Again, he stood there, just looking around. I thought, "Darn, I must have missed again. I'll shoot again when he steps forward out of that thick stuff."

Then he did the most unusual thing I've ever seen a deer do. He began to quickly walk backwards, back down into the ravine. When he was in the bottom, he disappeared. This was strange. I said to myself, "I hit him with the second shot and he is down!" I began looking through my scope into the ravine, but couldn't see a thing. After more than five minutes of scouring the area, I saw an antler. Wow! I did get him. My trophy at last!

I made a double-lung hit with my 12-gauge saboted slug. When Al saw him he exclaimed, "That is the same buck we saw yesterday when we set the stands!" As we looked at him longer, I determined that it was indeed him. His wide, heavy rack had lots of character and plenty of sticker points. He weighed 192 pounds and had 16 points. His molars were worn flat and there was little left to them.

It was hard to believe it was now over. It seems unbelievable, and it all happened so quickly. Yet there is a great story to this hunt and it took a lot longer to develop than most successful hunts. Still, it is hard to believe that after more than 25 years of dreaming of getting a big one to hang on the wall, it has finally happened.

— *Russ Nitchman*
New York

Wisconsin Man Ends 20-Year Big-Buck Drought

Life isn't always fair. Sometimes it seems everywhere you look, people are slapping their tags on big bucks, and you wonder when or if it'll ever be your turn.

Kent Lodholz, of Weston, Wis., wasn't complaining, but after nearly 20 years of hunting, he had never killed a big buck, although he'd had a couple of chances. Meanwhile, every three or four years, one of his hunting buddies scored with a big buck. Lodholz knew there were big bucks out there. It was just a matter of getting another chance at one.

In 2004, it was his turn.

On Nov. 21, Lodholz was hunting on the second day of Wisconsin's rifle season. The area he hunted was in a tag alder thicket. He'd been hunting this land for three years. During the last two seasons, Lodholz had found a large rub line through the alders, but he hadn't met up with the buck that made the rubs yet.

The first day of deer season his son accompanied him, but they only saw a buck fawn, and Lodholz didn't shoot.

The second day would turn out to be his day in the sun. Unfortunately, his son didn't tag along that day.

Lodholz didn't see anything that morning, and returned to his tree stand about 1 p.m. for an afternoon hunt.

Lodholz is a big fan of rattling and calling on his grunt tube because he's been very successful in the past. He called about four or five times between 1:00 and 3:30.

At 3:30, he heard a deer coming

After nearly 20 years of hunting, Kent Lodholz still hadn't killed a big buck. That changed when he bagged this 10-pointer with a 20-inch spread.

out of some tall, brown grass. The buck emerged from some alders only 30 yards from Lodholz. Lodholz was about to get another chance to finally tag a big buck.

He raised his .30-06 and found the deer in his scope. When he fired, the buck kicked up its legs, and Lodholz knew he'd made a good shot. The buck ran hard for 40 yards before dying of a heart-shot.

Lodholz's long-awaited big buck was a dandy. The deer had a 20-inch spread and sported 10 long tines.

— *Joe Shead*

Buckeye Hunter Arrows Deer of Local Legends

Aaron Ireland, of Okeana, Ohio, arrowed "Sling Blade" on Nov. 1, 2004. The giant nontypical sported 24 points and netted 219⁴/₈ inches.

During the 2001 and 2002 Ohio deer season, my friend asked me to go hunting on his property in Hocking County. The property is about 240 acres, and in 1997, 60 acres were clear-cut. My friend's mother lives on the property and has taken several photos of a drop-tined buck. We named the large nontypical "Sling Blade," due to the large drop tine and the main beam that curves down. After viewing the photos, I determined the deer was definitely a shooter.

I was always asking my friend to take me hunting. He has taken me several times during the last four archery seasons. During the four years of hunting Sling Blade, I have hunted all over the 240 acres. My friend has allowed about 20 people to hunt this buck, but the deer has only been seen from a tree maybe two or three times.

Over the years, my friend showed off the photos of Sling Blade to local sportsmen, and of course, everyone asked to hunt his

A scouting camera captured a photo of "Sling Blade," and another good buck, while they were still in velvet.

property. The deer was almost a legend in the Cincinnati area. Through the years, I have tried to look for his sheds, but was unsuccessful in my attempts. My friend was fortunate to find two of his sheds during different seasons.

During the spring of 2004, I went with my buddy to hang tree stands. I decided to hang my stand next to the clear-cut, adjacent to a power line. This was a bedding area, and there was tons of deer sign. I hung my stand in a pine tree about 20 feet off the ground. After clearing several shooting lanes, I was ready to hunt.

A month before season, I advised my buddy that I needed to cut a few more branches in one of my shooting lanes. That would be one of the best decisions I ever made.

On Oct. 31, 2004, my buddy and I arrived at his cabin for an evening hunt. On the way to my stand, I put out some deer scent. After letting the woods calm down, I proceeded to rattle and use my deer calls. Shortly after rattling and calling, I noticed a few does coming out of the clear-cut. I thought there might be a buck close behind. I saw a few more does, but I didn't see any bucks.

On Nov. 1, I began my hunt at 6 a.m. After getting my hunting gear on, I had my friend drive me to my stand on his ATV because the sun was rising quickly. After he dropped me off, I still had to walk about 100 yards. When I was about 50 yards from my stand, I heard a deer snort and run off. After spooking that deer I thought to myself, "I will never see anything this morning." As I continued to my stand, only 25 yards away, I heard a second deer snort and run in the same direction as the first deer. Now, I was very discouraged, but after all, it was Nov. 1 and the rut was on.

After getting my safety belt on and pulling my bow up, I began to think about the big nontypical we'd been hunting for years.

After letting the woods calm down for an hour, I decided to use my deer calls. I conducted several series of calls with a grunt tube and an estrous call. I waited 30 minutes and didn't see anything, so I did another series of calls. Shortly after the second series of calls, I noticed a small 8-point in the clear-cut about 50 yards away. I let out two soft grunts, thinking he might come closer so I could get a better look at him, and maybe a bigger one would be with him. As quickly as the 8-point appeared, he vanished.

Ten minutes went by before I heard a noise in the clear-cut. I noticed a sapling moving, apparently because a buck was rubbing it. I grabbed my bow and came to a shooting position. It seemed like the buck rubbed the sapling forever. The deer was only 50 yards from me, but I couldn't tell if it was the 8-point or not. The buck quit rubbing the sapling and began to walk my way. As it came closer, I could hear his antlers hitting the small saplings. Now the buck was only 40 yards from me, but I still couldn't tell if he was a shooter. The buck stopped

and began rubbing another sapling. At this point I could see his antlers, and I knew it was not the 8-point I had observed earlier.

After he rubbed a sapling for about two minutes, he continued my way. When the buck was 30 yards from me, I saw that it was Sling Blade. As soon as I saw him, I began to shake, but quickly regained my composure.

The monarch finally came out of the thicket and onto a deer trail. He had his nose to the ground and was quickly approaching the shooting lane I had trimmed earlier. I drew my bow and shot when he was 20 yards away. The buck ran 20 yards and stopped. I thought I had a good hit, but after he stopped, I thought that maybe I had missed him.

He stood for what seemed like forever, then walked another 20 yards and lay down. I knew I had hit him, but I wasn't sure where. I looked through my range-finder and located my arrow, which was covered in blood. I had so many thoughts going through my head, and my knees were shaking. I sat down and started looking for him from my stand.

I had just located him through my range-finder when I heard a truck coming down the road. As the truck came closer, the buck raised his head, then quickly lay it back down. After waiting for 1½ hours, I decided to sneak down from my stand and give the buck a few hours. I went back to the cabin and told my friend I had shot Sling Blade. My buddy didn't believe me, because Sling Blade has only been seen from a tree stand a few times.

It took a while, but I finally convinced him. When we took up the trail, the buck jumped up and ran. I advised my friend that we had to let him go until morning.

After making that decision, we went back and retrieved my arrow. There was a good blood trail, and I was certain we would find him in the morning.

Needless to say, the rest of the day was stressful. After a good home-cooked meal, I tried to get some sleep. I was tossing and turning all night, along with my friend, who claims it was because he was hot. I don't think so.

Finally the moment of truth came. At 6:30 a.m., the next day, the alarm went off. My friend made coffee and had doughnuts for me, but I couldn't think about eating or drinking; I was ready to go find my deer. We picked up the trail from where we had last seen him, and I spotted him only 60 yards down the trail.

After many joyful words, I began to realize just how big the monarch was. The deer had one large drop tine and several flyers coming off his G-2s. I did a quick count and came up with 24 scorable points.

After a 75-yard drag up a steep hill, we loaded the deer and took it back to the cabin. After several photos and informing my friend's mom (the landowner) that I had shot Sling Blade, the celebration began. Once the deer was back to the cabin, I closely examined the entrance wound. It appeared that I shot him through both lungs. I could not believe how far he had traveled.

The 24-pointer grossed 224 inches and netted 219⁴/₈ inches.
— *Aaron Ireland*
Okeana, Ohio

You Can't Always Get What You Want ...

Did you ever have your heart set on getting a certain Christmas present, but then on Christmas morning when you looked underneath the Christmas tree, it wasn't there?

Chad Thompson, of Mondovi, Wis., must have harbored a few of those thoughts during Wisconsin's 2004 bow-season. However, sometimes the best presents are unexpected ones, and that's exactly what Thompson got when he went bow-hunting on Nov. 12.

Thompson, who hunts in Buffalo County, had his heart set on a certain large 8-pointer that was roaming his father-in-law's farm, and the 50 acres that

Chad Thompson of Mondovi, Wis., didn't bag the big 8-pointer he was after, but he wasn't disappointed when he arrowed this 170-class 11-pointer instead.

Thompson had purchased from him.

Thompson takes vacation during the first two weeks of November so he can bow-hunt during the rut, and in fact, on the way to his stand on Nov. 11, Thompson jumped that big 8-pointer. The buck was with a doe, and its attention was so focused on her that it allowed Thompson to enter his stand, while it stayed in the vicinity, and it hung around within 60 yards of Thompson all night, but it never got close enough for a shot.

Thompson's stand was situated in a narrow strip of woods between a river and a cornfield. He'd been saving this spot for the rut. However, he was starting to get frustrated after seeing nothing but small bucks. But his neighbor knew large bucks cruised the river bottom in search of estrous does, and told him to plant himself in the area and stay put. It turned out to be great advice. During Thompson's three sits in this river bottom stand, he saw seven different bucks.

On Nov. 12, Thompson entered the woods about 1 p.m. An hour before dark, he heard a deer moving through the tall weeds that surround his stand. He soon spotted a huge buck drinking from the river. Thompson has scouting cameras in the woods and shares information with other deer hunters in the area, and feels like he has a pretty good idea of which bucks are roaming the area, but he'd never seen a deer the likes of the one he was now intently staring at.

The buck began working its way toward Thompson at a snail's pace, taking one step, then stopping for about 5 minutes. Meanwhile, Thompson was hanging on to his cold bow, getting colder by the minute and trying hard not to shake.

After many intense minutes, finally, the buck was standing 38 yards away. Thompson brought his bow to full draw, took careful aim and shot. However, he didn't hear the telltale "thwack" he usually hears when he hits a deer, making him think he'd missed the giant buck. The deer trotted off 40 yards, then bedded down, and Thompson heard the deer making its final kicks in the tall grass.

Thompson carefully slipped out of his stand, and went across the road for help with the field dressing and dragging chores. When he returned, he found his arrow covered with blood, and he found the dead buck right where he'd seen it bed down.

He was amazed at the size of the deer, which was the biggest buck he'd ever seen in the woods. The monster whitetail sported 11 scorable points and had split brow tines. It grossed $170^2/_8$ inches and dressed out at 200 pounds. And the best thing is, when Thompson looked at the deer in the daylight the next day, it appeared even bigger.

Is Thompson disappointed that he didn't shoot the big 8? It's safe to say that he's not. But he hasn't forgotten about it. He knows that it survived the gun season. Maybe that will be his Christmas present next year.

— *Joe Shead*

Tall Antlers are Massachusetts Buck's Demise

Robert Heyes of Palmer, Mass., was leaving his stand during a heavy downpour when he spotted this 190-class buck bedded in tall grass.

Some days are camp days; you know, those times when the weather is so extreme you'd rather stay in camp than venture outdoors. After all, the deer probably are not moving around much, either.

That is often sound advice, but last Dec. 1, Robert Heyes of Palmer, Mass., took to the woods during a downpour with his father, Donald, and shot the buck of a lifetime.

"We were only in the woods for an hour and a half or so when my dad called me on the radio," Robert Heyes said. "He told me he was soaking wet and was going to head back to the truck. I gathered up my belongings and starting walking back along the edge of a swamp. Suddenly, I saw what looked like antlers in the tall grass. I quickly found a solid rest, and whistled. The buck started moving his head all around, looking for the source of the whistle, but it was windy and rainy and he didn't have a clue where it was coming from. I didn't waste any time, and shot three times with my open-sighted 12-gauge, killing the bedded buck where it lay.

"I radioed back to my dad and told him I had just shot a big deer. He told me he had heard that before, thinking I was kidding. Five minutes later, however, he was standing next to me admiring my buck. Only then did I realize how big the buck really was!"

The 12-point Worcester County, Mass., buck dressed out at 175 pounds. The buck scored 192$^5/_8$ inches as a nontypical.

— *Bill Vaznis*

Aaron Davis hunted hard for this 20-point Michigan monster. He finally arrowed the buck on Nov. 14, 2004 — the day before the firearms season opened. The giant nontypical from southern Michigan netted 225⁷/₈ inches, despite a broken tine.

Persistent Archer Arrows 20-Point Nontypical

A lot of the largest bucks in Michigan come from the southern counties. This area consists of rich farmland, and is largely responsible for the upswing in Boone and Crockett entries from Michigan in the last 10 years. With an abundance of food and easy winters, bucks in southern Michigan enter the growing season in great shape for antler production and body growth.

The majority of the land in the region is privately owned, with limited access. An abundance of swampland intertwined with farm fields and hardwood ridges provides security cover for deer, allowing big bucks to escape heavy hunting pressure and attain a ripe old age.

Genetics in southern Michigan deer seem to be prime for growing some real whopper bucks. One county that in recent years has risen to the forefront of big-buck production is Hillsdale County, which is located on the Indiana-Michigan border. In 2001, Hillsdale County produced a world-record 8-point buck for Victor Bulliner. That buck netted $180^3/_8$ inches as an 8-pointer (see the November 2002 issue of *Deer & Deer Hunting*). In 2004, the county added another buck to the record books — a $225^7/_8$-inch nontypical 20-point monster. The lucky hunter, Aaron Davis of Holland, Mich., knew the potential for big bucks existed where he hunted, but never dreamed of killing a buck of such monstrous proportions.

Davis has hunted the farm where he killed the buck for the past five years. He had previously spotted the wall-hanger buck twice during the 2004 archery season. Both sightings occurred in the same area where Davis eventually killed the buck.

Davis was hunting a woodlot that was almost impenetrable to human intrusion. The tangles of briers, thorns and dense brush provided a sanctuary for the great buck to escape intense hunting pressure and hide virtually undetected. The close proximity of corn, soybean and alfalfa fields, combined with superior genetics, greatly aided antler development, thus, producing one of the highest-scoring whitetails in Michigan history.

Nov. 14, 2004, dawned with a slight breeze from the west and the mercury hovering at 24 degrees. Davis was situated in his tree stand, hoping to get a another chance at the big buck that kept eluding him.

He had been bow-hunting diligently all season and was down to the wire. The Michigan firearms deer season would begin the following morning, and Davis knew that any chances he had of catching the buck off-guard would drop drastically after gun-hunters took to the woods. It was now or never. Armed with his bow, rattling antlers and grunt call, he was ready to pull out all the stops if an encounter with the big nontypical materialized.

The sound of oak leaves shuffling in the thicket brought Davis to full attention. A deer was on the move and heading in his direction. A doe came down the lane, and Davis noticed that she was acting peculiar. She kept looking behind her when she stopped to survey her surroundings.

"I stared into the thicket, just trying to see what she was staring at," Davis recalled. "At first I thought I was imagining things. It was one of those times where you want to see something so bad that when you do see it, you don't believe it."

A huge rack was following the doe on a path that would lead right past Davis' tree stand. The doe was very cautious as she approached the woods edge that Davis was situated on. The woods became more open just inside the fringe and the fields had been harvested, so other than the thicket, there was not a lot of cover for the deer to hide in.

The big buck pursued the doe, staying within a 30-yard area around Davis' stand. But every time Davis started to draw his bow, the doe looked in his direction. The buck was oblivious to his presence and never saw him. The doe, however, knew something was amiss, but just couldn't figure out what.

For nearly 15 minutes, Davis played this cat-and-mouse game of trying to draw without being detected by the doe. Finally, after one of the buck's advances, the doe trotted past Davis at 20 yards with the giant buck right behind her. Davis came to full draw and settled his 20-yard pin behind the mammoth's shoulder before touching off the shot. The arrow ended the reign of the mega-buck and sent Davis into Michigan bow-hunting history.

The 20-point buck field dressed at 215 pounds and sported a 26-inch inside spread. The giant 10-point typical frame sits atop 25-inch main beams with tremendous mass measurements from the bases all the way to the tips. The brow tines sport multiple points, and both beams possess heavy palmation toward the ends. The rack netted $225^7/_8$ nontypical inches and ranks as the new No. 1 Michigan nontypical bow-kill. If the buck had not broken a point off of his left beam between the brow tine and the G-2, (the matching point on the right beam is more than 10 inches long), this amazing buck would have scored even higher!

Has Davis' newfound recognition changed this quiet, humble hunter?

"No, not really," says Davis. "My phone rang off the hook for weeks on end and people I didn't even know stopped by to see the buck. I did some TV appearances and quite a few interviews. Now it seems as though my life is getting back to normal, somewhat."

What are Davis' future plans for deer hunting, now that he has killed a once-in-a-lifetime buck? Davis plans to keep hunting the same general location where he killed the mega-buck, and he will definitely be sending the landowner a Christmas gift!

— *Troy Spooner*
Holland, Mich.

Veteran Hunter Sneaks Up on Windfall Buck

On Labor Day 2004, I was walking around on the 80 acres we hunt in central Wisconsin. As I made my way through the cedar swamp, I jumped a large buck from a windfall 25 yards from a permanent stand I had built 12 years ago. I bow-hunted the property nearly every weekend during the fall, but never spotted that buck again.

On opening day of the 2004 gun season, I hunted out of a ladder stand 200 yards from the edge of the swamp. At 10:30 a.m., I radioed my hunting partners that I was heading for the "sanctuary" in the swamp and informed them to be alert for anything I might push out as I headed for the permanent stand in the swamp.

It was very windy and rainy that morning, so I approached the stand and windfall very slowly, hoping to sneak up on a deer. As I entered the cedar swamp, I tripped and fell. At that point, I figured that every deer in the swamp had probably ran for the next county. I regrouped and proceeded to sneak toward the stand. When I was within about 25 yards of the windfall, I thought I saw a huge antler amongst the tangle of brush above the two large fallen trees. "I must be hallucinating from too much beer at camp the night before," I surmised. After further review, I convinced myself they were indeed huge antlers.

Strangely, I couldn't see ears, a head, nose or eyes; just antlers. I put the pail down I was carrying and took the shotgun off my shoulder. I peered through the scope: definitely antlers. Now, how do I get a shot? Do I walk around the windfall? No, stupid, the deer will be gone in a flash.

Dave Batten was walking through the woods to switch stands when he saw a large antler, which turned out to be this 10-pointer.

Based on the height of the antlers, the buck was obviously standing. I noticed a small 6-inch gap in the large trees. I looked through the scope at this area and could now see deer hide. Looking out my left eye to judge where the chest of the beast should be based on where the antlers were, I slowly squeezed the trigger. The buck dropped to the ground, and then all I could see through the windfall was antlers and legs thrashing. I stumbled around the windfall and to my amazement, this buck actually had ground swelling, not shrinkage as so often happens.

I have hunted with family since I was 5 years old and carried a weapon to hunt since I was 12. I am now 44 years old. This buck was well worth the 32-year wait. It had 10 points, a 21½-inch spread and field dressed at 197 pounds. The buck of a lifetime!

— *Dave Batten*
Wisconsin Rapids, Wis.

Surgery Can't Keep Woman Out of the Woods

Debbie Grizzell underwent surgery in 2003, and as a result, had to skip bow season. This was especially difficult after she spotted a huge 8-pointer near her home. She finally met up with the 158²/₈-inch buck during the firearms season, and downed it with one shot from her .45 pistol.

Debbie Grizzell's friends say she is obsessed with deer hunting. But it wasn't always that way.

Grizzell, of Laurel, Ind., grew up in the country, where she and her brother frequently hunted squirrels with their .22s. Grizzell became an excellent shot, honing her shooting skills by shooting walnuts out of trees. But she didn't take up deer hunting until 16 years ago.

Grizzell's husband asked her if she wanted to go deer hunting, but she didn't like the idea of walking to her stand in the dark, so her husband escorted her to her stand.

After seeing eight does that morning, she was hooked on deer hunting, and the next morning when her husband offered to walk her to her stand, she replied, "I can do it myself."

Now, 16 years later, and with several filled deer tags to her credit, the Indiana woman thinks about deer and deer hunting all year long. But things really got interesting during her roller-coaster 2003 season.

That fall, Grizzell underwent surgery. This kept her out of the woods for six weeks, and she missed bow-season. During her recovery, every morning she'd look longingly out the window of her country home, wishing she could be in the woods. One morning as she did this, she saw a tremendous 8-pointer breeding a doe. Grizzell couldn't believe the size of the buck. She phoned her daughter, and told her to rush over with her video camera and videotape the amazing buck. Grizzell's daughter was reluctant, as she was somewhat busy, but gave in to her adamant mother, and got footage of the giant buck.

Grizzell wouldn't forget this buck anytime soon. For one thing, it carried a tremendous 8-point rack. The buck also had a noticeable limp.

Bow-season was winding down, and gun-season loomed. Grizzell talked to her doctor about the possibility of going deer hunting, but the doctor said it wasn't a good idea. However, you don't keep a die-hard hunter out of the woods, and Grizzell wasn't taking no for an answer. Her doctor finally consented that she could go deer hunting.

Opening day was a trying one for Grizzell. She didn't see much for deer activity, and in her post-surgery condition, the hunt took its toll on her physically; so much so, that the next morning, she told her husband that she wasn't going hunting.

However, passion for deer hunting and stubbornness seem to run in the Grizzell family, and now *he* wasn't taking no for an answer. Debbie eventually gave in and decided to go hunting.

That morning, she saw three does come in behind her. One of them saw her, and the three deer moved off behind a hill. Soon after that she saw another deer. As soon as she saw that it was walking with a limp, she knew it was the huge 8-pointer that she'd seen out her window and her daughter had videotaped!

The buck was coming in Grizzell's direction, and worked to within 25 yards of her. The buck continued walking, and Grizzell waited for a good shot. When the deer was 50 yards away, Grizzell was worried the buck was going to walk off without presenting a good shot, so she whistled. The buck stopped, and Grizzell lined up the open sights of her .45 pistol on the buck and fired. The buck ran off and disappeared.

Grizzell waited impatiently for a half-hour before exiting the stand and looking for signs of a hit. When she reached the spot where the deer had been standing when she shot, she found no sign of a hit, so she went to get her husband and son for help.

Grizzell's son quickly found a blood trail, and after following it for only 50 yards, they found the incredible 8-pointer piled up on the ground!

The Indiana monster grossed $164^1/_8$ inches and netted $158^2/_8$ inches. The buck's main beams measured $27^2/_8$ inches and $28^4/_8$ inches, and the inside spread measured 23 inches. Grizzell believes her big 8-pointer may be the largest buck ever killed by a woman with a pistol in the Hoosier State.

— *Joe Shead*

Marshall Simmons and his hunting party strive to kill deer that dress out at 200 pounds or more. This 220-pound 18-pointer was not only Simmons' heaviest buck, but the rack, which grossed 183 inches, was also his highest-scoring.

Maine Heavyweight Dresses Out at 220 Pounds

For many deer hunters in the Northeast, rack size is really secondary to body size. In many circles the dressed weight of a whitetail buck is more indicative of trophy status that the width, length or number of tines on the rack. As one old-timer once told me years ago, a heavyweight buck is simply more indicative of a mature animal.

Indeed, any deer that field dresses at 200 pounds or more *is* a big animal! Marshall Simmons of New Jersey agrees. In his 30-odd years of deer hunting, he has tagged 71 bucks from Maine, Pennsylvania and New Jersey, and four of those bucks have dressed out in excess of 200 pounds: 209, 210, 212 and 220! And at least one buck, a fat 12-pointer, just missed the mark by dressing out at 196 pounds.

That alone is a very impressive record. But over the last 10 years, the 14-member gang Simmons hunts with in northern Maine has tagged 12 bucks that tipped the scales at more than 200 pounds dressed! These guys obviously know what they are doing.

Last autumn Simmons not only tagged his fourth heavyweight — the 220-pounder mentioned above — but also his highest-scoring rack; a gnarly nontypical that easily qualified for the Maine Antler and Skull Trophy Club.

"Chris Johnson and I left the cabin early," Simmons said. "It was only 8 degrees out, and the 2 inches of snow was old and crunchy. We walked 2 miles down a gated road, then split up. I wanted to check out a spot where I had shot a big buck the previous season. When I got there, however, there was no deer sign. I decided to look elsewhere and soon found a lot of deer sign along the edge of a new clear-cut. I jumped two deer nearby, so I called Johnson and told him what I'd found.

"When Johnson arrived, we planned a strategy so that at least one of us would see a deer. As it turned out, I soon jumped two more deer that ran off in my friend's direction. I sat down to cool off a bit, as it was hot walking. I casually looked off to my right and saw a doe standing there. I heard a buck grunt and turned to see a rack come over a small knoll. He was following that doe!

"I quickly put the cross-hairs in the middle of his chest and touched off my .30-06.

"He was by far the biggest deer I had ever seen. When he ran past me, I gave chase for some reason instead of just shooting him again. I fell down and saw lots of blood in the snow. That's when I realized he was dead on his feet. Sure enough, he collapsed 40 yards from where I shot him. I couldn't keep my eyes off of him. I must have said 'Oh my God' a hundred times!"

The 18-point nontypical buck grossed $183^2/_8$ inches and netted 176. It was later estimated to be $6^1/_2$ or $7^1/_2$ years old. The best part, however, is that it dressed out at 220 pounds, making it Simmons' largest buck both in terms of antlers and body weight.

— *Bill Vaznis*

Missouri Brothers Share a Hunt and a Nice Buck

Jason Brown and his brother Shawn teamed up to push this Missouri buck into bow-range. This memorable hunt has brought the pair closer than ever before.

My brother Shawn and I do not consider ourselves expert hunters. I have been bow-hunting for only five years and gun-hunting for just as long. Shawn has been a gun-hunter since age 12, but only a bow-hunter for three years.

Our idea of trophy deer are very different than those of most trophy hunters. We shoot does, many small bucks and a few nice ones.

In December 2002, I met a man who would change my view on what is good hunting and what isn't. Now a good friend, Dave Butterworth kept telling me how great hunting was in central Missouri about a 30-minute drive

north of Springfield. I always argued with him that southwest Missouri where I live was just as good as anywhere. This went on through 2003 and into 2004. Finally, in May of 2004, I decided to listen to the "all-knowing" Dave.

I started by calling the Missouri Department of Conservation agent in that region and asked if she could give me names of any farmers in the area. Surprisingly, she gave me the name of one farmer who turned out to be the nicest man my brother and I have ever met. He farmed thousands of acres in the county, so he had plenty of deer. I called Duke (the farmer) and told him our intentions. Without hesitation he said, "Come on up and I will put you on some property." Again I was shocked, and after I told my brother, he was too. We had plenty of phone conversations with Duke over the summer and finally got to meet him. The drive took two hours and it seemed like it wouldn't be worth the drive. We were dead wrong.

Duke is a crop farmer who has a lot of soybean and cornfields. He said on this one particular property, he and his hired hands had seen some very nice bucks. I decided that on our next trip to Duke's, which was in late August, I would put a trail camera up were Duke said deer seem to congregate.

We didn't come back until the first weekend of archery season. We retrieved the film from the camera after our morning hunt and took it to a one-hour photo center. The pictures we got back made my brother and I both believers in the area we were hunting, as well as the camera itself. All through September and October we saw a lot of great bucks, and the rut was still on its way.

As luck would have it, Shawn and I had requested our vacation at the same time. Our wonderful wives were kind enough to let us camp for a week away from our two young children.

The first day of our hunt, Shawn had picked a ladder stand we placed in a finger of woods. He shot a 115-class buck that morning, but lost it. This was not how either of us wanted our week to start.

As the week went on, we saw several nice bucks. By Friday, we knew that at any time, one of us would shoot a dandy. I started that morning by taking a button buck, which was the second deer that we shot for Duke. By 10 a.m., Shawn and I were getting restless, so we decided to change to different stands.

I went into the beanfield and glassed it. The secluded 160-acre field is rimmed by brush and trees. I was glassing an area about 600 yards away when I noticed something was different about the brush. When I saw a buck move, I came unglued.

I radioed my brother and told him what I had just seen. We decided to meet around 11:30 for lunch. Around noon, we went to pick up my button buck from earlier. As we drove to the spot where I'd glassed the buck, I looked again, and lo and behold, he was still there. Shawn agreed this was a great buck. We both thought, "we have to try for this buck."

We were able to walk the field line, due to a small point coming out of the edge of the field. We were now 80 to 100 yards from the bedded buck. Shawn and I argued, like brothers do, who was going to stand and who was going to push. Shawn had already pushed me a button buck earlier in the year. I really wanted the shot, but I was going to push for Shawn, when he decided to go around and push me the buck. We both thought this might work.

I waited for about five minutes

when I noticed Shawn walking the field edge with his bow in hand. I decided to move to the middle of the 40-yard-wide tree line. I was waiting for some kind of movement when all of a sudden I heard Shawn's familiar whistle. Then out of the thick brush came the big buck!

He was running at a light trot right at me. I felt my heart sink into my boots. Here he was, running straight to me, and the only thing I could think was, "draw your bow!" I was sure this huge buck was about to bowl me over.

Amazingly, the buck stopped 13 yards up the small path and turned broadside to look back at my brother. I aimed and let the arrow fly. It found the exact spot I aimed at. The buck leaped about 20 yards across a small ditch and ran into the beanfield. I watched as the beautiful creature expired 50 yards from me.

When I saw my brother, I could tell he knew it had worked. He was so happy for me! We said a prayer and went to the buck. He turned out to be a beautiful heavy 8-point with the body of a cow! The deer made me happy, but knowing that Shawn did this for me was even better. The buck scored $125^1/_8$ inches.

I can never say this is my buck because my brother gave his rights to this deer to me. He proved to me that he is the best sportsman and hunter I know by allowing me to take this buck. We are now closer because of this past archery season than we ever have been. I now know out of all the hunters I am acquainted with, Shawn will always get my vote for the best, no matter what.

Thank you, Shawn!
— *Jason Brown*
Aurora, Mo.

Lady Hunter Bags First Deer on Mississippi Hunt

My husband and I have been bow-hunting at Tara Hunt Club in Mississippi since 1999, and it is our favorite out-of-state hunting spot. The last three years we have been going in December, during the rut. I find this is the most exciting time to hunt.

My husband has been successful almost every year, but I had yet to kill a deer in my eight years of hunting. But I never gave up, and always kept a positive attitude.

This year when we got to Tara, the weather was a bit finicky: nice one day and pouring rain and lightning the next. But we were here to hunt, and hunt we did for 10 hours a day. This year my guide for the most part was Neil. He was taking me to an area where he had seen some really big bucks and good deer sign.

The first three mornings I was seeing a big 8- and a 10-pointer just as it turned light, and then again an hour or two later, but they weren't close enough for me to shoot. So I just watched, waited and tried to take in any little detail that might help me take these bucks later.

Patsy Hahn, of Boyertown, Pa., had been traveling to Mississippi to bow-hunt whitetails with her husband since 1999. For years, she had never killed a deer, but in 2004, on a morning she usually rests, she took her first deer — this 130-class 8-pointer. She said sharing the experience with her husband was even better than shooting the buck.

Wednesday morning Neil did not take me to that spot, as the wind was not in my favor, but I knew I would go back the next day if the wind was right, and in my heart I knew I would see one of those bucks again.

I normally take off Thursday mornings. It is kind of an "over the hump" day for me, as by now I have hunted 34 hours in 3½ days. This particular morning it was raining, and I thought it would be the perfect morning to stay in and not hunt.

We got up at 4 a.m., and my husband asked me if I was going to take the morning off. My body wanted to, but my mind kept thinking about the 8- and 10-pointer I had been seeing, so I dragged myself out of bed and went hunting.

I was in my tree stand around 5:15. About 6:30, it was still fairly dark when I heard something. Then I could faintly see antlers going past me about 20 yards away. I watched where the buck was going and waited.

Around 6:50, I was watching straight ahead of me, and starting to pull back the peel on my banana when I saw a buck coming toward me. The banana went back in my pack, and I stood, got my bow up, and watched as the buck came in toward me. I had my range-finder on him, so I knew he was legal.

When he was at 27 yards, I prayed for wisdom and straight shooting, and shot. The buck whirled around and took off 10 yards to my right. He looked up at me and just stared for what seemed like hours, but in fact was about a minute. He then walked another 8 to 10 yards and started bucking his head as he walked. "Oh great, now he has winded me," I thought. He went about 15 more yards and then slowly laid down in the brush.

I was just a little excited to say the least, and the first thing I did was thank the Lord about 20 times. Then I just sat and watched my buck to make sure he was definitely down for good.

Around 8 a.m., I got out of my stand and went over to where my arrow lay. Then I walked around 10 yards farther, just to make sure the buck was still there. I did not go right over, as I wanted to make sure I did not jump him if he was not dead. I went back up into my stand and waited patiently until 10:30, then I got down and walked over to pick up my arrow and went over to the buck. Oh, my, was he big! I went up to him and rubbed his horns with joy!

I walked out to the road to wait for Neil, and was reading my book when he pulled up. Anyone who knows Neil can tell you he is pretty laid back, and when he got out of the truck and briefly looked at my bow, he just looked at me and said something to the effect of, "Did you see anything?"

"Yes, I did. I shot one."

He had heard that before, and he knew it could mean many things. Then he asked me what it was, and I told him that I had shot a big buck.

He just looked at me, and I thought he might be thinking "yeah right." So, calmly, I said, "Yeah, I shot an 8-point buck. He is down and I can take you right to him."

"God dang, girl," he said, and hugged me.

I took Neil into the woods and showed him where I picked up the arrow, then I took him to the buck. He was just a little bit excited to say the least! He said it was a great buck, and he thought that it would qualify for the Pope and Young record book.

Needless to say, when I got back to camp, I could not wait until my husband got back from hunting. I was waiting outside the lodge when his truck came in, and I just smiled and did a little warrior dance so he knew I had gotten something, but I don't think he was prepared for what he saw in the truck. He laid down his bow, came over to me and hugged me. He told me he was so proud of me, and let me tell you, that meant more to me than shooting that buck. There is nothing like hunting with your spouse and sharing the victory with him.

My buck weighed 210 pounds, had an almost perfect 8-point rack and a 20-inch spread. It officially scored $132^{2}/_{8}$ inches. It is truly my trophy of a lifetime, and I will never forget it.

— *Patsy Hahn*
Boyertown, Pa.

Wisconsin Hunter Waylays Buck From Ice Shack

Ron Knitter Jr., left, hunted from his ice-fishing shack when the forecast called for rain on opening day of deer season. The result was this 12-pointer.

I bought an ice-fishing shack, and while I was fixing it up a little, I thought that it would be a good roof for deer season because the forecast called for rain. My buddies gave me a hard time about using a fishing shack for a deer stand, but I hauled it out to my 40 acres anyway.

It was about noon on opening day, and my dad stopped by to see what was moving. Just then we heard shots from my uncle's field, so we waited to see if any deer were coming. After 20 minutes nothing had showed, so my dad walked through some pines to see if he could stir something up.

After a few minutes, I saw a doe running from the swamp. Then I saw a buck. I shot and he went down. It was an 80-yard shot on a dead run.

My dad came running when he heard me shoot, and I gave him a high-five that was so hard, he said it nearly broke his fingers.

To my surprise, when I retrieved the deer, I discovered that it was a trophy buck. It had 12 points, a 17-inch spread and $6^5/_8$-inch bases.

I want to thank my hunting buddies for helping me remodel the shack. I hope the luck is as good ice-fishing from the shack as it was while I was hunting from it.

— *Ron Knitter Jr.*
Wittenberg, Wis.

Pennsylvania Hunter Intercepts the 'Big Boy'

The story about this deer starts in the summer of 2004, in the fields behind my house in western Pennsylvania near the town of Volant. In July, while walking a small wood-lot, I spotted a nice buck in velvet. When he saw me, he ran off, giving me only a brief glimpse, but I knew that this would be a big deer.

Summer progressed with a few more sightings. Each time I saw him, he was bigger, with tines seemingly everywhere. Every time I saw him, it was just a quick look.

Fall arrived and spotlighting increased. Many people saw the deer, but only for quick glimpses.

A week before archery season, the farmer posted his land where the deer was seen. Because I was a local, I was able to hunt the lot, but could not because of knee surgery.

I figured the deer surely would be killed by a bow-hunter. I even tried to set up my friend with a probable area to kill the buck, just so I would know who got it. He never saw the deer, nor did anyone else.

On the first day of rifle season on Nov. 29, I stuck to my traditional hunting area in Butler County. My son, who is 14 and loves the outdoors as much as I do, hunts with me at our first-day spot. I'm ready to call it his spot because as usual, he filled his tags, harvesting a 4-point and a doe.

The next few days we saw deer, but no big ones. Each day I thought of the big boy. I wondered if he was still out there.

Hunting around the house is hard because of posted land, and because there was a big buck in the area made access even harder. Word of this buck

Larry McConahy bagged this 17-point Keystone State buck. Many people in the area had seen it before season, and the buck was heavily hunted.

had spread like his rack, and most of the ground that once could be hunted, could not now.

On Dec. 1, my friend called and asked if I had heard anything about the buck. I told him I hadn't. He asked if I wanted to hunt the next day. Because I did not get out during archery season, I was ready to spend as much time as possible in the woods during rifle season.

We made plans to start hunting around 7 a.m., as I figured if we were going to get deer, we would have to push them. Deer get like rabbits after the first day or so; they hold tight and you have to work for them.

Morning came with high hopes of getting a few does. My friends arrived and we drove to the spot where I wanted to start. It also happened to be one of the last areas where the big boy was seen.

I posted my friends, then I walked the length of the field to where a fence line corner and a woodlot joined. I radioed the rest of the party that I would push the lot at 8 a.m.

At 7:15, someone in our group saw two deer go into the woodlot, and we got excited, knowing there were deer in the lot to push. I had sat my .300 Mag. against a tree and was thinking of starting the drive sooner when I heard the telltale sound of a deer trotting in the leaves. I studied the surroundings, but saw nothing, and the sound soon disappeared. Knowing the habits of deer in the area, I knew we were in a prime escape route for deer, so I stayed put.

Just then, I heard traffic on the small back road and turned to see three trucks of hunters headed for the woodlot we were hunting. As soon as the trucks disappeared, I heard the footsteps again, only this time they were getting louder.

I bent down to grab my gun, and as I turned in the direction of the sounds, I saw a deer sneaking down the field edge at me. As I raised the rifle to waist height, the deer spotted me and froze. I slowly shouldered my rifle, but the deer was standing in brush and had a direct lock on me.

I waited, still not knowing what I was looking at. The deer turned and started to run back the way it had come from, and I decided that if I were to get a shot, I had to do something now, so I stepped to the side toward the field and saw that it was a shooter buck. I raised the gun and fired. I missed, but the shot scared him and he turned to the open field. When he turned I saw rack — lots of rack — and it clicked that it was

"him." Now the big boy was running full-tilt. My second shot hit him, and turned him so he was now broadside. Now, instead of running away, he was running toward me. The next shot was a miss and I started to sweat. I had one shot left — then my gun would be empty. At the report of my last shot, the mighty deer dropped in his tracks with a barrel roll.

My radio cracked and my friend said, "You got lucky. I had that deer in my sights and was ready to shoot just as you dropped him."

I radioed back with a quivering voice, "I think that's him; the big boy from behind the house."

I walked up to the deer and was speechless. His rack was big even bigger than I thought. I radioed the rest of the guys to come take a look.

He was impressive! He had 17 points, with the two smallest being broken tines an inch long, one of which was a drop tine. His spread was $19^5/8$ inches, and he weighed an estimated 205 pounds live.

Over the next four days, word spread about the buck, and many people came to my home to see him. At least two other hunters had seen him during gun season. One hunter had seen him on the first day but could not scope him, and the other had seen him the second day, but had already filled his buck tag and could not shoot him.

This deer managed to dodge hunters for four days until I was in a natural funnel of an escape route to intercept him. The big boy that I wanted a chance at is truly the biggest deer of my hunting career — a once-in-a-lifetime trophy.

— *Larry McConahy*
Volant, Pa.

Cancer Survivor Uses Bow-Hunting as Therapy

Most of us, without even thinking about it, take for granted the sights, sounds and smells of the deer woods. If we don't get a deer, there's always tomorrow, right? But what if we suddenly found ourselves too sick to take a stand in the woods — or worse — what if there *wasn't* a tomorrow?

It would be a scary and brutal reality. Just ask Neil Callahan of Merrill, Wis.

Callahan, a self-employed auto parts dealer, is also a deer hunting nut. But like most people, his busy lifestyle left him with limited time in the woods, and he usually did most of his hunting on the weekends or on his vacation during the rut. But the world as he knew it departed like a startled whitetail in spring 2001 — May 17, to be exact, he told me. "You don't forget a day like that."

On that day, Callahan was diagnosed with chronic lymphocytic leukemia.

For weeks before the diagnosis, Callahan wasn't feeling like himself. He was constantly tired, and his body was bruising from no apparent injuries. His wife suggested that he go to the doctor for a physical.

During the physical, he learned that his white blood cell count, which, for him, should be about 5,000 to 10,000, was a staggering 385,000! Something was definitely wrong, and Callahan was soon diagnosed with leukemia.

The diagnosis changed his life immediately. At first he was depressed. Callahan would have to undergo chemotherapy, and the chance of survival was only about 40 to 50 percent.

"When you're gambling, that seems like pretty good odds, but when it's your life, that doesn't sound so good," he said.

These sessions last for three to five hours and are physically grueling. Callahan took the treatment intravenously, via a needle in his hand. During these sessions, Callahan tried to focus on something he loved — deer hunting.

"They turn on some crappy daytime TV that you can watch, or you can read hunting magazines. To me it was a no-brainer. I read a lot of hunting magazines," he said. "You have to be totally interested in something while you're undergoing chemo for hours. Hunting kept me going."

Callahan underwent 29 treatments of chemotherapy, which left him nauseous and sleepy. As a result, he missed most of the gun season that first year, and when he did go hunting, he was limited to short sits because the chemotherapy also hurts the muscles in his feet and buttocks.

To undergo a treatment that makes you sick as it tries to make you healthy is bad enough, but when it prevents you from doing something you love — hunting — it hurts all the more. But Callahan had no choice. He was fighting for his life.

Fortunately, the treatment was working, and by late 2002, he was starting to feel better.

He took up bow-hunting again and found his quiet sits in the woods to be very therapeutic. He enjoyed everything, whether he was watching deer, coyotes, bobcats or just sitting in the woods. Simply being able to hunt again made every sit worth-

Neil Callahan was diagnosed with leukemia in 2001. When his health began improving, he took up bow-hunting with renewed vigor, using his time in the woods as "therapy." He arrowed this 8-pointer after more than 40 days of hunting.

while, and he took nothing for granted.

Now semi-retired, Callahan's hunts have become much more frequent, and he hunts during the week as often as he can. Even though he owns his own hunting land, he has been amazed by the increased deer activity he sees when other hunters aren't in the woods during the week.

As his time in the woods increased, Callahan's family noticed positive changes in his health. So did his doctor. "Whatever you're doing, keep doing it," he told Callahan. His family agreed.

"My wife and family were very supportive," he said. "They just said 'Go!'"

So he did. In 2004, he took his passion for hunting to a new level.

That season, he bow-hunted nearly every day, only missing a day afield when he took his granddaughter Kendra to her first deer hunting banquet, and another day when he attended another banquet. (Callahan is a strong advocate for getting youths involved in hunting.)

Callahan felt somewhat guilty by leaving his wife to cover the business deliveries while he went bow-hunting every afternoon, but she knew he was not only enjoying his time in the stand, but it was also doing him good. Callahan told his friends he was "taking out parts" every afternoon at 2:30 or 3:00, but everyone knew he was going bow-hunting.

At first, Callahan was getting to his stand around 3:15 each day. He only wanted to hunt a few hours, because he was battling a sinus infection and "doesn't have the wind that he used to." Plus, he had coughing spells and he got cold easily because the chemotherapy weakened his immune system. However, he began bumping deer off his food plot when he got to his stand, so he began heading out at 2 p.m., and frequently saw deer from 3:00 to 4:00.

In early October, Callahan got a photo of a large buck on his scouting camera. Knowing this buck was in the area inspired him to hunt, even when hunting so hard became long and tiring.

"It gives you the drive," he said.

During the season, he passed up seven or eight bucks. The thought that a bigger one was around kept entering his mind. On Nov. 2 — after hunting more than 40 days — he finally saw the big buck.

That afternoon, Callahan was perched in one of his five or six stands. These stands are short — only about 6 feet off the ground — and enclosed in a tent. He'd been sitting a while when a large 7-pointer came in, chasing a doe around on a brassica food plot. The doe would run into the woods and the buck lip-curled. When she re-entered the plot, he would chase her again. All this activity was taking place on Callahan's right side, and being right-handed, it would have been hard for him to shoot.

Suddenly, the big deer that appeared in his scouting-camera photos appeared, perhaps attracted by the smell of the estrous doe. The buck came from his left, giving Callahan a perfect shot opportunity.

Callahan stood up, drew his bow, and shot. The buck ran off with its tail held high, making Callahan think he'd missed. However, when he climbed down from his stand, Callahan discovered he'd gotten a pass-through, and the buck only ran 60 yards before piling up. The 8-pointer has a 20-inch spread and $8^1/_2$-inch brow tines.

Although shooting this buck after hunting so hard was the highlight of his season, Callahan is just thankful to be out hunting once again.

"Not everyone gets the opportunity I got. (Chemo) doesn't work for a lot of people. I'm just lucky."

Callahan's last chemo treatment was in late 2002, and now he is in "clinical remission," meaning the number of abnormal cells in his body is knocked down to a low level. He merely takes a pill a day to keep abnormal cells from increasing.

Soon after shooting his buck, Callahan got more good news. His doctor told him that his health had improved to the point where he only needed checkups once every four months — compared to once a week in the early stages of his treatment.

"That's the best Christmas present I've gotten in a long time," he said.

Callahan has been through a lot the last few years, but for the most part, he's taken it in stride. And you can be sure this cancer survivor will be back in the woods this fall. Whether he shoots a deer or not, you can bet he'll be appreciating his time afield. He hopes others do the same.

"You can fight this stuff and live a fairly normal life. I'd like to see more cancer patients get out there," he said.

Let's hope more people follow his inspirational example.

— Joe Shead

Grunt Call Lures 34-Pointer Into Bow Range

Cade Bump of El Dorado, Kan., connected with this buck while bow-hunting in Kansas. The 34-point monster scored 198³/₈ inches.

Big bucks don't make many mistakes, but they're not infallible. In fact, sometimes they even give you second chances. Just ask Cade Bump of El Dorado, Kan.

On Nov. 4, 2004, Bump went to the farm he'd been hunting all his life to help his brother set up a tree stand. It was about 2:30 p.m.

After setting up the stand, Bump planned to bow-hunt from a tree stand where he'd been seeing a large 10-pointer. However, by the time the stand was hung and Bump had changed into his hunting clothes, he decided it was too late to hunt this stand, because the 10-

pointer consistently arrived early in the evening. Bump decided to hunt from another stand that he'd only hunted from about four or five times that season.

He quietly walked into the timber near the stand when a hawk jumped into the air and fluttered away. Suddenly, a huge buck with a gnarly rack jumped up from its bed and sprinted across a river near the tree stand. Bump quickly pulled out his grunt call and grunted at the buck, hoping to disguise himself as another buck, but it didn't work.

Bump was upset that he'd

spooked the huge buck, but there was nothing he could've done differently, so he headed for his stand and climbed in.

Soon after he got situated, he noticed movement. Before he identified it, he grunted. Seconds later, he realized that the movement was from a doe that was bedded right next to where the buck jumped up. She rose to her feet and walked into a beanfield.

A half-hour later, Bump heard grunting from across the river. When he looked, he saw the same buck. There was no mistaking the huge nontypical rack.

The buck was facing away, but when Bump grunted, the buck turned toward him. Then it stood still for 15 minutes, giving Bump time to look at the amazing rack through his binoculars. When he gave another grunt on his call, the buck walked across a grass field, then forded the river, grunting all the way. It stopped broadside at 40 yards, and Bump made the shot. The mortally wounded deer ran back across the river, falling 40 yards from the water.

Bump called his brother and told him he'd shot his biggest buck ever. The brothers had to secure permission from the neighboring landowner to recover the giant deer. When they did, they discovered just how huge the buck was. The "Second Chance Buck" sported 34 points and scored $198^{3}/_{8}$ nontypical inches.

— *Joe Shead*

Scouting Camera Betrays Mississippi 12-Pointer

Carl Bourgeois was invited to join a hunt club in Jefferson County, Miss., after a relatively poor season of hunting in a wildlife management area. He and his uncle, Terry, had been hunting together for many years. As a matter of fact, it was Terry who had introduced 10-year-old Carl and Carl Sr. to deer hunting. Carl and Terry got into the Jefferson County club with two parcels of land, each one about 1,100 acres. Both properties were located along the banks of the Mississippi River in an area that has produced some of the finest deer hunting in the South over the past 10 to 15 years.

Carl scouted the lay of the land, erected hunting stands, established his sleeping quar-

Carl Bourgeois got a photo of this 160-class 12-pointer with his scouting camera, but never told a soul. He met up with the Mississippi monster on a January morning.

ters, got to know the other members of the club and put in his required workdays (mostly planting food plots). But his main energy was focused on finding deer to hunt. Carl's new hunting terrain included ravine after ravine, many 100 to 200 feet deep, with sheer vertical walls. Scout this area in the summer with the mercury at 95 degrees and humidity to match, and the challenge quickly becomes clear.

Carl chose to cut some corners by purchasing scouting cameras. Although it required numerous trips from camp to the cameras to collect film and move the cameras, the effort paid off. There were many photos of opossums, raccoons, turkeys and squirrels, but the most rewarding were the deer.

The benefit of the many hours spent using the scouting cameras was clear on opening weekend. Carl's uncle Terry harvested a respectable 8-pointer that the camera had recorded near the stand. Next was a fine 10-pointer in the 200-pound category in the 125-inch class — also a previously filmed deer. The scouting work also helped Carl set up a "payback dad" hunt for all Carl Sr. had done to teach him the many facets of deer hunting.

Carl placed his dad in a tripod stand in a cow pasture with a 100-yard strip of trees running down the middle. "Pop," Carl said, "I've filmed a real fine buck in that field." After two sittings in the stand, Carl Sr. harvested an admirable 9-pointer weighing 195 pounds. If it wasn't the buck Carl had on film, it must have been his twin.

The season was wearing on onto the rut — that's around Christmas in south Mississippi — and Carl decided to get serious about a picture he had chosen not to share with anyone. Carl awoke on Jan. 3, 2003, and retrieved from under his pillow the secret photo of the big 12-pointer. He decided to hunt the end of a long ridge that nearly touched an adjacent ridge where I had already planned to hunt. A finger off of my ridge, about 300 yards long, ended about 200 yards from the end of Carl's ridge. When I hadn't seen a deer by 9 a.m., I decided to climb down from my stand and stalk hunt the $2^1/_4$-inch hoof prints along a well-rubbed tree line.

This stalk, following the giant hoof prints, took me down to the bottom of the ridges Carl and I were hunting. Unbeknownst to me, Carl was positioned on the ground and spotted my orange; I didn't detect his presence a mere 200 yards away. Carl decided to make a move and backed off around the other end of the ridge. He flushed a flock of turkeys, which flew across the bottom and over to my side. A few minutes later the roar of Carl's rifle echoed in the bottom. A second report told me he had administered a final shot to put down his deer.

A couple of hours later I was greeted back at the camp by Carl and a piano keyboard-sized smile that told me everything. Carl had the huge-hoofed buck up on the meat pole. He had his secret photograph to prove his story of the 225-pound 12-pointer that scored $160^4/_8$ inches.

Carl's story goes to show what hard work and a lot of scouting can do for you. And to illustrate what a scouting camera or two can add to the enjoyment.

— *Bryan Zeringue*
Norco, La.

Joke Gets Hunter Into Suburban Deer Hideout

Ramin Ansari joked that he'd take care of problem deer on his boss' land. However, these deer were no joke to his boss, and Ansari had a new place to hunt. The result was this wide-racked 9-pointer.

Ramin Ansari of West Lafayette, Ind., must have a knack for good timing.

Ansari, who started bow-hunting four years ago, used to bow-hunt on public land until a casual conversation with his boss landed him a hunting spot on private land.

Ansari and his boss were flying on company business when the boss started complaining about deer eating the plants on his 15-acre suburban property.

"I'll take care of those deer for you," Ansari joked.

"It's a deal," his boss replied.

Ansari was surprised by his boss' response, but he was tickled to have a place to hunt.

In 2003, he began bow-hunting the small property, which consists of about 10 wooded acres, with a narrow strip of woods located at the bottom of a ravine.

After three or four weeks of bow-hunting Ansari didn't have much to show for his efforts. But then, one day in late October, the story of his amazing 2003 deer season began unfolding.

That day, Ansari was perched in his climbing stand when he heard crashing in the bottom of the ravine. He saw squirrels scatter and it was obvious something was creating a lot of commotion. Seconds later he saw two does running through the woods. Ansari wondered what could have startled them like that. Could it have been a person on a walk?

Fifteen minutes later, he heard the answer. Something was slowly walking in his direction. As it came closer, Ansari thought it sounded like a horse or a cow walking, but he knew that couldn't be right, however, the gait just didn't seem like it could be a deer. When the animal was about 40 or 50 yards away, Ansari could make out the body of a large deer. It was heading in his general direction.

When it was about 25 yards away, it turned 45 degrees and started coming directly at the tree Ansari was sitting in. By now, the hunter knew he was not only looking at a buck, but a very large one. The only problem was, the deer was coming head-on, providing no shot opportunity.

The buck stopped when it was 15 yards away, and all the while, Ansari was "shaking like you wouldn't believe." Then the buck continued even closer, finally stopping right at the bottom of Ansari's tree!

The buck was now partially obscured by the foot of the tree stand, but Ansari didn't dare move as the buck sniffed the tree. The next thing the excited bow-hunter saw was the buck's antlers tipping back, and then the buck looked right at Ansari. The buck sniffed the air like a dog, knowing something wasn't quite right. Then it took two steps backward, turned 90 degrees and started walking away.

After 10 yards, it stopped and looked back. Ansari and the buck made eye contact for about 15 seconds. Then the buck walked 10 more yards and looked back again. Then it seemingly walked off and out of Ansari's life forever.

A few weeks later, gun season opened. Ansari returned to hunt from the same spot where he'd had the encounter with the big buck during bow season. The memory of that deer still haunted him. Should he have shot? Some of his friends said yes. But others agreed that he never had a good shot at the buck, and he did the right thing by not shooting.

It's doubtful Ansari held any hope of ever seeing that buck again, but then, sometimes things just seem to work out.

By 8 a.m. on the opening morning of Indiana's 2003 gun season, Ansari had heard no shooting, likely due to the drizzly weather conditions. Ansari was wet and cold, but he stuck it out, and was rewarded when he spotted a deer taking the same path he'd seen the big buck take weeks earlier.

Once again, the deer came to a point in the trail where it had to turn 45 degrees, and Ansari saw that it was the same big buck! He raised his smoothbore shotgun. The buck caught his movement, but it was too late. Ansari's shot was on its way, and the buck dropped on the spot.

After dressing out the huge 9-pointer, which later weighed in at 216 pounds, Ansari tried to drag his buck, but soon decided to call his friends for help, as he needed to drag the deer up an 80-foot rise.

Upon inspection of the deer, he noticed the deer had a deformed hoof, which may explain the unusual way the deer walked when Ansari saw the deer during bow-season.

Although all of Ansari's friends were amazed by the fact that he got the buck after seeing the deer a few weeks earlier, the real surprise came after Ansari tagged the buck. Before the season, Ansari had made a promise that the first deer he killed, he would donate to Food Finders — a venison-donation program. And that's exactly what he did!

— *Joe Shead*

Oklahoma Newcomer Shoots Odd Nontypical

Heath Herje of Duncan, Okla., is new to deer hunting, but he's quickly making up for lost time. With the help of some scouting cameras and a sound QDM program, he downed this 14-point nontypical.

I am a 24-year-old Oklahoma native who is a newcomer to deer hunting. I had mostly hunted quail and waterfowl until I was 22. Then, in 2003, I set up tripod stands in a few CRP fields on my family's properties in southwestern Oklahoma. That year I harvested a 145-inch 11-point and caught the fever I'd heard so much about.

I began studying whitetails, joined the Quality Deer Management Association and implemented a solid QDM program. After planting warm- and cool-season food plots, along with providing mineral supplements, I purchased three game cameras to assist with my management objectives. I caught numerous large-racked typicals on film, but knew that many still needed time to grow trophy-class racks. It was not until mid-October that one of the most bizarre nontypicals I had ever seen graced my cameras.

I developed four photographs of this Oklahoma giant, and on opening morning of the 2004 firearms season, I caught up with him. The buck carried a massive 8x6 nontypical rack with a 12-inch drop tine. The 4½-year-old deer weighed 210 pounds.

I scored after making a 265-yard shot. I lured the buck out of dense CRP grass using a doe bleat and a decoy. I speculate that the buck may have injured its rack, which caused the unusual formation.

— *Heath Herje*
Duncan, Okla.

Bow-Season Phantom Shows During Gun Season

After spotting this 11-pointer several times during bow-season, Allen Lee Fish finally got a shot at it on opening day of Ohio's firearms season.

It was the opening morning of shotgun season in Ohio, which to many hunters is a state holiday. I decided to go to one of my favorite tree stands that morning, hoping that it would bring me luck. I had hunted this tree stand during bow-season and saw a few nice bucks, including one with a huge body and a large rack, but he always stayed just out of bow range.

Opening morning began uneventfully for me. I heard shots around my property, but I wasn't seeing any deer. Around 8 a.m., I saw a nice 8-pointer walking toward me. He met all the requirements that my twin brother, Lee Allen, and I have set. He had a spread wider than his ears, he had 8 points or more and appeared to

be fairly old. The 8-pointer walked within 20 yards of me and then laid down, facing away from me. I decided to wait to see if a bigger buck would show up.

About 8:20, I saw movement to my left. It was two does walking along a brier patch 75 yards away. They were looking behind them as if looking at another deer, and that's when I saw him! He was walking about 20 feet behind the does, making his way around a large brier patch. With his large body size, I was pretty certain it was the big buck I'd seen during bow-season. I made sure it was him with the binoculars and hoped that he would give me a shot.

He was slowly moving down a faint deer path. I saw a small open-

42

ing just in front of him, and I waited until he gave me a clean shot. The big buck was about 70 yards away when I placed the sights of my .50-caliber muzzle-loader on his vitals and squeezed the trigger. He leaped up and never regained his feet. He went down about 10 feet from where I shot him.

I reloaded and thanked God for letting me get such a fine trophy. The field-dressed weight was 238 pounds. The buck was a large 11-pointer with a split brow tine on his right side. It is the largest deer I've ever taken.

We are doing quality deer management on our property, and it is sure making a big difference in the quality of deer we are taking. My brother and I started about five years ago, and within two years, we both took two big 10-pointers. I am certain this was a direct result of QDM.

After seeing the results on our property, the neighbors are now starting to do QDM on their own properties, which is helping all of the hunters get bigger bucks and healthier, larger does.

My wife, Sharla, shot a very large doe this year, and the meat processor said that it weighed 179½ pounds! This was Sharla's first year hunting, and she is already hooked. She wants to go out next year and go for a big buck. That's all right with me, as long as it's not bigger than the one I get!

— *Allen Lee Fish*
Newcomerstown, Ohio

Ohio Man Encounters 30-Pointer on Hike to Stand

The second weekend of bow-season was one I will never forget. We had started to do quality deer management on our property about five years ago, and it didn't take long to start seeing results. My twin brother Allen Lee had filmed several large bucks, and noticed that one buck seemed to be growing faster and bigger then the rest of them, with points in every direction. Watching the big buck on film, I knew he was the one that I wanted. The week before bow-season, all I could think about was how I could get that big nontypical buck.

The first week of bow-season was very warm, and I didn't hunt very hard because the heat limited deer movement. The following few days a slight rain and cold front brought temperatures down, and deer started moving.

The next week I decided to hunt after work for a few hours each night to see if I could get within bow-range of the big nontypical. On Thursday evening, after getting my camo clothes on and spraying myself with a scent-killing spray, I decided to head for a climbing tree stand in a grove of large oak trees. I was walking slowly to my tree stand so I would not scare any deer when I spotted two deer — a doe and a fawn — walking parallel to me. They didn't seem to notice me because their attention was fixed on something up ahead. I decided that I would stand still beside a large oak tree until they passed me or until I saw what they were looking at.

That is when I spotted the big nontypical moving just ahead of me

Lee Allen Fish hoped to get a shot at the 30-point nontypical his brother had filmed, but he didn't expect to see it on the walk to his stand.

less then 20 yards away! I couldn't believe what I was seeing! His massive rack made my heart skip a beat, and I knew that I would have to calm down or I would mess this up and not get him. His attention was fixed on the two other deer. He was not even looking at me or worried about anything but those two deer.

He was making his way toward the deer very slowly. I decided that the next time he stepped behind a tree, I would get my bow ready. As he stepped from the tree, I focused on exactly where I wanted to place my shot, and shot. He took off, but I knew that I hit him where I was aiming and that I had made a good shot. I just stood there for a few minutes and I couldn't believe it. I decided to go back to the house and

get my brother to help track the buck.

We returned to the place where I'd shot him, and my brother could hardly believe that I'd gotten this close to him. The blood trail was very hard to trace, but after following it for about 40 yards I saw the buck lying in a brier patch. I could not believe my eyes. He was even bigger then I could have imagined!

The buck had 30 points, with three drop tines. I couldn't even put my hands around the antlers. I had seen this buck on my brother's video, but to actually hold this buck and to know I'd shot him was incredible. Words could not describe how happy I was to take such a fine trophy.

— *Lee Allen Fish*
Newcomerstown, Ohio

12-Pointer Escapes Once, But Hunter Prevails

It was Sept. 15, 2003 — the bow-hunting opener. For the past month, my friend Mark and I had scouted a chunk of land that borders a major interstate in the neighborhood where we live. We had placed five stands that we could rotate between, depending on wind direction. I had two stands about 80 yards apart that I would spend most of my time in. One stand was in plain view of the free-way, overlooking a tall grass area with several small water holes. The other was in the woods along a small opening in which several scrapes and rubs were visible. Opening evening, I chose to sit near the freeway, due to the wind direction and the fact that we had seen several deer crossing there the previous few nights.

I arrived in my stand around 5 p.m. Last light would be about 7:40. By 6:30, I had several deer in front of me, including two small 8-pointers, a 4-pointer and two does. I was paying special attention to one of the 8-pointers, when movement caught my eye. Two larger bucks were browsing about 70 yards straight in front of me! This was only my second year of bow-hunting, and I could barely contain my excitement. I watched, trying to take slow, deep breaths as the biggest buck I'd seen in 22 years of hunting began to cross the swamp toward me. As I drew my broadhead, I estimated his distance to be about 30 yards. But my estimation was off, and my arrow missed his backbone by inches and stuck in the mud behind him. Still, I remained calm, as all the white flags disappeared into the woods. Hey, this was opening night, and that was one of the most exciting hunts of my life. I shared my story with Mark, who has bow-hunted for many years, and we came to the conclusion that we may not see that large of a buck again.

Sept. 18 was an important day for me, not just because I was going hunting, but because I had harvested my first deer with a bow the previous year on that evening. I had an agree-ment with myself that no matter what the weather was like, I would be in my stand. When I arrived home, I called Mark, who informed me that he had no intention of hunting, due to the rain and drizzle and 45-degree temperature. I told him that I would come get him to help drag my buck, and we both chuckled. Little did I know that I would be back in his driveway within the hour.

I dressed for the weather and was in my stand by 5:15 p.m. I decided to sit in the stand I had placed in the woods, as it gave me some cover from the rain. After about 45 minutes of sitting motionless, I was cold and miserable, and I decided to still-hunt through the woods to my other stand.

After walking slowly about 40 yards, I realized that I was seeing the motion of a set of large antlers right near my other stand. The wind was straight in my face, and the noise of rush-hour traffic on the freeway allowed me to move without being heard. My only option would be to belly crawl in the tall grass to a lone tree about 40 yards in front of me.

Once I'd reached the tree, I noticed that there were two bucks thrashing their heavy antlers in the brush. One looked to be a large 8-point buck, and the other had at least 11 points. I

Rick Runberg, of North Branch, Minn., got a second chance on this 12-pointer, after missing it three days earlier. Pictured with him are Runberg's future hunting partners, his sons Gavin, 12, and Nathan, 7.

couldn't believe that the same giant buck would give me another chance.

Both bucks remained out of bow-range, although I knew in my heart I was only going to draw on the bigger buck. Cars continued to pass by, and the time seemed to be in slow motion. After about 10 minutes, I was still undetected, and the giant buck started to move to my left.

"Oh no," I thought, "I'm not even going to get a shot if he goes that way." Suddenly, and for no apparent reason, he turned and headed right in front of me at about 10 yards. I didn't have time to be nervous. I drew my arrow and released, taking notice that about 6 inches of my arrow was still showing from his chest. The buck spun around from the impact, got back up and ran about 20 yards before falling over dead.

I threw my arms in the air, and then broke my personal-best time in the 300-yard dash as I headed for my four-wheeler. The look on Mark's face as I pulled into his driveway, only an hour after we had spoken, brought a sense of reality to what had just happened.

Mark and I retrieved the buck about an hour later. The buck had 12 points, with the G-2s measuring $13\frac{1}{2}$ inches, and the brow tines almost 9 inches. The deer had a dressed weight of 225 pounds. It was a day I will never forget. What a hunt!

This hunt happened at a great time for me, as this coming year, my son Gavin will be going on his first bow-hunt. My efforts will now be focused on my favorite hunting partner.

— Rick Runberg
North Branch, Minn.

Shed Hunter Finally Gathers Up His Buck

My usual deer season begins in late February or early March. Every weekend in those months is the same old thing if you ask my wife. At 6 a.m., I kiss her goodbye and tell her I'll be home in a couple hours. I think she knows by now a couple hours usually means five to 10. I grab my coffee and out the door I go to meet my long-time hunting partner and good friend Nick Mastenbrook.

We shed hunt every year, and finding sheds is almost as exciting as sitting on stand, waiting to see how much bigger those deer have grown since last year.

Last year on the third Sunday in March, I decided to take a little walk. I didn't call Nick that day because I knew he was spending time with his family. So I walked about 100 yards into the timber and found my first shed. It was a dandy, and after examining it for a few minutes, I concluded that I had found the shed to a deer I had seen the year before. I also had a set of his sheds from the previous year. I took another hundred steps or so, and to my surprise, there lay the other half.

I must tell you that I had many encounters with this deer over the last three years, but I never could close the deal. After finding the other half, I decided it was probably worth walking for a few more minutes. To my surprise, I found another shed within another 50 yards.

At that point I couldn't leave Nick out of this. I called him and within 10 minutes, he, his wife and their 6-month-old daughter had arrived.

The day ended with my partner finding a shed from a deer killed this year that scored 195 nontypical.

Needless to say, we were both very excited about the upcoming archery season. After some intense scouting and many discussions about stand placement, we hung our stands. Now the only thing we had trouble deciding was who was going to sit where opening day.

We had chosen one stand that we thought would be our best place to kill a buck. We decided the only fair way to decide who would sit where was to get a third party involved.

I won opening morning in the stand I wanted, which was not all that good. I didn't see a deer in six hours. Nick saw eight deer, all within bow-range, and seven were bucks.

The deal we made was to swap stands on the second morning, which I gladly did. Rain and wind were going to put a damper on this hunt, or so I thought. Not even a half-hour after legal shouting time, Nick called me on the radio. He had shot a monster. It was not a deer we even knew was around. I was extremely excited for him, and was very happy with the way the season had started.

As bow-season pushed on, I spent many hours in the field, and had many opportunities to kill deer, but just not the one I had two sets of sheds from. By Nov. 14, I had decided that the deer I was hunting must have gotten hit by car or not made it through the winter.

On Nov. 15, opening day of firearms season, I decided to take my brother along. My brother, Nick and I set up so a deer could not make it onto our property without being seen.

By 10 a.m., I was thinking maybe

Ed Hardesty had found two sets of sheds from this buck. He finally downed the 162-inch bruiser during Michigan's 2004 firearms season.

we didn't know deer as well as we thought. Then, a half-hour later, Nick called me on the radio and said he'd seen deer moving behind him. Then I heard two shots.

Nick came back on the radio and said he had the biggest buck he had ever seen at 125 yards, standing broadside, but he couldn't hit it. Four shots later, he was back on the radio. The buck was still standing there, and he was out of shells.

I rounded up my brother and we headed to Nick's stand to see if we could find blood. After finding nothing, and after Nick explained where the deer had gone, I set up a stalk.

That deer was smart. He knew exactly what we were doing. Ten minutes into the stalk, Nick spotted him bedded down in a waist-high field of grass. I set up in a fallen tree,

and had it not been for the advantage I had of being elevated, I don't think I would have gotten a shot. The buck kept his head down and tried to sneak through the grass, keeping his antlers below the top of the grass. Little did he know I was waiting at the end of the field for him.

He got about 40 yards in front of me and stopped. There was an area in the field that was just thin enough that his vitals were exposed, and I sealed the deal with one pull of my shotgun's trigger.

As I approached the deer, I realized it was the same deer I had two sets of sheds from, and had so many encounters with. The deer scored 162$^{7}/_{8}$ inches, and is the biggest buck I have ever killed.

— *Ed Hardesty*
South Lyon, Mich.

Youth Bagged First Deer With a Minute to Spare

It was Thanksgiving weekend of 1994, and the Ohio gun-season opener was approaching. I was 18, and a senior in high school. This would be my sixth year hunting deer. I had not harvested a deer yet, and was eager to shoot my first deer.

It was finally Sunday evening, and my excitement for the Monday morning opener was growing. I had my shotgun sighted in, and my hunting equipment was ready to go. As I lay down to sleep that night, all I could think about was going deer hunting. The excitement and anticipation I felt made it seem like it was the night before Christmas. I finally fell asleep, and the next thing I knew, I was waking up to my alarm clock. After eating breakfast, it was time to get ready for the hunt.

I was decked out in my camouflage in no time and I had all my hunting gear ready to go. My dad and I left and headed for our hunting spot.

We were in our tree stands well before daylight. As I waited for daylight to break, I could not help picturing a buck walking into shooting range.

Daylight finally approached and legal shooting time began. My dad was in his tree stand about 35 yards down the hill from me. We were within looking distance of each other for safety reasons, and also so we could let one another know when we wanted to get down.

As time passed I heard plenty of shots close.by, and I was on full alert for any kind of movement in the woods. All of a sudden, I heard a loud crash coming from downhill. When I looked, I saw deer running full-speed in my direction. They went right in front of my dad, but he didn't have a shot because they were running.

As the deer made their way in front of me, my dad let out a loud whistle. The three deer stopped right in front of me about 50 yards away. I noticed that one of the deer had a set of antlers, so I quickly got my gun up, clicked the safety off and aimed. Boom! The three deer just stood there, so I shot again. Boom!

They all took off running straight toward me, then turned up the hillside to my left. As the deer got up the hillside, they stopped. So I quickly aimed at the buck and fired again ... boom! Still, the deer took off running up and over the hill.

I couldn't believe what just happened. I was in shock! Things just happened so fast. Surely, I could not have missed all three times!

I motioned to my dad that I was getting down. I made my way over to where the deer were and looked around for blood. To my amazement, I found no trace of blood. All three shots had been clean misses.

As my dad walked up, he could see that I was all shook up. I told him all three shots had missed, and I complained that I had just blown my opportunity to harvest my first deer. I was very upset and disap-

Adam Smallridge, right, of Chillicothe, Ohio, had a roller coaster ride of a season, en route to killing his first deer, this 10-point monster, with one minute to spare during Ohio's 1994 firearms season.

pointed. I decided it was best to go home to gather my thoughts and regroup.

I was so disappointed about what had happened that morning that I couldn't bring myself to go hunting that afternoon. I couldn't get the thought that I had blown my opportunity at harvesting my first buck out of my head. That afternoon I sat back at the house, dwelling on what I'd done wrong. I concluded that I shot too quickly instead of taking my time. Hard lesson learned ...

The next day I had school and wouldn't be able to hunt until that evening. I couldn't wait to be back up in my tree stand in hopes of redeeming myself. I couldn't let missing a deer bother me too much. I had to get back out there and keep trying.

The school day finally ended, and I found myself back up in my tree stand. I had less than two hours to hunt. As I sat in my stand, I couldn't help but run yesterday's events through my head.

All of a sudden I heard a noise up the hillside to my left. I kept a watchful eye in that direction.

Finally I saw some movement and made it out to be a deer. I got my gun up and ready. Four does made their way past my stand at about 30 yards. I aimed at the lead doe and squeezed the trigger. Boom! The doe fell down. She started to get back up, and I fired again. She was still rising to her feet. I fired again with the same result. As she got to her feet, I fired one last time. She made it to her feet and fled. All I could do was watch this doe run out of sight.

I couldn't believe I'd just shot four times at a deer and still watched her run out of sight. I sat for a good 30 minutes before motioning to my dad that I was getting down.

As we walked up to where I had first shot, I saw lots of blood and a good blood trail. I was in high hopes of finding this deer. But about 50 yards into the trail, the blood started to grow faint until there was nothing at all. My dad and I were both puzzled on how this deer just stopped bleeding. We walked around in hopes of finding the deer. Needless to say, my hopes of finding the doe were now diminishing. We walked around for quite a while before calling it quits.

Once again I was heartbroken. Instead of celebrating my first deer, I was experiencing a hunter's worst nightmare — wounding an animal and not being able to find it. I was very upset with myself over doing what I hoped I would never have to witness, but I knew what I had to do: I had to take this experience and learn from it, and hopefully never have to experience it again. It was another hard lesson learned.

I couldn't hunt the next three days because of school and other after-school activities. That left me only Saturday to hunt, which was the final day of the gun-deer season.

I was up extra early Saturday morning, in hopes of still making this gun season my first to harvest a deer. I was in good spirits early that morning of turning my luck around, but that early morning quickly turned into late morning with no sign of any deer. I decided to go home for lunch before going out to hunt one last time that evening.

My dad and I reached our stands for the last hunt of the season around 3 p.m. This would be my last opportunity to harvest my first deer this season. My confidence was low because of all that had happened to me that week, but I knew I had to stay positive. While I sat, I couldn't help but reflect on the events of the past week and how close I had been to harvesting my first deer.

Just then, I happened to notice movement in front of me. I got ready for a deer to jump out of the brush. To my surprise, a brown dog jumped out of the brush instead, and ran down the hill.

Talk about being disappointed! I thought for sure I was going to get another shot at a deer. I looked at my watch and it read 4:33 p.m., and legal shooting time was up at 5:01 p.m. I had less than 30 minutes left, and my spirits were down after seeing the dog run past.

As I waited while the clock ticked down, I looked over at my dad, and he motioned to see if I was ready to get down. Right at that moment I heard something up the hillside to my right. I motioned to my dad that there was something walking down the hill. I kept my eyes peeled, looking in the direction from which I'd heard the noise. Finally, I could make out a deer, and it was a buck!

I made a hand signal to my dad that there was a buck because I didn't want him trying to get down while I was watching this big buck walk my way. As the buck made its way closer, my heart started to beat faster and faster. I started to breathe harder and harder, and then my legs started to shake. I was experiencing buck fever.

I knew I had to try to calm myself down to make it through this. I told myself not to look at the antlers and to pick out a spot behind the buck's front shoulder to aim at. The buck was almost into shooting range now, and I quickly positioned myself for the shot. I stuck the butt of the gun into my right shoulder and clicked off the safety. It was now or never as the buck walked into my shooting lane at 40 yards. I aimed for the spot behind the right shoulder that I had been concentrating on and said a little prayer. Then I squeezed the trigger. Boom! The buck dropped in its tracks!

I sat with my gun aimed right at the buck, just in case it tried to get up, but thankfully it didn't. I looked at my watch and it read 5:00. I sat for a few minutes to gather my composure.

After a few minutes, I motioned to my dad that I was getting down.

I was careful climbing down because I was still shaking a little and breathing hard. When I reached the ground, I looked up to where the buck was laying to make sure he was still there. Indeed he was, and I made my way over to my dad.

My dad was just reaching the ground as I reached his tree stand. When I told him I got one, he was surprised. He thought I had missed, so I told him to look up the hill right between two trees where I could see the big rack sticking up. As my dad's eyes focused on the deer, his eyes lit up with excitement.

We quickly made our way up to the deer. I picked up the buck's rack and admired it. It turned out to be a 10-pointer. My dad gave me a high five and congratulated me on harvesting my first deer. I think he was more excited than I was!

I had my buck officially scored. It grossed $146^3/_8$ inches and netted $141^4/_8$ inches. I now have it mounted on my wall.

Every time I look at it, I remember sharing that special moment with my dad and hanging in there and not giving up when things went bad. I believe everything happens for a reason, and that's why I didn't harvest the buck that I shot at on Monday morning or the doe on Tuesday evening. That week of the 1994 Ohio deer gun season I harvested my first deer on the last day of gun season with one minute of legal shooting time to spare.

— *Adam Smallridge*
Chillicothe, Ohio

Virginia Man Solves 'Spooky House Buck' Mystery

I was dissatisfied with my 2003-2004 hunting season, so I decided to purchase a game camera to aid in my quest to bag the ultimate deer. Determined to get a true trophy-size buck, I planted food plots where I knew a particular buck lived, which I have since dubbed the "Spooky House Buck." This particular animal had been sighted many times during the past several years, but had somehow managed to escape numerous close calls with many skilled local hunters.

In Southside Virginia, hunting deer with hounds is permitted during regular gun season, which can be quite an experience. Much work and time is spent with our beloved hounds year-round, and the sound of your faithful dogs hot on the track of a deer is really awe-inspiring and a source of great pride and joy for the dog owner. But it seemed that every time our hounds jumped the Spooky House Buck and drive him toward us, he would somehow elude everyone in the end. Only minutes into the chase, the crafty buck would somehow get away from the hounds, but not before someone got a fleeting glimpse of him as he disappeared like a ghost into the woods.

The deer's moniker is an interesting story. There is a huge abandoned two-story farmhouse in the general vicinity where the deer was thought to spend most of his time. Two hunting companions of mine, Owen and John, often tease that the dwelling is haunted. Many times, they would still-hunt inside the house on rainy days, and as it grew darker outside, the eerie noises coming from the old house would grow louder and creepier. I guess it is befitting that we named the deer the Spooky House Buck.

During August 2004, I began to obtain some really great pictures of several nice deer with my new game camera. Finally, around September, I was awe-struck when I had my film developed and there he was at last: the famed Spooky House Buck. The photo seemed to take on an other-worldly appearance when placed alongside the other photos I had taken. He only cooperated to have his photo taken once. I also managed to photograph another nice buck several times, an 11-pointer, but he wasn't quite as large as my desired trophy.

Hoping to get the Spooky House Buck during bow-season, I placed two stands near the food plot on opposite ends of the field. I knew that bow-season would be my best opportunity to bag the deer because few people bow-hunt the area.

I did see the Spooky House Buck one evening at about 75 yards, and I achingly watched him for more than 10 minutes! The rut had not gotten fully underway yet, and neither grunt calls nor scent seemed to interest him. I was determined to wait until dark before leaving the stand so as not to alarm him, but he bolted seconds after being startled by a covey of quail going to roost.

Soon, bow-season had come and gone, leaving me with only a doe for my freezer and nothing for my wall.

I didn't see the Spooky House Buck during the black-powder season, but I couldn't hunt the whole season, due to a family vacation.

Ricky Vernon Moser caught up with the "Spooky House Buck" on a dreary November day, just before nightfall.

Regular gun season started after I returned from vacation, and I was worried that I wouldn't see the Spooky House Buck again because of the tremendous hunting pressure. As I mentioned earlier, we hunt with hounds during regular gun season, and the number of hunters in the field greatly increases. I knew this would only push the buck further into hiding and make him even more elusive.

On Nov. 24, after a two-day deluge of nonstop rain, the weather took a peculiar turn. It would rain very hard and then stop, with the temperature dropping quickly immediately after the rain stopped. Remembering my

then, a single doe entered another corner of the same field. With only minutes of light left, I was determined to watch her back trail. I paid so much attention to her, that I almost failed to check over the rest of the area. Suddenly, out of the corner of my eye, like a specter, the Spooky House Buck materialized!

He had entered the field where the two smaller bucks had left. With his head down at approximately 150 yards, I could not determine yet if it was a buck or doe in the failing light. Raising my trusty .270 to check the animal in my scope, he then lifted his head, showing his glorious 10-point rack and revealing his identity. Wanting to take a clean shot, I waited for him to turn broadside. After several heart-pounding, adrenalin-filled minutes of telling myself not to make any mistakes, he finally turned! "Now or never," I said to myself as I gently squeezed the trigger. The .270 sounded off, and the buck dropped to the ground where he had stood.

After calming myself down and watching to see if he would try to get up, I silently thanked the Good Lord for smiling down upon me, and thought of my daddy. I somehow knew he was somewhere up above watching down on me and smiling, and no doubt had a hand in this glorious moment.

The Spooky House Buck had 6-inch bases, a 17-inch spread, 25-inch main beams and a perfect 10-point rack. My game camera had provided me the extra edge, and along with some determination and hard work, had made this single moment worth all the effort.

— *Ricky Vernon Moser*
Java, Va.

daddy saying "You can't kill him if you ain't out there," I decided to give it a try, despite the foul weather conditions. I felt it could prove to be the chance I needed. After spending many hours in the cold with rain dropping off the brim of my soaked cap, I began to question my sanity.

Shortly thereafter, my hopes grew after spotting a 3-pointer, accompanied by a button buck, entering the edge of the field. Sitting there being up close to these magnificent animals gave me a feeling of success and made the burdensome rain not so bad after all.

Soon after feeding, both deer left the field. Some time passed, and I knew it would be dark soon. Just

Rainy-Day 8-Pointer Appears in the Nick of Time

Elwood Burtt is an expert bow-hunter, having tagged more than 30 whitetails. Last year, however, his experience was put to the test when he learned where the buck of a lifetime was rutting.

Elwood Burtt has killed more than 30 whitetails, but none like this 237-pounder he arrowed in 2004.

"I first saw the buck last year (in 2003). I was walking to my tree stand about 2:00 in the afternoon when I jumped him as he fed within sight of my stand! All I saw was his big rack going over a nearby hill. I never had a chance to nock an arrow, and I never saw him again that season.

"Then last year a friend was working in the area and he told me he saw a big buck standing in a field just prior to the hunting season. I knew then the buck was still alive and had not been shot, hit by a truck or poached.

"I found his scrape in the same area as last season. There was no missing his big tracks and there were plenty of big rubs nearby to confirm it was him working the area.

"On Nov. 4, I heard a storm was brewing and decided to hunt that afternoon before the storm hit. I went up a tree that overlooked his primary scrape with my climber, but it soon started to rain. When the rain became a downpour, I got down out of the tree, packed my stuff and started walking back to my vehicle when three does ran out in front of me.

"I knew something was up, so I fumbled around and got my release ready. Suddenly, I saw the big buck appear behind the does, obviously chasing them. When he stopped 15 yards in front of me, I calmly brought my bow to full draw. I picked a spot, held steady and then sent an arrow toward his vitals. My aim was true and the buck bolted less then 30 yards before dropping to the ground.

The Hampshire County, Mass., buck dressed out at 237 pounds. A taxidermist estimated it to be $5\frac{1}{2}$ years old. When scored by the Northeast Big Buck Club, the typical 8-pointer tallied $162\frac{1}{8}$ inches.

— *Bill Vaznis*

Dog Man Bags Hefty Canadian 8-Point Buck

Hunting with dogs is my favorite way of deer hunting. I also enjoy the quietness of bow-hunting in early and late season, but during the rifle season, nothing is more exciting than to hear the beautiful voice of your own beagle echoing through the mountains.

My hunting party is located in Whitney, Ontario, where the rut usually kicks off during the second week of rifle season. The rifle hunt always starts on the first Monday of November and goes on for two weeks.

The hunt had been on for nearly a full week, and all we had to account for was a small buck and a fawn on our pole.

Friday of the first week it was snowy and windy, so the boys decided to tell stories inside camp with warm cups of coffee and a great late breakfast. My long-time friend, Claude, and I decided to drive the four hours to Ottawa to pick up my brother so he could join us for the second week of the hunt. We left early the following day and were back at camp by 11 a.m.

After lunch, Claude decided to change our plan a little and attack an area where we hadn't given much chase previously. Because I was the dog man, Claude explained to me how I should run the chase with his dog, Brinkley. The boys would be lined up on the hilltop, and I would walk the bottom and follow the contour of the lake until I reached the last man posted.

I had my young cousin, Eric,

join me for the long walk. As we stopped to take a breather, I found a nice shed.

"It would be nice to see this one," I said, "but what are your chances when you are the dog man, right?"

After two minutes of watching the beagle work on an old track, we resumed our walk. We came upon a little creek that came from the top of the hill and connected to the lake.

We had been working the edge of the lake for the last $3/4$ mile. I was thinking "How far do we have to go?"

I grabbed my radio and called Claude. He told me to keep going for another 100 yards on the other side of the creek and then call it quits.

So Eric and I hopped over the small creek and kept on walking. After going about 100 yards, we turned around and started making our way back to camp. We had just crossed the creek when a voice came on the radio. It was my cousin, Steve, who was standing on the hilltop above me. He notified me that I hadn't gone far enough. After going 100 yards across the creek, I had ended up just below him. He could hear the dog barking. But there were still two hunters past him, Claude being the last one. Tired and exhausted, I looked at Eric, and confirmed to the other boys that we were on our way. So for the second time, we crossed the creek and kept going.

Suddenly, two shots rang out in

front of me. Claude got on the radio and confirmed that he had shot at two deer and believed he had missed. The deer actually had come from the opposite side of where Claude was looking. He wanted me to come over with the dog.

Stephane Lepage was the dog man for his party of Ontario deer hunters. Toward the end of a hunt, this 8-pointer burst from its bed, and Lepage dropped it.

When I got to Claude, Brinkley picked up the deer's scent immediately and gave a 15-minute chase.

We looked for blood or any trace of a wounded deer, but came up empty. It was indeed a miss.

When Brinkley came back, I was happy to realize that the chase was over and we were headed back to camp.

But Claude had something else in mind. He was looking in the direction of where the deer had come from, and I could clearly see what he wanted. The shoreline is full of fingers, with bays in between.

It seems like the two deer had come out of one of the two fingers in front of Claude. I told him to move over a little bit, and I would try to get something out of the fingers. I told Eric, who was now very tired, to stay with Claude and I would keep going alone with Brinkley.

I was 20 yards inside the first finger when Brinkley took off like a bullet. A deer ran out of the finger, taking the dog for a short chase. I realized that there were a lot of rabbit tracks in the area, and I was worried that the dog might chase a rabbit instead, so I decided to call the chase quits. It was 4 p.m. and the sun was getting low on the horizon.

As I got on the radio to announce that the chase was over, I heard a loud splash 10 yards away from me. Brinkley lost his mind. He got up on his back legs and moved like lightning. His voice was low and almost growling at the same time.

I knew Brinkley saw the deer and was really close to it. The deer took the dog to the point of the finger, jumped in the bay and onto an island about 160-180 yards from shore.

I made my way through thick pines, spruces and cedars, to the bay and stepped into the marshy grass.

Brinkley was barking nonstop, and I'm sure that everyone was on their toes. My eyes were scanning the island, which is about 8 acres in size. The deer had to come out one way or another.

There he was, standing beside the island, with the dog quickly approaching. The rack was sticking out of the grass and the sunset shone on it, making it bright yellow. How did he get there? I never saw him step off of the island.

There was no time to crank up the power of the 3x9 scope on my .30-06. I had to shoot right now. I was sinking in the marshy, mossy wet grass and I would be trying a 170-yard freehand shot. Good luck.

My first shot was a miss. It didn't take much time to put in another round and fire a second shot.

This time, the 180-grain bullet found its mark on his neck. To my surprise, the deer turned my way and ran straight at me. He was closing the distance quickly. I fired a third shot, which landed in his back.

Amazingly, he kept running, and my pulse kept increasing. He stopped broadside at 60 yards to analyze what was going on. He had no idea where the shots were coming from. The fourth shot was the final shot. He managed to disappear at the tip of a finger. I immediately called Claude on the radio, who was only about 80 yards behind me. Claude and Brinkley reached me at the same time.

We tied the dog on a leash and checked for blood. I really thought there would've been more blood. After the final shot, the deer went 20 yards before crashing in the brush.

I was concentrating so hard on hitting the kill zone that I never realized how big the buck's rack was. I knew he was a wall-hanger, but never in my wildest dreams had I thought about shooting a grey ghost while I was the dog man.

It's amazing that I was standing 10 yards from a bedded monster, and he never moved in the five minutes I stood there until I spoke on the radio.

When we brought the deer to the check-in station in Arnprior, Ontario, I found out that they don't weigh deer there anymore. But by their experience and the taxidermist's experience, they estimated my buck would weigh more than 240 pounds field dressed. I weigh 205 pounds myself, so you can make the comparison.

The buck is an 8-point with a 22-inch inside spread.

Where we hunt there are no fields, no farmland, no food plots and no acorns. Just cedars, pines and maples, and miles and miles of swamps and hardwoods. Deer don't get much bigger than this in my area.

— *Stephane Lepage*
Cumberland, Ontario

Giant Illinois Buck Pulls Annual Houdini Act

You can never underestimate the elusive nature of mature bucks. Any deer that's grown more than a couple sets of antlers has also developed an ability to hide from hunters.

Just ask Matt Baalman of Hardin, Ill. In 2001, he began getting photos of a large buck on his scouting camera. Baalman and his four brothers saw the deer several times a week in a field less than 200 yards from his house. But when hunting season drew near, the buck vanished. The following spring it reappeared.

The buck has repeated the same scenario every year since. Despite their best efforts, the Baalman brothers have yet to even see the buck during hunting season. Meanwhile, the buck has only grown larger, and in 2004 sported a massive rack.

How long will the buck keep reappearing, and will it ever show up during hunting season? The Baalmans are eager to find out.

— *Joe Shead*

California Boy's Reward is a Texas 8-Pointer

Jacob Siefke of Watsonville, Calif., couldn't wait until he turned 12 to go deer hunting, so he and his father traveled to Texas to hunt whitetails. He downed this 8-pointer on his first deer hunt.

"Patience, son, patience," I kept whispering to my 11-year-old son, Jacob, as we sat motionless, afraid to draw a breath. We were sitting in an elevated box blind overlooking a sparse two-track road in South Texas. Standing in the middle of it, a mere 70 yards away, was an 8-point whitetail, not very tall, both brow tines broken, but wide, with good mass and character. A good deer for the free-roam area we were hunting in and a

great first deer for any new hunter. I watched the deer through the lens of my camcorder. Jacob was watching through the scope of a whittled-down .243 and he was anxious to squeeze the trigger. Suddenly, the buck jerked in alarm. He took a step to his right, then immediately turned left, exposing his vitals. The rifle blast produced a deafening echo in the blind and shattered the calmness of the morning.

We were in south Texas the day after Christmas in 2004 on the sprawling E Tom ranch, a 5,000-acre spread covered with mesquite trees and every thorny bush known to man. Jacob and I had come from California on a mission: to bag his first buck, a South Texas whitetail. Jacob got his hunting license last year, but in California you must be 12 years old to hunt big game, and he was not about to wait another long year.

After arriving and getting settled, we ate, and then bedded down for a restless night's sleep, anticipating the next morning's hunt. At 5 a.m. only darkness greeted us, and after a quick bite, our guide drove us to an elevated box blind overlooking a dirt road cut into miles of brush country. I learned later, locals call them *senderos*, a Spanish word for road. The weather was cloudy and cold, but there was no fog to hamper our vision. A slight wind pushed from behind us. It was not long before the sun began to break the horizon and our hunt began.

We watched several does emerge from the dense brush to feed. A short time later, two small bucks appeared, but we had been warned not to shoot the first one we saw, because there would be more around. An hour went by and three javalinas came out on the other side of the stand. Several cottontails darted from bush to bush. We watched all this action with great appreciation for the amount of wildlife on the ranch. We were loving every minute.

Just then, a small 6-point buck with a noticeable limp appeared 100 yards out and was coming our way. The buck didn't know it, but a coyote was trailing him. Every time the buck stopped to feed, the coyote would close the gap. Just when it appeared the coyote would prevail, the buck's head snapped alert and whipped around to see the danger. Despite his bad leg, the buck bounded into the high brush with the coyote in feverish pursuit. We watched with delight and anticipation as this stalk played out below us. We soon lost sight of them and just sat marveling at nature's way of keeping everything in balance.

After another hour, the morning sun started poking through the clouds, revealing a crystal-blue sky above. Out in the distance, a small shape was visible on the road, hastily making its way toward us. As it drew closer, we saw it was a coyote, possibly the same one we had watched earlier, and he was nervous, frequently glancing over his shoulder. Coming up behind him was a much larger buck, and this one was not limping. Both animals were trotting, and at any moment a full-blown chase was about to erupt.

The buck appeared angry, nose to the ground with steam emitting from each nostril. He was focused on the coyote. We quietly laughed at this coyote's misfortune to be the hunter one minute and prey the next. Suddenly, the buck stopped in his tracks about 100 yards out, put his nose in the wind and looked directly toward our stand. A brief second later he took two steps and disappeared into the thick brush. He was obviously no dummy; he smelled danger and pursuing a coyote was not worth it.

Jacob and I had momentarily forgotten we were hunting. A buck like the one that just got away was the reason we had traveled to Texas in the first place. We continued our silent vigil over the *sendero* with the solemn feeling the morning's hunt was over. It was already past 9 a.m., and the guide would be driving up soon to take us back to the bunkhouse for breakfast.

Just then, Jacob whispered, "Dad look behind us. There's a buck." I swiveled my seat around, expecting to see another young buck. To my surprise, it was the same wide 8-pointer that had been chasing the coyote, and he was again in the middle of the *sendero*, and close. Apparently he had circled around our stand and could no longer smell us.

I got out my binoculars and took a good look at him. I wanted this hunt to be successful for my son. Here was a nice buck, standing in the open, and the shot distance was just right. Far enough to still be a challenge, yet close enough that he would have a good chance of hitting the mark. I asked Jacob what he thought, and of course he wanted this buck. I told him to get ready.

"Patience, son, patience," I kept repeating. The tension was almost unbearable. The buck had his head down and was directly facing us, a poor shot by any hunter's standard. This had been going on for 20 minutes. Jacob was waiting, eye glued to the scope, safety off, waiting for the deer to turn, waiting for what seemed like an eternity. My camcorder was almost out of disc space. Worse yet, I looked at my watch: 9:30 a.m. The guide was due to pick us up. I strained to hear a truck's engine approaching. I could hear my son's shallow breathing. I knew our hunt was only minutes from ending. Then, in a blink of an eye, it happened. Looking back on the video, I saw the buck come alert, step, and then the comes a sharp flash and the roar of the rifle. A red dot appears behind the buck's shoulder. The buck's legs disappear from under him and he smashes to the *sendero* with a thud.

My son had his first buck. I don't know who was more excited, him or me. After unloading his rifle, we climbed down from the stand, reloaded and Jacob put the majestic animal out of its misery. Just then, our guide drove up, and after some congratulations and pictures, we hoisted the bruiser onto the rack and returned to camp. That night, all of the hunters in camp feasted on fresh chicken fried venison back straps, cut into medallions, with mashed potatoes and gravy. I never saw my son eat so much. Later, we sat around the campfire and told the story of the hunt and how the buck was chasing the coyote. Nobody felt sorry for either the coyote or the buck. All the hunters told Jacob he had a lot of patience to wait so long for a clean shot, and said he'd done a great job. Jacob soon drifted off to sleep with a proud grin on his face. I think he likes hunting ... a lot.

— *Paul Siefke*
Watsonville, Calif.

Man Tags 191-Inch Buck Via Wife's Suggestion

When it comes to deer hunting, James Kenney has learned to listen to his wife. After all, her comments helped him shoot the buck of a lifetime.

"I've been a meat hunter most of my life," Kenney said, "although I have recently passed up several deer with my bow. About six or seven years ago I took up black powder hunting, taking a modest 8-pointer so far for my efforts.

"Then this past season I got a shot at a wide-racked buck. He was only 50 yards away, but the buck escaped unscathed. I looked for a couple of hours that evening and most of the next day without any luck. I couldn't believe I had missed, so I shot the gun again and found it to be shooting six or seven inches high at 50 yards. It was then I remembered knocking the gun down while riding on my ATV a week earlier.

When James Kenney's wife told him to go hunting, he listened. The result was this 191-inch 18-pointer — which Kenney had missed three weeks earlier.

"I immediately re-sighted the gun. Then three Saturdays later, I was moping around the house when my wife told me to go hunting. "'You'll probably shoot a real big buck this afternoon,' she said.

"There was a storm approaching, so I took her advice, grabbed my muzzleloader, and headed to my tree stand across the road. I was only a short distance from where I had missed the big buck earlier when I saw a buck walking past me some 50-60 yards away. Without hesitation, I found him in my scope and fired. I immediately ran a patch and reloaded, but it was not necessary. The shot had felled the buck.

"When I turned the buck over to do the field-dressing chores, I found where a bullet had grazed the buck's back. That's when I realized it was the same buck I had missed three weeks earlier!"

Kenney's monster buck was indeed special. The 18-pointer dressed out at 190 pounds with the heart and liver, and was thought to be $4^{1}/_{2}$ years old. It had an inside spread of $21^{7}/_{8}$ inches, with main beams measuring $26^{2}/_{8}$ and $26^{4}/_{8}$ inches. After adding in $18^{3}/_{8}$ inches of abnormal points, the final net non-typical tally was a whopping $191^{2}/_{8}$ inches.

— *Bill Vaznis*

Illinois Duck Hunter Finds 'River Bank Warriors'

I'm an avid deer and waterfowl hunter. I live very close to the Kaskaskia River in Randolph County, Ill. When I was younger, I used to hunt every chance I could on the river. About 15 years ago, I started hunting different spots throughout southern Illinois, and I didn't really spend much time on the river until Dec. 27, 2004.

On that morning, several hunting buddies talked me into duck hunting on the river, which I had no faith in, because of the declining waterfowl population there. I hadn't hunted ducks on the river in 15 years.

We put out a nice spread of duck decoys and only four goose decoys, in case we lucked into seeing geese that morning. About 8:30 a.m., we heard other waterfowl hunters calling geese, and soon noticed that a single goose was coming up the river.

In all of my previous hunting trips on the river, I'd never killed a goose here. My buddies and I started calling and soon convinced the goose to take a look. The goose came in and we broke its wing, causing it to fall in the river. The injured goose swam to the other side, so we got in the boat to track it down. I drove the boat across and soon flushed the bird about 20 yards downriver.

While backing the boat up to pursue the goose, something caught my attention. It appeared to be part of a deer's hindquarter, floating in the river. We quickly recovered the goose, and then went back to investigate the deer.

We discovered that what we thought was one deer turned out to be two big bucks locked together, floating in the river. Apparently a 10-pointer and an 11-pointer had

Kent Wall found two floating objects in the Kaskaskia River in Illinois. At first they looked like rocks, but when he poked them with his paddle, he discovered a 10-point and an 11-point buck.

become locked up in battle near the riverbank and fell in. I realize this discovery isn't the first of its kind, but the way that I found the deer was almost as if it was meant to be.

First, I haven't hunted the Kaskaskia River in more than 15 years. Second, I've never killed a goose on that river, and third, the goose led me right to the bucks.

I received two permits from a conservation officer to keep the racks, and returned to the bucks with a saw. I removed the heads (which was a rather smelly task) and took them to a taxidermist. Two friends gave me capes from their bucks to use in the mount. I am getting them mounted together with a nameplate that reads "River Bank Warriors."

I haven't had them scored yet, but I plan to as soon as possible.

— Kent Wall
Evansville, Ill.

Strange Shirt Proves Lucky for Virginia Brothers

Mike is my younger brother. We grew up hunting and shooting together. We first enjoyed hunting rabbits, squirrels and doves, but as we began stepping up to centerfire rifles, our focus shifted toward whitetails. Mike harvested his first deer, an 8-point buck, at the age of 9. I was quite a bit older when I first experienced big-game success.

Chasing eastern whitetails in Virginia began to dominate all of our hunting over the years, but we had never harvested a buck more than $2^1/_2$ years old. I began researching possible out-of-state destinations a couple of years ago in hopes of getting a real wall-hanger in our houses.

Fast-forward to Nov. 19, 2003. I took a great buck in Macon County, Missouri that grossed $187^3/_8$ nontypical inches. It was my lifetime buck for sure. Neither of us had ever killed anything in Virginia over 92 inches.

Mike didn't harvest anything on this trip, but wanted another try. We rebooked again with Darrin Bradley at IMB Outfitters, but moved to Pike County, Ill., for the 2004 hunt.

We arrived in Pike County on Dec. 1, 2004. The second gun season didn't begin until the following day, so we sat around, joking a lot, checking our guns and packing and re-packing our back-packs about four times that day. I was going through my clothes and then asked Mike, "Do you believe in lucky things?"

"No, not really," he said.

"Try something this hunt. Put my spent shell in your backpack from my Missouri monster last year. Also, put on this obnoxious purple/blue-colored Thermax turtleneck that I had on at the time." I threw him my shell and shirt and he said, "Whatever. I'll try anything once."

On Dec. 4, the third day of our four-day hunt, Mike's luck was about to change. At 6:30 that evening, I was the last to be picked up by the guide. Mike rolled out of the pickup with his arms raised up in the air.

"I got one!" he yelled. He ran over to me with his digital camera in hand. I looked at the images and immediately started the back slaps. "He's a 9-point and I think he'll go 150, and he has a pretty big body too," Mike said.

The buck was with a doe in the second rut. It took him 25 minutes to reach the edge of the field where Mike was hunting. At one point he had a 50-yard shot at the buck, but his bouncing cross-hairs caused him to wait. "He was weaving through the thick brush, but very slow and diligent. He was very alert and did not want to come out!" Mike related. Ten minutes and 20 yards later, Mike made a perfect 30-yard shot at 4:25 p.m.

We went back to the lodge for supper and to get the four-wheeler. On the way back for the recovery, Mike had a revelation. "It worked!" he exclaimed. I asked him what he was talking about. "The shell and the turtleneck brought me good luck!" I guess they did.

Mike's buck grossed $156^1/_8$

Kenny and Mike Meyers killed their bucks of a lifetime in Missouri and Illinois, respectively. Kenny shot his 180-class nontypical in 2003, and Kenny shot his 150-class typical in 2004.

inches as a main-frame typical 8-point, with one G-3 broken. The deer was huge and weighed 276 pounds live weight.

A long series of pictures and celebration consumed the rest of the evening and part of the next morning. I had just picked up my buck from the taxidermist, and now we had more than 343 inches of antler on two deer, for two brothers with two lifetime bucks. I broke out my "backup blue turtleneck" for joint pictures. We get many questions about these blue shirts. All I can say is, "It worked for us!"

Mike and I compared score cards, and my buck beats his by only a half-inch on beam length,

but his has more than 2 inches more in mass circumference measurements. Both are high racks and are similarly framed, which is unique, considering the locations were at least two hours away, and across the Mississippi River. And, it looks like both will make the big bucks club in each respective state. Not bad for two brothers, on two hunts, with two lucky items and two lifetime bucks.

Now the shirt and two shells are in possession of our hunting buddy Jeff Phillips. Hopefully, they'll bring him luck on his Texas hunt. He said, "I'll try it. I believe!"

— *Kenny Myers*
Mt. Sidney, Va.

Ohio Woman Prayed Every Day She'd Get a Buck

I grew up in a hunting family and was fortunate enough to marry a wonderful man who is also an avid hunter. I've always loved the outdoors and especially being in the woods, but somehow never considered being a deer hunter until a few years ago, when I was almost 50.

I started going out in the woods with my husband, Jon, just to watch the wildlife and sometimes take videos of the hunt. It wasn't long before Jon bought me my own climbing stand so I could get a better view of the deer. He encouraged me to think about hunting, and the more I thought about it, the more I thought I'd like to give it a try. So we started practicing more with the gun and the crossbow, even though shooting is one of our favorite pastimes.

I bought my first hunting license in 1999 and saw quite a few deer, but didn't take a shot at anything that year. In 2000, I was determined to do better, and ended up shooting a nice 6-point with my crossbow. From that moment on, I was hooked for good. The following three years I took three more deer, all does — two with my shotgun and one with my crossbow.

In 2004, I really wanted to shoot another buck. Every day I would say a prayer that a buck would come within range. I saw several nice bucks during bow-season, but they were never close enough for a shot.

Days turned into weeks as I continued to pray for a buck. I was in the woods every chance I got. Because I had two tags this year, I shot a big doe with my crossbow in October. She offered me a perfect 20-yard shot from a stand that was in just the right spot. The other tag I saved for the buck I was hoping would come my way.

Gun season arrived, and although we hunted every day, I passed on many does without ever seeing a buck. That week came and went quickly, and I pinned my hopes of getting a buck on muzzleloader season after Christmas.

I have a .50-caliber inline muzzleloader. I had shot it quite a bit before Christmas, and knew it was dead-on, so I felt very comfortable taking it out.

The evening before the first day of muzzleloader season we got an unexpected snowfall, and instead of flurries, we had 1 to 2 inches of snow on the ground by morning. The day dawned bright and sunny, but the temperature hovered around 9 degrees through the morning, with winds out of the north at 10 mph. It didn't take long for the cold to seep right through me, even though I had several layers of clothes on. By the time Jon called me on the radio at 11:15 a.m. to see if I wanted to meet him and my dad for some coffee, I was more than ready to climb out of my tree.

We were going to meet at the gate on the trail at noon, but my hands were so numb I decided to climb down early and slowly walk to our meeting point while I got my circulation going again. I got my gear gathered up and started out through the woods. Last night's snow had frozen enough that it sounded like I was walking on cornflakes. I kept my eyes peeled for any deer that might have come out to feed.

Kathleen McCrea, of East Palestine, Ohio, prayed every day that she would get a buck during the 2004 season. As the season waned, she decided to shoot any good-sized deer. As she walked toward the large "doe," she realized she'd killed a big 11-point.

I had already had my customary talk with God while I was on the tree stand and asked him to guide me this day when the cold weather would determine how long I could sit in the woods. I decided that I would shoot at the first nice-sized deer that presented itself, buck or doe.

I hadn't walked far before I looked across a hardwood flat and saw what I thought could be the body of a deer. It was about 150 yards away and not moving, so I brought my scope up for a better look. Sure enough, I could see a

deer's body, but its head was completely behind a large tree. It looked like a nice-sized deer, so I dropped down on one knee to see if I could get a shot.

There were too many limbs and saplings in the way, so I started sliding across the snow on my knees, looking for an opening and praying that the deer wouldn't hear me in the crunchy snow.

I finally had a clear shooting lane and the deer was still in the same spot feeding, so I steadied my elbow on my knee and squeezed the trigger. All I could see was smoke for a few moments, but I was trying to see across the hillside where I thought the deer would run. I didn't see any movement, so I looked back to where the deer had been standing and realized I had dropped it in its tracks. I watched for a couple more minutes, but it didn't move. I gave thanks to God for a nice doe and a clean kill, then pulled out my radio to call Jon.

He hadn't heard the shot and was surprised when I told him I had just shot a big doe. He told me he'd pick up my dad at his stand, and then they would bring the cart to where I was. I said I'd walk over to look at my deer and wait for them there.

Then, the funniest thing happened. As I started walking across the woods toward my deer, I thought I saw an antler sticking up in the snow. I quickened my pace and as I got closer, more antlers appeared. I got back on the radio to Jon. "Honey, you're not going to believe this, but my doe is actually a buck." He wanted to know how big and I told him I thought it was an 8-point.

By now I was almost running through the woods with excitement. I jumped across a little run and finally reached my deer. I couldn't believe my eyes. In front of me lay a beautiful 11-point buck!

I called Jon again. "Honey, it's an 11-point." The closer I got, the bigger the buck got. Jon was almost as excited as I was.

While I waited for them to meet me, I thought about what a sense of humor God has. I realized He had been listening to me all along through the whole hunting season, but God answers in His own time, and I sincerely gave thanks for my answered prayer.

— *Kathleen McCrea*
East Palestine, Ohio

Taking of Large Missouri Buck is a Family Affair

When my friend Mike handed me a new osage selfbow he had just made and asked me what I thought of it, I simply said, "Wow!" I noticed the back and how he had followed a single growth ring from tip to tip. I noticed that it had a larger handle, just like I like to have on a bow. But mostly I noticed that this one was shorter than most of the bows he makes, and would be nice to handle in a tree stand.

Then he said, "Turn it over." There, on the belly of the upper limb he had written Matthew 5:16 which says, "Let your light so shine before men, that they may see your good works, and glorify your father which is in heaven." It was sealed under the clearcoat of the bow. Then I looked down at the bottom limb and there was written, "A bow for Randy."

Instantly my heart leaped into my throat. Mike just smiled as I looked up at him with tears in my eyes. I knew how much work he had put into making the bow because I had seen the tree right after he cut it down. I also knew how much those kind of custom bows sell for. I told him there was no way I could accept it. He simply said, "Yes you can." He'd been working on it all summer to make it just right. It pulls 58 pounds at 28 inches and throws a full-length wooden shaft with some

Randy Eason used his homemade bow – a surprise gift from his friend Mike – to arrow this Missouri whitetail. Several family members helped him trail the buck.

serious punch.

I told him I wouldn't have time before that bow-season to become proficient enough to hunt with it. Besides, we were in the process of getting ready for an elk hunt, and had been for several months. He simply told me that was OK and that he just wanted me to have it. I looked at him with all the conviction I could muster and stated, "All right, then I'm going to kill a deer with it!" He just smiled and said, "I'm sure you will."

That season started with a few lows, but ended on a couple of high notes. The Lord blessed several of us with some nice bucks for the wall that year. When the summer rolled around, my conviction was starting to weigh heavily on me. With several months of practice and a couple of 3D shoots under my belt, I was starting to gain confidence in my new weapon.

Now, I'm no Myles Keller or Chuck Adams. I'm just a guy who feels 20 feet closer to God when I'm up a tree. I'm a guy who goes out to shoot a deer and finds myself thanking the Lord more for a beautiful sunrise or sunset. But I'm also a guy who likes to see some fruits for my labor. And after a few weeks of sitting and watching the squirrels and birds, I kind of need to at least see a deer.

My problem wasn't seeing one. I had several within what most would consider a competent compound shooter's range. But nothing came close to what I felt confidant was my personal longbow range.

Then, one Saturday morning in the rain, my feathers went flat and I cracked. I went home, screwed some broadheads on my aluminum arrows and dusted off my compound. You can probably guess where I started seeing deer then. That's right, outside of my effective rifle range!

I was beginning to pile a heap of pressure on myself to "get one down," so I could go back to my close-range wooden bow. And I stopped having fun.

Then, one morning as my 3-year-old daughter Rachel and I were lounging around the house flipping through the channels, we came across the movie *Robin Hood*. That did it for her. I wasn't allowed to change the channel again after that. Finally she turned and looked at me saying, "He's got a bow like you Daddy!" We rooted harder for the "merry men" that day than had been done since the days of King Richard! When it was over, I hugged her and said, "I'm going to be the first person to kill a deer with a Sytkowski bow."

The following Saturday found me back in the woods with my longbow. I only saw one deer that evening, but at least I enjoyed my evening sit.

Sunday morning I was up before the alarm and jumped in the shower with my unscented soap. After putting on some extra clothes to stave off the drop in temperature, I noticed a string hanging from the top of my closet. When I reached up and pulled on it, my rattling antlers came tumbling down. As an afterthought, I stuck them in my quiver and headed out the door.

It was a long, dark walk that morning. After I settled into my stand, I said a prayer for the landowner whose husband had passed away only a week before. He was one of the happiest men I ever knew and was always genuinely excited when I had any kind of luck while hunting there. I only wished

I'd known him longer. I couldn't help but think that if something good was going to happen with my stickbow, I wanted it to be there on the place that Forrest had loved so much.

As the sky started to lighten, I could hear the critters moving around. The leaves were dry and I'd been settled in for more than 30 minutes, so things had already settled back down. When you sit like a stone day after day, eventually you get fidgety; at least I do. I'd lost several hours of sleep over the last three weeks and my body didn't want to pretend to be a piece of vegetation any longer.

Then I remembered the antlers. I had draped them over a limb above me and to my left. I could only reach one of them, so I picked it up and just kind of tickled it against the other one for a few seconds and let it rest back against the tree. My urge to fidget had subsided and I felt I hadn't made too much noise.

About 15 minutes later my legs started to go to sleep. I tried tightening and relaxing the muscles to wake them up, and reached for the antler again. I'd just started to tickle them together when I heard what sounded like a freight train crashing through the woods in my direction. As I dropped the antler and turned to look, all I could see were antlers; big ones! They were attached to an angry buck with wild eyes and flaring nostrils.

He charged in and stopped 8 feet in front of me, but his vitals were covered by limbs. I barely remember doing it, but somehow I managed to get to my feet. The buck only stood there for about the count of three before deciding that something wasn't right and turning to flee. His last bad decision was to turn and run under my stand. As he passed at a trot, I drew and released. The tapered pine shaft struck the buck midship, angling forward. I watched him trot out of sight with most of my arrow inside him. I was worried that I might not have gotten an exit wound, but I felt good about the hit.

That's when the shakes set in. I had to grab the tree with both hands to keep from falling out of my stand. It was 7:53 a.m. I heard the buck's hoofs hit the rocks in the creek, and I thought I heard him go down. I waited 30 minutes, climbed down, and tiptoed out of there.

I pulled out my cell phone and called Mike. I wanted him to be the first to know. He was beside himself, relaying my every word to everyone at his house while I hoofed it out of the woods.

I knew my oldest daughter, Danielle, was spending the night with my folks, and I wanted all the eyes I could get to help look for blood. As it turned out, my brother's two girls were there too, and my brother showed up shortly after I got there.

It had taken me an hour to walk out of the woods, and we waited another hour for good measure. I paced the whole time. Before long though, me, my dad, my brother, his girls and Danielle were scanning the leaves. I don't know if it's because they are closest to the ground or what, but those kids were seeing things that I couldn't. It was my brother that the Lord blessed with vision that day. He was picking out little spots that my racing heart wouldn't allow me to slow down and see. He got us on the right track, found where the buck crossed the fence, and kept us pointed in the right direction.

Then it started. A splash here and a splash there, with my dad leading the way. The three girls were right on his heels, as excited as a pack of young beagles after a rabbit. "Here's some. There's some. He went this way," they would say. Then dad stopped and pointed up the hill. I couldn't see the deer, but I charged forward, ahead of the pack. As tears welled up in my eyes I stood over my prize. I tilted my head back and yelled, "Thank you, Lord! And thank you, Mike!" Never in my wildest dreams did I imagine taking an animal like this. Especially with a true stick and string. And a home-made wooden arrow to boot.

The greatest thing about the whole day was the fact that I got to share the experience with everyone, and the fact that so many had a hand in it. Mike has given me so much more than just a bow. What I got to share with my family that day is priceless. And to accomplish it this way is a blessing from God that few will ever realize.

As I reflect on my life, I have received some tremendous gifts. My parents' gift of birth, and into a hunting heritage. God's gift of my children. But most of all, the Father's unmatchable gift of His only begotten Son.

I've always felt blessed just by Mike's friendship and the adventures that we've shared together. Thanks, Mike!

— *Randy Eason*
Freeman, Mo.

Troy Stephens had to borrow a shotgun, shells and hunting clothes, but he didn't let his unfamiliar equipment handicap him. He killed this 16-pointer on Nov. 25, 1996. The buck netted 198 inches and stands as the Michigan state-record typical.

Hunter Takes Record Buck With Borrowed Gun

Luck often plays an important role in the taking of some of the largest bucks. A case in point is Michigan's current state record typical — a massive 16-pointer that grosses 214$^3/_8$ inches, with a net score of 198.

That whitetail was the highest-scoring typical known taken in North America in 1996. Troy Stephens of Jackson, Mich., shot the world-class buck on the morning of Nov. 25 that year. Stephens shot the buck with a borrowed shotgun and shells while wearing borrowed hunting clothes, and hunting in an area he had never hunted before.

Stephens had been unemployed for a while, which is why he had to borrow the gun and accessories he used on the hunt. William Gregory, who was his mother's boyfriend at the time, had a gun collection, and he was kind enough to lend Stephens shotguns and other deer hunting equipment over for several years. During his record-breaking hunt, Stephens was using a smoothbore 12-gauge with a bead sight.

On the evening of Nov. 24, 1996, one of Stephens' friends invited him to go deer hunting the following morning in Jackson County, Mich. Stephens gratefully accepted because he still had an unfilled tag.

There were 2 inches of fresh snow on the ground by the following morning, and the white blanket set the stage for Stephens' success.

As Stephens and his host drove, looking for a spot to hunt, they saw a well-used deer trail marked by numerous fresh tracks, coming out of a cornfield. A wedge of woods extended into the cornfield where the trail was. It was a logical place for whitetails to move from the field into the woods without exposing themselves any more than necessary.

Failing to find anything that looked better, Stephens decided to watch the well-used runway leaving the cornfield. He set up a folding chair about 10 feet into the woods so he would have some cover between him and any deer that exited the cornfield, reducing the chances he would be seen. He was in position before first light on that chilly morning, with the temperature in the teens.

"Just as it started to get light, I saw two deer come out of the cornfield," Stephens said. "I could see shadows over one deer's head, so I knew it was a buck. The sun started to come up as they got closer, and I could see a little bit of rack on the buck's head.

"I was wearing real thick gloves due to the cold. I had to take the glove on my shooting hand off before I could shoot so I could slip my finger into the trigger guard. I wasn't sure how good the buck was, but I was going to make him look at me. I dropped the glove hard on the snow. It was a still morning, so the sound of the glove hitting the ground was easy to hear.

"The buck looked my way, then put his head down and kept walking. He was following a doe. I put the gun up and took my time, carefully putting the sights on him. The gun was loaded with buckshot and slugs, with buckshot in the chamber.

"My first shot hit him in the front leg and he started limping. After I shot, he started heading for the woods. I jumped up and ran after him. Then I took another shot, but I couldn't tell if that one hit him. Right before he got in the woods, I took one more shot and he dropped right there."

A copper-plated 00 buckshot pellet to the brain stopped the book buck. Stephens' taxidermist found the fatal chunk of lead when removing the buck's skull plate prior to mounting the head. Based on examination of the carcass, it appeared as though Stephens' second shot, a slug, also connected.

After waiting 15 to 20 minutes, Stephens walked up to the fallen buck and confirmed it was dead. It wasn't until he lifted the enormous rack that he saw how big it was.

"I was pretty excited when I saw how big the horns were," Stephens said. "They didn't look that big when I first saw the deer. I could tell he had horns, but I didn't know how many points there were. I thought maybe there were 8 or 10 points."

The state-record deer was only the third whitetail that Stephens had taken. He shot an 8-pointer when he was 15 or 16, and a 9-pointer in 1995.

The story behind the Stephens Buck should serve as inspiration for every whitetail hunter who dreams of shooting a big buck. If Stephens could bag a state-record buck with borrowed equipment in a spot he had never hunted before, there's hope for everyone. It's simply a matter of being in the right place at the right time. Sometimes a whim or taking advantage of an unexpected opportunity can be the most important factor in the big-buck equation.

The rack from the Stephens Buck has a typical 12-point frame and four sticker points. Total length of the sticker points is $6^6/8$ inches. If they had been absent, the net score of the antlers would have broken the 200 mark, putting the final tally at $204^6/8$ inches.

Exceptional tine and beam length and good mass contributed to the rack's tremendous score. The right beam measured $29^2/8$ inches, and the left beam was $^2/8$ inch longer. The inside spread was $20^2/8$ inches.

Brow tines were outstanding, measuring 10 and $11^3/8$ inches. The G-2s on each side were the longest, taping $13^2/8$ and $13^4/8$ inches. G-3s and G-4s were between 9 and 11 inches.

Two of the four circumferences on the right beam were more than 5 inches. Three of those measurements exceeded 5 inches on the left beam. Interestingly, the greatest circumference of $5^4/8$ inches was recorded between the G-3 and G-4 on the right side.

The Stephens Buck, along with other exceptional whitetails from Michigan and across North America, are on display at the Michigan Whitetail Hall of Fame Museum east of Jackson.

— *Richard P. Smith*

Hunter Slips Into Stand Only 50 Yards From Buck

Brian Cozzolino of Holden, Mass., slipped into his stand very quietly on Nov. 8, 2004. In fact, he climbed into his stand without alerting this 166-inch 10-pointer, which was bedded about 50 yards away. He arrowed the buck minutes later.

Brian Cozzolino of Holden, Mass., is an avid deer hunter, choosing to hunt exclusively with archery tackle on a 120-acre lot near his home. Over the years he has taken several nice bucks from the property, including five 8-pointers, one of which scored in the mid-120s.

"The lot is a natural buck magnet," explains Cozzolino.

"Bucks consistently funnel in from the surrounding area, making it a real hot spot for the entire season. In fact, the area is so good I often sit in my stand all day long, knowing that at any moment I might tag a monster trophy buck."

On Nov. 8, 2004, Cozzolino's persistence paid off when he arrowed his best buck ever, and one of the best bucks to ever come out of Massachusetts.

"I hunted a stand at first light on the far side of the property with the intention of hanging a new stand in the same area after the morning hunt," Cozzolino said. "Nothing was moving, so I got down out of my stand around 10:00, went back to my truck and gathered up my equipment, then returned to the woodlot and positioned a new stand. I completed the task by noon, went home and showered. I returned to the woodlot later in the afternoon and climbed into a different stand on the other side of the lot around 3:15. It was clear and sunny that afternoon, although a bit windy. It was a good day to be in the woods.

"This stand is only 70 yards or so off the road. Nonetheless, I made it a point to sneak in quietly because I knew does have a tendency to bed nearby in the late afternoon. Normally, I finish dressing in my stand, but because I was so close to my vehicle, I arrived ready for action. I quickly ascended into the stand and hooked on my safety harness.

"I was only in position a few minutes when something caught my attention. I thought it was a deer's eye. I looked and looked and suddenly I realized a doe was bedded in the laurels only 35 yards away! She must have been there when I climbed into my stand. All I could think was 'you've got to be kidding!'

"I thought everything would be OK as long as I didn't spook her, so I settled down and waited. I kept looking in her direction when I suddenly saw a giant rack sway-ing back and forth in a figure-8 pattern about 15 yards behind her. Unbelievable! He must have been bedded there all along, too!

"This buck sure had my attention. The rack was just massive! I couldn't keep my eyes off that patch of laurel now.

"About 15 minutes later, the doe got up and starting coming down the hill, taking her time. She stopped in the middle of one of my shooting lanes about 32 yards out, urinated, and then moved on down the hill, eventually disappearing into some thick stuff.

"That's when the buck rose from his bed and meandered down behind the doe along the same trail she used. I could see his long tines clearly now, and I prepared myself for a shot. He soon entered my shooting lane, stopping right where the doe urinated. It was perfect. I drew back, held steady and released. The arrow hit with a resounding 'whack,' and the buck ran off with my arrow sticking out of his shoulder.

"The blood trail was spotty and it was getting dark, so I returned to my truck and enlisted the help of one of my good friends, Jeff Zottoli. We eventually found the 175-pound 10-pointer piled up only 50 yards from where I shot, with a feathered arrow buried deep in his left lung. I had the $4^1/_2$-year-old buck scored by Jeff Brown, co-founder of the Northeast Big Buck Club. It netted $166^3/_8$ inches, making it my best buck to date, and one of the top-five archery bucks to ever come out of the Bay State!"

— *Bill Vaznis*

N.Y. Traditional Archer Arrows Big 6-Pointer

It was a rainy November afternoon in 2004 as I bow-hunted for whitetails along the famous Grand Canyon of the East — the famed Genesee River Valley of New York. This area consists of rich farmlands and hardwoods ideally suited to whitetails.

I was sitting in my tree stand, located along a hayfield just inside a mixed pine and hardwood stand. The smells of fresh, wet earth scents drifted on the air currents as west winds picked up. This is the magical time of year for bow-hunters. The whitetail rut was about to explode at any time.

The afternoon was passing without much activity, and I didn't see a deer until about 3 p.m. Then, I glassed a few does and fawns moving from heavy cover out into the hayfields to feed.

Kirk Schroeder, of Castile, N.Y., was bow-hunting with his recurve when a doe, a 4-pointer and a 6-pointer cruised past his stand. He arrowed the 6-pointer at 10 yards.

Without warning, a doe came crashing down one of the three trails near my setup. Right behind her was a yearling 4-pointer, with a heavy-racked 6-pointer hot on his tail, grunting and trying to get ahead of the younger buck. They went wide to my left, breaking pine branches as they darted through the dense cover and out of sight.

Moments later, the loud grunting headed in my direction again. This time the bigger buck was alone. It hit me that he had lost the doe and was trying to pick up her scent again. I quickly pulled out my can call and tipped it three times. The buck came crashing through the pines on a straight line to me. I grabbed my recurve and swung it in the stand. The buck was only 10 yards to my left. I came to full draw and grunted with my mouth, stopping the buck long enough to watch my broadhead disappear into his side. After watching this great buck running straight away with my arrow buried up to the orange-and-white feathers, the fear came over me that I may have gotten only one lung. As darkness began to fall, I decided to wait until morning and hopefully pick up a good blood trail.

After a very long night of little sleep, at first light I was back at my stand. I picked up a good blood trail within 20 yards of my shot. Only 40 yards farther lay my trophy, with antlers sticking up high. As I held the heavy-racked 6-point in my hands, I gave thanks to our Creator for this great River Valley whitetail.

— *Kirk Schroeder*
Castile, N.Y.

Darrell Daigre shot this 168-inch whopper after his hunting partner rattled it in on Jan. 18, 2005. They were hunting on a 15,000-acre parcel in Alabama.

Alabama Landholding Coughs Up 168-Incher

Although 160-inch bucks are rare all across whitetail country, they are especially uncommon in the South. But Darrell Daigre discovered one such monster in Alabama.

Mossy Oak, in cooperation with International Paper, has been aggressively managing a 15,000-acre tract of land west of Montgomery, Ala., known as Portland Landing. The holding is split into two sections; 9,000 acres are dedicated to gun hunting, with the remaining 6,000 acres set aside for archers.

Prior to the partnership between Mossy Oak and International Paper, which is now in its fourth year, Portland Landing was a commercial hunting lease known for its abundant deer, but lacking in the quality of the animals inhabiting the range.

Today, with International Paper's sound timber-management and tree-harvesting schedule, along with Mossy Oak's aggressive wildlife plan, which includes several varieties of food plots, trophy-class deer have become a reality.

Daigre pointed out, "We are not a trophy-hunting operation. Our herd is managed for quality, balance and age structure. With hundreds of stands scattered throughout the property, any hunter visiting Portland Landing has an equal opportunity in harvesting a quality buck."

After dropping off hunters at their stands on the afternoon of Jan. 18, Daigre and Mossy Oak co-worker Lannie Wallace set out to lure this buck, which they had seen the evening before, into shooting range. Due to wind direction, the two hunters had to cautiously slip halfway across a huge clear-cut in order to set up within a narrow finger of woods jutting into the expanse.

By mutual agreement, Daigre would be the shooter, and he hung his stand 20 yards in front of Wallace, who remained on the ground, concealed within a huge deadfall. It wasn't long after Wallace began to rattle that things heated up. A young buck came instantly to the antlers. Once the juvenile finally wandered off, Wallace became a lot more aggressive with his mock buck fight. He violently banged the antlers together, raked nearby trees and scraped the ground. His performance was so convincing that a 140-class 8-pointer brazenly waltzed onto the scene, obviously looking for a piece of the action. According to Wallace, "This buck was so convinced my mock battle was the real deal that he actually walked within 10 feet of me and stood staring into my hideout."

With one eye on the buck, and his other on Daigre, Wallace wondered, "Why isn't Darrell shooting this buck?" What Wallace didn't know was his comrade was now staring at the biggest buck of his life, which was sauntering out of a streamside management area and toward their position. Fortunately, the 8-pointer became disinterested and took off, allowing Daigre to visibly communicate to his partner to rattle again.

Once the antlers came together, the buck closed the distance. Confidently locked on target, Daigre's .280 roared, and before the echo from the shot disappeared, the buck folded.

The 11-pointer grossed $168^{6}/_{8}$ inches and had a live weight of 176 pounds.

— *R.G. Bernier*

Keystone Man Witnesses Fury of Rut Activity

I hunt with a crossbow because I have a bad arthritic right shoulder. I obtained a disabled crossbow permit from the Pennsylvania Game Commission several years ago. For a year and a half, I gave up bow-hunting because of the pain I had, until I got the permit. I would still rather be able to hunt with a regular bow.

It was Saturday, Nov. 1, 2003, in Craley, Pa. I usually get up between 2 a.m. and 4 a.m., as I have for 40-odd years. Rarely do I plan what I'm going to do from one day to the next since I retired more than five years ago.

I bought my house and 4.52 acres 12 years ago. My wife and I have taken a half-dozen deer on the property, even though she doesn't bow-hunt and I usually go elsewhere to deer hunt. It's very thick, steep terrain below the house, and deer bed and feed on wild grapes and paw-paws.

A few years ago, I cut some trails through the bush, and most of the time deer just travel past my land, but I have permission to hunt all the neighbor's land. I just have to be careful of the kids, pets and horses, and respect the safety laws.

I normally hunt the last week in October, as it's usually cooler weather. I'd started to find some rubs and some big tracks.

Just before daylight, I sneaked down and looked for the best spot to stand (I don't hunt from tree stands). I tried five places, then finally went back to the fourth place I tried. I backed up against a double tree, from which I could shoot from either side. I settled in about 7:10 a.m.

It was a bit warmer and more humid than I would have liked, and I didn't really expect deer to be moving.

I was hunting close to the edge of my property, which connects with land owned by a farmer whom I know well. He told me about a nice buck he had seen near the creek.

About 8 a.m., I heard, "grunt, grunt, grunt," really quick and I kept hearing it. I thought someone was using a grunt call and didn't know how to use it. I thought, "that's getting closer," and all of a sudden, here they came: a huge doe, followed by a big buck. There was also another doe, a spike buck and four fawns, all within 25 yards. All of their tongues were hanging out, and the huge buck's hair was standing up from his neck to his tail.

I was just above a narrow bench, which the big doe slipped on and fell down. The spike buck (which was about six steps in front of me, but wasn't legal) was walking toward the big doe when the big buck charged it and knocked it down.

When I first saw the big 10-point, I thought to myself, "I'm never going to get a shot at that big boy." I was just about to shoot the big doe when she took off with the big buck in hot pursuit. The spike got back up and limped away with its tail between its legs. The spike, the smaller doe and her fawn went off to the right, into the thick stuff. The big doe, her three fawns and the big buck went to my left, then up the hill and out of sight.

I slowly looked around me and couldn't hear or see anything, so I thought, "I'm never going to get a shot at that big buck again!"

Bob Shultz of Wrightsville, Pa., was hunting on his 4½-acre parcel when he saw this buck chasing other deer. Shultz made the 22-yard shot on the 10-pointer.

All at once, about 70 yards away, I saw the three fawns run straight down the hill. I waited. Right behind them came the big doe, with the big buck still after her.

When they were about 30 yards away, I whistled two sharp blasts. The buck stopped on a dime, facing away from me at 22 steps. I had about 4 inches of vitals showing for a perfect shot. I held my breath and squeezed the trigger. I watched the fletching disappear into the buck. The big buck lunged and took off down the steep hill, and I heard it crash.

Below me was Fishing Creek and a field. I never saw the buck cross the creek. Then I saw a white half-circle going around. When it stopped moving, it hit me that the buck was down and out. (It took me three days after seeing this before my heart rate settled back down.)

It was incredible, because I am far from being a trophy hunter. The 10-point buck was 216 pounds hog dressed and netted 156⅛ inches. The longest tine is 11 inches and the inside spread is 18⅞ inches.

Probably from the time I first heard the grunting until I saw the buck's tail stop moving was less than 2 minutes. The 10-point buck was dead within 20 seconds. I have never experienced all that chasing and grunting in such a short time. I'd like to thank the buck that gave up his life for a die-hard hunter.

I still refuse to be a trophy hunter. I don't think I'll ever reach that caliber! The thrill of the hunt is more important to me!

— *Bob Shultz*
Wrightsville, Pa.

Pennsylvania Man Has Mature Bucks Diagnosed

I have a theory on hunting mature bucks that other hunters often frown upon. While my buddies are heading for the deep woods to set up their stands, I prefer to hit the corner of my favorite goldenrod field. Sometimes I even set up in big oak trees right in the middle of goldenrod fields.

I have listened to my comrades discuss their strategy of cutting off bucks as they leave their bedding area, or setting up in bottlenecks to ambush bucks on their way to a feeding spot. As a matter of fact, those were my exact hunting strategies for many years. I have never had difficulty harvesting a buck during the archery season. I have, however, had great difficulty harvesting mature bucks, as most of us have, until a change in hunting habits resulted in three success stories.

My open-field theory works best when small-game or turkey season coincides with archery season. Turkey hunters penetrate the woods well before daylight, pushing deer and changing their normal movement pattern. In the past, I'd seen bucks move to open fields and planned my hunting strategy accordingly. It's not uncommon for me to see more than one buck bedded in an open field, cautiously watching the woods. The following hunting stories describe my open-field hunting strategy, and how hunting open fields has provided me the opportunity to successfully bag mature bucks three years in a row.

The afternoon of Oct. 30, 1999, in northwestern Pennsylvania was clear, crisp and cool. After seemingly endless unexpected delays, I was finally at my favorite hunting spot.

The day had been hectic, and by afternoon, I had virtually given up hope of making it out to hunt. Usually, nothing would keep me from an evening hunt, but my wife's car broke down, and she needed to get to work. Some things, even a dedicated hunter like myself knows, must take precedence over hunting time.

As one aggravating thing led to another, I tried to convince myself that missing one evening of hunting wouldn't be so bad, but in the back of my mind a little voice was screaming, "Why me? Why now? I live to hunt and all I ask is to have archery season for myself. I work hard to fulfill all of my obligations to family, friends and my job before archery season. Those who are nearest and dearest respect the fact that for a few precious weeks I am totally committed to archery."

Just after 3 p.m., things calmed down. However, another crisis had erupted in my mind — do I hunt? There was time, but I wasn't totally prepared for hunting. I was wearing my leather work boots and I might spook deer if I wore them. I was tired, frustrated, close to being angry and feeling a little sorry for myself. I knew the chances of seeing a buck were slim, but I couldn't throw in the towel and call it a day. I decided to hunt, just to let Mother Nature

Don Baker, of Centerville, Pa., poses with a 9-point buck he shot in 1999. He killed it using his "open-field" hunting method.

work her magic on my troubled heart. Nothing can lighten my heart or calm my spirit like being in the woods. A trip to the tree stand would be therapeutic, even if it was unproductive.

The plan worked. Mother Nature worked her spell on me. As the day wore on and the afternoon sun began to drop in the autumn sky, I felt more relaxed than ever. In fact, I was in a Zen-like state, staring at one spot, half asleep. But my trance quickly vanished. I can't recall if I had heard a noise, but for whatever reason, I glanced over my shoulder, feeling an over-whelming sense of anticipation.

A doe stepped out and proceeded in my direction. I cautiously and quietly rose from my seat, not expecting to see a buck because the rut wouldn't begin for about another week. A deep grunt from the corner of the field immediately sent a rush of adrenaline coursing through my veins, increasing my heart rate to a deep thudding in my chest. Large antlers magically appeared behind the doe, slowly trailing her through the field. That magnificent rack became my main focus; everything else was a blur.

My thoughts were soon inter-rupted by the sound of hoofs approaching the bottom of my tree stand. The doe stopped and nervously sniffed the leaf-covered ground near the base of my tree. As I stood in the old oak tree, a suffocating anxiety swept over me. The doe may have picked up on my scent from the path I had walked on. The doe reared up, eyes filled with fear, as she bucked backwards and scurried around the trunk of the tree and into the densely wooded lot.

I knew the buck would be on red alert. My mind overflowed with strategies. I tried to turn and face the buck's direction, but no matter how hard I tried, my safety belt prevented me from turning around. Panic filled my body as the buck moved closer to my tree. Should I stay still? Should I risk spooking this magnificent creature? Deciding on a daring move, I turned completely around to see a familiar face, the elusive "Snow Buck."

Even in this intense situation, I could recall my first encounter with this beautiful creature. The previous year, 1998, the buck had circled my stand, and after picking up my scent, vanished like a ghost. Earl Snow's farm had provided a virtual safe haven for the buck for at least two seasons. A few hunters had seen the elusive buck, and he had become almost a legend in the area.

I was overcome with delight when I saw him again while scouting in June 1999. I had crawled along a blackberry trail to catch a glimpse of a lone deer feeding in the woods. I began to tremble like a crying baby as I got my first close-up look at the magnificent creature. The "Snow Buck" had survived the previous hunting season and was standing before me oblivious to my presence. I watched the deer until he was gone from sight. Yet, for fear of over-scouting the area, I had not seen the buck, a majestic 9-point, until this fateful day.

As the buck drew near, I brought my bow to full draw. The deer was about 25 yards away, well within range, but unfortunately, a small branch blocked my shot. Patiently I waited for him to step out, clearing the branch and giving me a clear shot. The buck finally took half a step forward. Just as my pin was settling on the mark, the deer turned to bolt. In the heat of the moment, I pulled the trigger on my release. As the arrow pierced the buck's chest, the buck took off like a jet plane. After running 80 yards, the buck crumbled in the thick sea of goldenrod.

I felt incredible, knowing that I had just accomplished a lifetime goal. After waiting for what felt like an eternity, I descended from my tree stand and entered the ocean of goldenrod that had engulfed my trophy buck. With pride pulsing in my chest, I walked in the direction the deer had fallen. When the beautiful 9-point rack came into sight, I fell to my knees and thanked God for the wonderful buck.

The $3^1/_2$-year-old buck weighed 200 pounds, and the antlers grossed 133 inches. After taking some pictures, I noticed something unusual. The buck had a double throat patch.

As months went by and the excitement of killing the buck

Don Baker hunted exclusively for this 7-point buck during Pennsylvania's 2000 bow-season. He missed it twice, then finally bagged it on the last day of the season.

wore down, I was hoping to harvest another big buck in the upcoming season. My hunting partners tried to stifle my spirits, saying the odds of taking another mature buck would be almost impossible. Due to the high concentration of hunters, most bucks only live 1½ years in our area. If a buck does have the opportunity to mature, he is often hard to pattern and usually nocturnal, due to hunting pressure. In

hoping to prove them wrong, in 2000, I would embark on another all-out battle with a magnificent whitetail.

Third Time's a Charm on Lucky 7

My archery season was winding down on a cloudy November day in northwestern Pennsylvania. I found myself sitting on my stand at 8 a.m. with only one day left to hunt. The temperature hovered at 40 degrees. I reflected on this season and how I had dedicated all my efforts to harvesting a particular 7-point buck. My persistence had given me two opportunities to draw my bow on this magnificent creature, only to have my arrows be deflected by tiny limbs. I knew that having these two chances was good fortune and the probability of another shot was slim. However, after all of the time and effort put into hunting this buck, I was committed to finish the season in the buck's territory.

With the rut in full swing, it looked as if the buck was the official king of the hill, having made it to the end of the season despite local hunters' attempts to outsmart him. Daydreaming a bit on my stand, I recalled the highlights of the season. It felt like yesterday when I caught my first glimpse of the 7-point. I was amazed how this animal managed to keep his presence a secret to area archers until just before the season began.

The endless hours of scouting and patterning had panned out, and the buck's secrets were no longer his own. I had become a part of the animal's domain. For my labors, I was granted the opportunity to have the buck within my grasp, only to have fate intervene and the buck slip from my reach. Standing high on the platform of the tree stand, I realized that this was the final morning that I would be able to enjoy this passion until next year. Was it worth it?

I had passed up several smaller bucks in hopes of bagging the king of the hill. Only in the few hours remaining would the answer to my question become evident.

A slight movement in the corner of the swamp caught my eye and redirected my attention. A small buck was rapidly approaching my stand from the corner of the swamp. He looked to be a little 6-point and paid no attention to what was ahead of him. He seemed to be retreating from a nemesis stalking him from behind.

Then, out of the shadows of the swamp emerged the force he was fleeing. There, in all his glory, was the magnificent 7-point buck I had been pursuing this entire season. I stared in disbelief as the chase drew near. It was barely possible to believe the surreal scenario unfolding below my stand.

The smaller buck worked his way directly toward my tree stand in his attempt to flee the ghostly presence that pursued him. The larger, more aggressive deer fearlessly stalked the weaker deer. Both were oblivious to the shadowy figure high above them in a hemlock tree.

As the pair of rutting bucks drew near, the innate hunter instinct within me quickly emptied my mind of all emotion. Instinctively my grip on the bow handle tightened as I quickly, yet quietly, shifted into proper stance. My mind focused on aiming and following through with the shot.

As the buck approached an opening in the twisted thicket, I knew the moment of truth was near. With my bow at full draw, I settled the pin on the buck's chest. The beautiful 7-point looked straight up as I released the shot. The arrow humanely hit its mark and I knew that the diligence, hard

Don Baker spotted this buck with a hot doe, then slipped in on it the following day. He grunted in the 8-pointer while hunting on the ground.

work and persistence had paid off. I immediately gave thanks for the blessing that had been bestowed upon me.

The buck ran 100 yards before staggering and crashing to the ground. I could hardly contain my excitement. While waiting, thoughts of the season once again raced through my mind. The hours of scouting and patterning the buck now seem like only minutes. The previous two encounters, when fate had so cruelly intervened, now became fleeting images as I waited to claim my trophy.

My knees began to shake and my heart soared as I climbed down from the hemlock tree. In my heart, I knew the well-deserved trophy was mine, and the third time had truly been a charm.

Today, this magnificent 7-point buck is proudly displayed in my home. Field dressed, the 3½-year-old buck weighed 160 pounds — a fine buck for such a heavily hunted area.

Ground Attack on the Tree Warrior

Standing on a Crawford County, Pa., hillside in my ground blind the last week of the 2003 archery season, I was contemplating my final week of vacation and the prospect that the best part of bowseason was about to close. All at once a gust of wind from the north ripped through the dried, dead leaves attached to the small oak saplings scattered on the hillside. In the blink of an eye, rain came pouring down, pelting me in the face like June bugs slapping into a motorcycle helmet. Even though I was dressed in layers, my aging camouflaged body wouldn't stop shivering. I stood frozen like Santa Claus watching the hillside for a rutting Rudolph.

A north wind had come up in the night, bringing the promise of winter over my curve of the world. The morning sun was lost in the black, rainy sky, with the prospect of snow sure to follow. Deer seemed to all but vanish, probably hunkering down in some steep ravine sheltered from the storm.

With time running out and all the elements against me, I was playing mind games as a last resort to keep from giving in. I don't know what it is about steep ravines, but I don't like hunting them. I often get busted when the wind changes. I've found it's best to hunt in a draw only if the wind is light and steady, and blowing in the same direction as the draw. Still mornings present the best opportunity to hunt in a ravine. Thermal breezes go down the slope in the morning until well in the day, when the sun warms the area.

After three hours of hunting, my fingers and toes were getting cold, but I didn't want to leave because past experience had taught me that during the rut is the best time to see a buck. Mature bucks often bed down before daylight and wait until late morning or midday to cruise the edges and interior of bedding areas and scent-check for estrous does.

After following a huge set of tracks the day before into a steep, brushy ravine on the back side of a standing cornfield, I located a big buck guarding a doe next to a treetop. Time was a factor because I didn't know how much longer the buck would stay with the doe before moving on, looking for the next receptive doe. I had no choice but to get in there and hunt, even though high winds were against me.

The next morning, I decided against trying to climb a tree with my climbing stand. The wind would probably blow my scent all around, and climbing a tree would be too noisy. Instead, I slipped in silently, close to the treetop. I stood with my back against a birch tree just above a small stream in the valley. A small pine tree in front of me helped break up my outline and keep me hidden in the shadows. A small trail through the blackberries a few yards above me snaked its way past a nearby beech tree, then turned toward the bottom of the ravine. The bend in the trail was about 60 yards away, near the treetop where the buck was holed up.

After three hours of standing with zero sightings, my patience was all but used up. If I stayed much longer, I would probably look like Frosty the Snowman stuck to the side of the tree.

When the rain suddenly let up, I decided to blow on my grunt tube before giving up. All at once, two small bucks poked their heads up from a blackberry patch and started moving along the side of the ravine. A big buck charged out of the treetop, chasing off the immature bucks, then turned around, walking back into the treetop. I gave another call and the warrior once again came walking around the bend toward me.

I thought to myself, "If the buck gets to the big beech tree, I'll draw my bow." The buck was half-stepping and really fired up, wanting to know where the grunting was coming from. Afraid to move for fear he would see me, I stood like a soldier patiently waiting. When the gray-faced buck made it to the tree, he quickly turned around and headed back to the treetop. I swung my bow with him to try to get a shot through a small opening as he passed by, but couldn't.

I reached for my grunt tube in desperation and called again. Within seconds, he reappeared around the bend. Hair bristled on his back, and his eyes were fire red as he walked stiff-legged my way. He stopped right in my opening and started making a scrape. My heart was pounding as I came to full draw. My first impulse was to hammer the trigger on my release, but I calmed down and squeezed the trigger. The arrow found its mark. The buck wheeled around and ran back down the ravine where he stumbled sideways and almost went down.

As I stood shaking after the deer disappeared, a course of adrenaline flowed through my veins. Every fiber in my body was a live wire ready to explode. Suddenly, Mr. Frosty was no longer cold. I felt like the man of steel, who had just captured a once-in-a-lifetime moment. I replayed the scene over and over in my mind to make sure it was real and not a dream.

The last place I remember seeing the deer was 80 yards away beside three trees that grew close together in a small clearing by the stream. The three trees would make a good reference point if I had a difficult blood trail to follow. It was also where the buck stumbled and almost went down before regaining his balance and turning uphill.

With the tracking job at hand, I knew it was too early to celebrate. Being too hasty when claiming your trophy is a serious mistake.

After waiting an hour, I began the search and soon spotted a piece of my broken arrow on the blackberry trail near the scrape. The 4-inch piece of arrow with the fletching must have broken after hitting bone.

I followed the trail to the three trees, then up the hill along the ravine. Just ahead, a deer jumped up from a treetop and ran down into the draw. Not taking any chances of pushing the deer, I decided to wait until the next morning before trying to recover the deer.

The next morning, after little sleep, I recovered the buck right where the other deer jumped up from the treetop. The other deer must have been the hot doe the buck had been with. Even though it wasn't necessary to wait until the next morning before taking up the trail again, it's better to be safe than sorry.

The big 8-pointer had 21-inch main beams and 5-inch bases. I was overwhelmed with joy, and thanked God for a wonderful trophy.

— *Donald J. Baker*
Centerville, Pa.

New Friendship Helps Iowa Man Bag a Monster

Saturday, Nov. 6, 2004, I was in my truck before sunup, heading toward an area that provides some excellent whitetail viewing. The sun was just beginning to come up, and the eastern sky was filled with different shades of red and orange. The sky looked like it was on fire.

I observed several deer moving across a picked cornfield. After stopping to glass the field, I moved on.

As I came to the next intersection, I noticed a silver pickup parked along the roadside. It looked like there was a video camera hanging out the window. I looked out into the field to see what was being filmed and observed a young doe walking along the fence line about 100 yards out. Behind her was a small buck.

My eyes were searching the ridgeline when I noticed something just breaking the horizon. I observed antlers, and then more antlers. This image was fast becoming the largest buck I had ever seen.

The buck topped the hill with the sun at his back, highlighting his massive rack. He was about 225 yards out and did not seem overly concerned with the vehicles on the road and continued about his business. I watched for about 10 minutes. I left not believing what I had just seen.

I regained my composure, pulled alongside the silver pickup and talked to the driver. I asked him if he had caught the buck on video, and he said he had. We both commented on the size of the buck, introduced ourselves and continued on our separate ways.

This chance meeting would repeat itself many more times over the next five weeks.

I stayed on my usual route for another hour or so and found myself repeating "what a buck" out loud. I had to tell my wife and son.

When I got home, I told my wife about the huge buck, and her reaction was "that's nice." Not the reaction I was looking for. I called my son, Jay, to see what his reaction would be. Jay was as excited as I was.

Over the next five weeks, Jay and I spent as much time as possible in the area, trying to get a handle on the buck's travel patterns. I talked to the farmer who owns the property adjacent to where I had first observed the buck, and asked his permission to hunt his property during the first shotgun season. Thankfully, the farmer said I could.

During my time in the area, I kept running into Roger Hill, the gentleman whom I had observed videotaping the buck. Roger is a professional wildlife photographer who spends a great deal of time in the fall and winter months looking for new subjects. In talking with Roger, I learned that he does not hunt with firearms anymore, but his camera work shows his skills in the field. I told Roger that I had not hunted for a very long time, but to have a chance to hunt this buck caused me to reconsider my

Roger Hill

Wayne Nelson first encountered this 207-inch 16-pointer while driving. That same day he met Roger Hill, who had been photographing the deer for years. And so began a new friendship and a long journey to patterning the giant buck.

position.

I learned that Roger had been filming this particular buck for the last three years. He had the buck on video in 2002 as a 12-pointer, in 2003 as a 14-pointer and in 2004 as a 16-pointer. I asked Roger if there was any way I could get a copy of the video. Without hesitation, Roger said he would make me a copy. After I watched the video for the first time, if I was

not totally consumed with hunting this buck before, I was now!

On Dec. 3, 2004, my son and I decided to take one more look at the area and make our final plans for our hunt the next morning. We planned to cover two of the four routes the buck used in his daily routine. The wind was supposed to be out of the south the next morning, and the two locations we picked would provide us with the best chance of getting a shot.

While we were in the area, we saw Roger again and told him what the plans were for the next morning. Roger gave me two phone numbers that he could be reached at if things came together for us in the morning. He wished us luck and was on his way.

After Jay and I returned home, we shot our muzzleloaders to make sure they were right on. They were, and hopefully they would be in the morning, too.

On opening day, Jay arrived at my house at about 5:30 a.m. We discussed our final plans. Jay thought that we should cover the area differently than we had first planned. He explained what he felt would increase our chances of one of us getting a shot. I am very glad that I listened to him.

As we were getting ready to leave, my wife wished us good luck and gave me a parting shot, saying, "I hope you don't get him; he is too beautiful to shoot." I thanked her for her support. We loaded the pickup and were on our way.

While driving to the area, we noticed several pickups parked off the roadway on the west side of the property. They were getting set up for their drive through the timber.

My son dropped me off at my spot and went down the road another 400 yards to his spot. I walked out into the field as quietly as I could. I set up on the fence line, in the tall grass. It was still dark, so I got comfortable and waited.

I had been there about 30 minutes when I heard something moving. I still couldn't see very far, but I picked up movement about 25 yards to my right. I observed a couple of does walking down the fence line toward me. The wind was out of the southwest, and they were coming from the south. All I could think was, "I hope the Scent-Blocker works." The two does passed by me undisturbed.

Another 10 minutes passed when the fence I was sitting by began to shake. I observed two more does coming out of the tall grass to the south. They had clipped the fence as they jumped it. If I wasn't completely awake before, I was now. These does came within 10 yards, and didn't seem to notice me. They continued about 100 yards out into the field and began to feed.

My eyes were searching the field for "my buck" when I observed movement to my left. There was a buck about 25 yards away. He was downwind from me and was walking slowly, headed toward the does in the field. I sat dead-still. I knew he was going to cross my scent stream in about five more steps. He took a few steps, turned and looked right at me. I thought, "That's it, I'm busted."

The buck continued looking at me for several minutes, then stomped his feet a couple of times, trying to make me move, but I was locked up.

The buck turned to his left, saw the does in the field, and must have decided that they looked better than I did and walked slowly toward them. This buck was a nice 8-pointer, and got my adrenaline pumping, but he was not the buck I was here for. As I sat there, I wondered if I had made the right decision.

Just then I heard a gunshot behind me and to the south. The shot sent the does and the buck over the ridge and out of view.

Time passed and I wondered if the shot I had heard might have been the end of my dream. The shot had come from an area where "the buck" bedded occasionally. I thought a hunter could have jumped him from his bed and made the shot.

It had been about 15 minutes since I heard the shot, but it seemed a lot longer. In that time, my mind covered just about everything bad that could have happened to "the buck."

Just then, I caught a glimpse of movement to my left. It was the buck I was after. He was moving through the tall grass, and walking slowly with his head held high. He was huge.

I had watched him with binoculars numerous times, and many more times on video. But nothing prepared me for this.

He was traveling the same path the 8-pointer had taken earlier. I knew that I would not get away with my scent stream again. I had to turn my body more to the left to get a shot before it was too late.

As I turned, the barrel of the muzzleloader touched the barbed-wire fence. That was all it took. The buck took off on a dead run, straight away from me, giving me no shot. To my surprise, he stopped about 125 yards away, turned broadside and looked back.

I put the cross-hairs on his shoulder and squeezed the trigger. The smoke from the muzzleloader blocked my view for several seconds. As the smoke cleared, I could see him going over the ridge and out of sight.

I tried to calm down. I sat for another 15 minutes, going over the shot in my mind. I was sure that I had a good hit on him; as sure as you can be when your buck of a lifetime is running out of sight. I decided to pack up and head to the truck, get my son, and give the buck a little more time.

I arrived at the truck, dropped off my gear, and headed toward where my son was set up. He was already walking toward the truck. I told him what had happened.

We decided to wait another 15 minutes, which seemed like a day and a half. We then went to find the buck. Jay was walking ahead of me, and I pointed him toward where I had last seen the buck. Jay found the buck just over the top of the hill and yelled, "Here he is, Dad!" What a feeling! No ground shrinkage here!

The first call was to my wife. The second call was to Roger. There is nothing like having a professional wildlife photographer take your field photos.

The rack officially scored 207$^4/_8$ inches, nontypical.

Sharing time with my son while hunting this buck was incredible. Plus, I was lucky enough to get a record-book whitetail and gain a new friend in the process. Thanks, Roger.

— *Wayne Nelson*
Madrid, Iowa

N.J. Hunter Passes Up 10-Pointer for 8-Pointer

I harvested my best archery buck to date during the first week of October 2003 while hunting on my farm in northwestern New Jersey.

I had entered the woods around 3:30 p.m. After climbing into my stand, I sat quietly 25 feet above the ground and let the woods settle down.

It wasn't long before a few does passed my stand and worked their way down the ridge toward some open fields. I watched closely to see if they were watching their back trail or acting unusual, but nothing seemed to be pressuring them.

An hour later, a buck came up the hill toward my stand. He was a nice yearling 7-point, but his rack was just a small basket, so I let him pass.

About 5:30, the silence was broken by the sound of deer walking down the ridge behind me. I slowly turned and was pleasantly surprised to see four does and two 3 1/2-year-old bucks about 60 yards away, coming directly toward me. As I waited for them to close the gap, adrenaline ran through my system as I prepared for the shot.

When the does were less than 20 yards from my perch, they stopped to look back at the bucks. It was an anxious few minutes as they stood right below me. Slowly, the bucks moved closer, eventually ending up 18 yards in front of me, but facing toward me. I didn't want to move, so I waited, trying to control my shaking as they stood there looking at each other. Suddenly, both bucks slammed into each other, creating a loud crack as their racks made contact.

As they backed away and stared at one another, I drew my bow. I decided to take the 8-pointer instead of the 10-pointer because he

Greg Wright, of Hamburg, N.J., passed up a 10-pointer for a taller-tined 8-pointer on his New Jersey farm.

presented a clean quartering-away shot, and had much longer tines.

Without hesitation, I released. The arrow took out both lungs.

The deer exploded from beneath me and raced down the draw. My buck bolted 40 yards and stood on the side of the ridge, looking around as if nothing had happened.

I quietly observed for about five minutes, questioning my shot as I played back the sequence in my mind. But then I felt a rush of exhilaration as the buck fell over and slid down the hill. This was truly the most exciting hunt I've ever experienced.

— *Greg Wright*
Hamburg, N.J.

Scouting Trip Reveals Warm-Weather Deer Trail

It was mid-November in Freestone County, Texas. It was warmer than usual, and hunting was slow. My brother, Cole, brother-in-law Rusty Harvey and I were out scouting when I found a creek bank all torn up. There was a heavy trail, and the sandy creek bottom was covered with tracks. After our discovery, we quietly left the area.

About 4 p.m. I returned with a folding chair and positioned it behind a big oak. At 4:30 or so I heard something moving behind me. I finally turned around, only to see a big hog — about 200 pounds — slowly headed my way. I watched him for a few minutes as he got closer and closer. I was pretty nervous by now because hogs are very unpredictable. I eased my rifle around to my lap, my heart beating in my throat, and took the safety off. After what seemed like forever, the hog moved deeper into the woods and out of sight, and I began to breath normally again.

It was now after 5 p.m., and all was silent. My light was fading when I saw movement in the creek bottom. I slowly raised my .270 and looked through my scope. In it I saw deer legs. A fallen tree was leaning over the creek bank, and a branch was blocking my line of sight.

The deer lifted his head for a second, and I could tell it was a nice buck. He looked like he might go up the creek bank, which would have left me without a shot, but after a few minutes, he turned around again and looked as if he was coming toward the open creek bottom.

I was holding my rifle free-hand the entire time, which was about 15

Sam Bradshaw Jr. found a heavy deer trail in a creek bottom after warm weather slowed deer movement. That afternoon, he set up near the trail and waylaid this 8-pointer.

minutes. The light was fading, but I could only see half of his neck, his shoulder and front legs.

It was now or never because my shooting light was almost gone. I placed the cross-hairs on his front shoulder and squeezed the trigger. I saw the muzzle flash, and I strained to listen for movement. Nothing!

I waited 10 minutes and headed for the creek bottom. I walked the 40 yards to the creek and looked down. There he was, lying in the bottom of the creek, right where he had stood. The buck had eight points, a heavy rack and great body mass. It was my most exciting hunt, and it will forever be etched in my mind.

— Sam Bradshaw Jr.
Houston, Texas

Kelly Raab was working on a central New York farm one summer when he met the woman of his dreams. One day as the two young lovers worked on the farm, they saw a large 10-point buck, which became the key to their relationship.

'Love Buck' Brings Together New York Couple

I was working on a farm in central New York when I met the girl of my dreams. She had a summer position on the farm and was leaving for another state at the end of the summer.

As the summer progressed, we developed strong feelings for each other, and we would work together whenever we got the chance.

One morning in late summer we were working together when three deer ran out of a nearby cornfield and passed within 40 yards of us. There was a doe, a nice 8-point and a beautiful 10-point.

Later that week I asked the girl what I had to do to keep her from moving away. Her response was, "Shoot that 10-point this fall and I will come back to you."

My heart sank. If she had told me to win the lottery, I felt I would have had a better chance of getting her back. In 13 years of hunting, I had only seen a couple of deer the size of that 10-point, let alone get a shot at one. I pretty much dismissed the thought of it ever happening.

Summer ended and the girl of my dreams moved more than 600 miles away. Thankfully, archery season was just around the corner. It was just what I needed to get my mind off of missing her.

I had to work the first evening of the season, but the second night I managed to hunt a small brush lot on the farm that I worked on. I was sitting in a multiple-trunked maple overlooking a couple of apple trees. The foliage was still on and I only had a couple of very narrow shooting lanes through the thick brush.

The evening progressed quietly with no sightings until about 15 minutes before dark. Suddenly, I heard the steady, unmistakable walk of a deer coming close. The deer was within 25 yards, but I could not see it because of the brush. Finally I caught just a glimpse of antler and my heart began to race. It did not matter to me what size the buck was; I was simply happy to have an opportunity as I prepared for a shot.

There was only one shooting lane in the direction the deer was headed, so I came to full draw and aimed down the lane. Before I knew what happened, the buck's head and neck were already through the opening, followed by its shoulder, and I touched the release. I heard a good thwack and the deer was instantly gone.

I waited about 10 minutes and I snuck out of the brush lot as quietly as I could. I drove to a nearby co-worker's house for some lanterns and tracking assistance. He was excited to help, and he asked how big I thought the buck was. I pointed to one of the many yearling bucks on his garage wall and said, "About like that 6-point."

After a long, two-hour wait we took up the blood trail. About 10 minutes and 100 yards into the trail I almost stepped on what was and still is the biggest buck I have taken. I could not believe my eyes when I saw how big the deer was; my yearling 6-point turned into a 3-year-old 10-point. After a couple of victory high fives, it dawned on me that this was the same deer I had seen that summer with my girlfriend, and you can bet I remembered what she had said about coming back to be with me if I got it.

The next day we took lots of pictures and I had them developed as quickly as possible. I sent several of the pictures to my girl and reminded her of her promise.

To make a long story short, my girl kept her promise. She moved back to be with me shortly after hunting season. We have now been happily married for more than seven years. We have two great children, and we all refer to the 10-point as the "Love Buck."
— *Kelly Raab*
Hammondsport, N.Y.

Indiana Man Surprises Hunter With Buck Photo

Kenny Henderson captured this 177-inch buck with his scouting camera in the summer of 2004. When a hunter killed the buck that fall, Henderson gave him an 8x11 photo of the deer in velvet.

I was glassing a soybean field in southern Indiana when I just had a gut feeling I should turn around and look behind me. When I did, I saw three big bucks about 250 to 300 yards away.

After seeing these dandy bucks, I put my camera on a fence row that separated a soybean field from a cornfield and came up with some awesome buck pictures.

My dad saw the deer pictured here during bow-season. A hunter shot the buck on opening day of shotgun season about 2 miles from where this photo was taken. It grossed 177 inches. I made an 8x11 print of this photo and gave it to the hunter who killed this buck. He was ecstatic!
— *Kenny Henderson*
Boonville, Ind.

Patience Brings Alabama Man an 11th-Hour Buck

J.W. Harville had to work on the last day of Alabama's 2004-05 deer season, but when it began to rain, he could work no longer. With time and Harville's hopes winding down, this 8-pointer appeared, and Harville concluded the season on a high note.

It was Jan. 31, 2005 — the last day of deer season in Alabama. It was also a Monday, and I had to work.

This particular day I was working in Montgomery, and it was raining. Luckily, the job I have won't allow me to work in wet weather. With my ATV and tree stand in tow just in case, I headed to work not knowing that I would actually get to sneak out that afternoon for one final hunt.

Like most hunters, I absolutely dread the last day of deer season. First, it means your favorite thing in the world is over. Second, if you were like me this season, you didn't have much success. I hunt

on my uncle's 2,000-acre farm in Covington County, just outside of Red Level. I've hunted there my entire life, and I've seen some tremendous bucks. I have one on my office wall that I killed more than 10 years ago. I always said I would never top it. Boy, was I wrong.

My friend Jonathan had killed a beautiful 8-point back in November. It had what we called "barnacles" from the base of the antlers to the tips. I saw a couple of smaller bucks during the year, but nothing compared to Jonathan's.

Around 2 p.m. on that final day of deer season, I decided there was no use in trying to work, so I went hunting one last time. I drove as quickly as possible to the farm, which is 1¹/₂ hours away. I called my cousin to see where everyone would be hunting, and he said nobody was hunting in the stand from which Jonathan had killed his buck. That was fine with me, because I had never hunted it. The stand is situated on a very small food plot in the middle of a clear-cut.

As time ticked away, I grew more anxious for a buck to appear. At about 5 p.m., I had given up. I only had about 20 more minutes, and deer season would be over. I said a little prayer and asked the Man Upstairs, if he would mind sending a buck my way. If not, I'd try again next year.

I looked to my left, then back to the right one last time, and there he was. I was overcome with excitement. He was a good buck. He was walking from right to left without a care in the world. It was as if he knew deer season was almost over.

I shouldered my .243, found him in my scope, and let one fly. After about 10 minutes, I climbed down and went to meet my trophy. He was a gorgeous 8-point with a crooked brow tine. He was almost a twin to Jonathan's buck. I thrust my hand to the sky and shouted, "Thank you, Lord!" and went to get the ATV.

I learned an important lesson that day — it's not over till it's over. That's how I got my 11th-hour buck.

— *J.W. Harville*
Dothan, Ala.

Woodcutter Cracks the Code of 200-Pound Bucks

Thomas Crews, a woodcutter from Skowhegan, Maine, is an expert woodsman and one of the Pine Tree State's most successful big-buck hunters. He has been chasing whitetails ever since he was old enough to lug a rifle, killing his first deer at age 10. Since then, Crews has tagged more than 20 whitetails, and nearly all of them were bucks. That would be an enviable record for any hunter, but five of those bucks tipped the scales at more than 200 pounds, including a giant 10-pointer that field dressed at 248 pounds and netted 158 inches. He also has tagged two more bucks that field dressed just under the 200-pound mark at 199 and 191 pounds.

On opening day last fall, Crews tagged yet another heavyweight, and his highest-scoring buck yet. In fact, the buck was so big, Crews needed help getting it back to civilization.

"The first time I saw this buck was during a scouting trip in early October. I was very impressed to say the least. Even at 500 yards his rack looked huge. I watched him for a while through a pair of binoculars while he browsed.

"The second time I laid eyes on the buck was just 10 days before the rifle season opener. He was with four does. I kept my distance and did not spook him.

"The third time I saw the buck was on the season opener. I was en route to hang a tree stand in a spot where I thought I had a chance of seeing that buck. Suddenly, I caught

Thomas Crews is a woodcutter, so he spends more time in the woods than most people. As a result, he has a lot of time to scout for bucks. He bagged this 165-inch buck on opening day of Maine's rifle season after first seeing it in October.

some does acting strangely. The last doe kept looking behind her, as if another hunter was in the area. It wasn't another hunter, however, it was the big buck! I could easily see his rack, even though he was 200 to 225 yards away.

"I didn't waste any time, but leaned up against the crotch of a nearby tree and rested my .30-06 carbine for a steady shot. As soon as I centered the cross-hairs, I squeezed off a shot, severing the buck's spine. The 9-pointer never knew what hit him, falling flat on his face the moment the bullet struck. I was so excited I ran right up to the buck. In fact, I think I could have outrun an Olympic sprinter!

"I tagged the deer, but I had all I could do to drag him 30 feet to a brush pile where I hid him until I could get some help. I went back to my truck and called some friends. As luck would have it, they were just about to go back into the woods, but they were willing to give up their hunt to help me drag."

Crews' Summerset County buck weighed 222 pounds field dressed, making it his sixth buck weighing more than 200 pounds. The buck grossed 169$^4/_8$ inches and netted 165 even — more than enough to place him high in the Maine Antler and Skull Trophy Club.

He just missed the Boone and Crockett record book, but Crews didn't mind. After all, he's only 39 years old, and he says he knows where there's plenty more of those big Maine bucks roaming around!

— *Bill Vaznis*

Steve Nessl's first deer was this 12-point Illinois monster. He shot the buck on the second afternoon of his first bow-hunting trip. The buck's rack grossed 178 inches.

Rookie Archer Worried Buck Wasn't Big Enough

As a lifelong resident of Orange County, Calif., Steve Nessl never encountered a whitetail at close range until he was an adult. However, despite growing up near Los Angeles, he was never an anti-hunter, just your classic American nonhunter — neither for, nor against wild pursuits.

That all changed when Nessl, 33, became public relations manager for Yamaha Motor Corp. and was asked to head up the firm's venture into the hunting market. He started by learning to shoot a shotgun and was soon chasing pheasants, turkeys, ducks and geese.

"I felt obligated to really learn what makes hunters tick," he said. "I knew there was no way I could fake it. You know what? I really enjoyed it and knew it was something I'd like to pursue."

Nessl didn't hesitate in learning the ropes. He got his first bow in August 2004 and enrolled in an archery school. One of his instructors was world-famous bow-hunter Jan Perry of Renegade Archery. "It was pretty intense," Nessl recalls. "We shot at pie plates, 3-D deer and every other kind of target you can think of. Jan worked with me on my shooting form for a whole day. By November, Nessl was ready and raring to go. Luckily for him, his first chance came when Jerry Peterson, president of Woods Wise Hunting Products, invited him on a rut-time hunt in Brown County, Ill. I was in camp with Nessl and actually hunted a stand just 400 yards from his on the first evening. As we compared notes at dinner, he explained how he saw — and passed up — "a basket-racked 10-pointer." Nessl's voice quivered with excitement as he described the close encounter.

"I didn't shoot because I was worried he might be too small — you know, not wide enough," he said, referring to the camp's 16-inch spread rule.

Nessl hunted the same stand the next evening and saw the same buck. This time, however, the buck walked within 25 yards, revealing a rack that was somewhat larger than Nessl thought he saw the previous day.

The buck was cruising for does but was alert. Nessl followed all of the instructions other hunters had offered over the previous three months ... stay calm, pick a spot and follow through on the shot ... and coolly delivered the arrow on target. Despite a blood-soaked arrow and confidence that his shot was true, Nessl's guides didn't take any chances. They marked the blood trail that night and decided to return in the morning.

"We found the buck very quickly the next morning," Nessl said. "He didn't go far. After they saw the deer up ahead, the guides let me approach it first. I knew it was a big one, but, honestly, I really didn't comprehend how big (it was) until they all started hooting and congratulating me."

The main-frame 10-pointer sported 11-inch G-2s, 10-inch G-3s, 23-inch main beams and an 8-inch dagger that grew straight out from the left G-2. Nessl's original fears that the buck "wasn't big enough" were technically correct, because the inside spread was 15³/₄ inches. Of course, the 4¹/₂-year-old buck was plenty big enough to meet the camp's antler standards — or any North American deer camp's standards for that matter! Well-known antler scorer Mike Handley was also in camp, and he gross-scored the deer's rack at a whopping 178 inches.

However, Nessl wasn't done yet. He recorded his second bow-kill later that week when he made an impressive shot on a mature doe. Talk about jumping on the fast track to success. However, through it all, Nessl expressed a humble, almost shellshocked attitude.

"I came from a family of nonhunters, and my wife was very hesitant with the whole thing. She held the stereotypical view. She didn't know that hunters are conservationists and now understands that hunters are doing good for the environment. In fact, we both see the big picture now. Hunting is a way to sustain yourself — we eat venison and have even eaten wild boar. I didn't understand those things until I started hunting."

Every hunter at camp made it a point to tell Nessl he'd have a hard time topping his Illinois buck. He was OK with that.

"The excitement is contagious," he said. "This has been a progression of appreciation, and there's no doubt it will get stronger over time."

— *Daniel E. Schmidt*

New Yorker Arrows 12-Pointer From the Ground

Big bucks often appear as if by magic, forcing the hunter to control his emotions and make the shot of a lifetime. Such was the case when Michael Abbruzzi, of New Rochelle, N.Y., had a 160-class Westchester County buck walk into his life.

Abbruzzi did not grow up in a hunting family, and in fact, didn't even consider hunting until he was in his early 20s. His first two years afield produced two bucks with firearms, but then the bow-hunting bug bit him, and he started racking up bucks with archery tackle. These included several 8-pointers and one 9-pointer that just missed the New York state record book. But he'd never killed a buck quite like the one he arrowed in 2004.

"I had no idea this buck was living in the area," Abbruzzi said of his 2004 buck. "I hunted there the day before and saw a couple of does, but no bucks. I returned the next day and moved 30 yards closer to where I had seen the does, but as luck would have it, the same does went past where I was sitting the day before!

"Suddenly I heard some noise off in the distance. I turned and saw a flock of turkeys coming my way. I also noticed a big buck with his head down following the flock, as if he were using the turkeys as some sort of sentinel.

"As he worked his way up a slight incline, I lost sight of him for several seconds. Then he reappeared in front of me, about to enter a break near the intersection of two stone walls about 22 yards away.

"He never winded me, and never

saw me sitting on the ground with my back to a tree. In fact, he seemed completely oblivious to my presence. I drew my bow and took the shot I had practiced a hundred times in my back yard at a deer target. I knew the arrow hit hard, and I watched the buck run off until he was out of sight.

"My adrenaline was really pumping hard, and I worried about losing the blood trail, as darkness was approaching. I waited what felt like 10 minutes, and

Michael Abbruzzi of New Rochelle, N.Y., arrowed this 160-class 12-pointer while hunting from the ground.

took up the trail. The buck had only traveled about 50 yards before falling down.

"I didn't realize at first how big this buck really was, even though it had an outside spread of 21 inches. As a consequence, I never had him weighed or aged, but we later estimated his dressed weight to be about 200 pounds, and his age to be 5½."

After the 60-day drying period, Abbruzzi had his 12-point buck scored. He was surprised that it tallied 168 even, and unless a bigger buck is brought to the attention of the New York State Big Buck Club, Abbruzzi's buck will be the biggest typical bow-kill of 2004.

— *Bill Vaznis*

John Bryant Stewart, age 7, desperately wanted to go deer hunting, even though his father hadn't hunted deer for years. During his first season, the Madison County, Miss., hunter shot two does and this 184-inch 15-pointer.

Mississippi Boy's First Buck Scored 184 Inches

When I drove into the driveway of his home in rural Madison County, Miss., my initial observation was that John Bryant Stewart was like any other 7-year-old kid. He was riding his bike in circles around his dog, which was tethered to a tree in the front yard. Between a barking dog and spinning bike wheels, he couldn't have cared less that some stranger was coming to talk about his deer hunting exploits.

His mind was nowhere near focused on the trophy buck he had collected just months earlier on the day after Christmas, 2004. And like any 7-year-old boy full of springtime vigor, his father Jeb had to yell several times to get him to part with his bike long enough to mind his Southern-bred manners that a guest had come to visit.

I found out about the young man's monster whitetail through a friend who lives just down the road from the Stewart family.

"Man you've got to come see the buck this little boy killed last December just a few miles from here," my friend excitedly told me. "I think the score is going to make it a state trophy-class deer, but the real story is that it was his first buck."

If Lady Luck ever really smiles on deer hunters, then she definitely had an ear-to-ear grin going for this young Mississippi hunter. To start with, John Bryant's father is not even a deer hunter. His preference is for bird and duck hunting.

"I had not deer hunted since I was a kid," Jeb said, "but my son kept after me to take him on a deer hunt. We didn't even own a deer rifle, so I asked around and ended up getting him a Remington bolt-action in .243. I wanted something easy on the recoil. He quickly became a good shot, even with the open sights."

Jeb and John Bryant went on a couple of deer hunts early in the season, and the boy took two does in the process. This contributed greatly to building the young hunter's shooting confidence, but it also contributed to his frustration. He desperately wanted to take his first buck, but after only two hunts, that simply hadn't happened.

"Dad got me several deer hunting magazines to look at so I could study the antlers and everything so I'd be ready when we went hunting. I had just about worn out the pages staring at all the big bucks in those stories," John Bryant explained. "Sure, I had already killed two does, but I had not seen a buck at all. I was disappointed that we had not even seen one buck, not even a small one when we were out hunting."

Just think of the frustration John Bryant is likely going to have while deer hunting in the years ahead!

"On the day after Christmas we took our places in a shooting house in the corner of a planted greenfield that was sheltered by woods and thickets," Jeb said. "A friend of ours offered to let John

Bryant hunt in his own favorite stand so the boy would maybe get a chance to see a buck. The landowner, though, put a harvest minimum of 6 points on any buck taken. I coached my son that we had to be real careful to make sure any buck we saw had that many points."

John Bryant continued to relate his amazing deer-hunting tale. "I was laying down in the stand, taking a nap, but Dad woke me up in time to watch the field for the rest of the day.

"The sun was already going down behind the far trees when I saw a doe come out to start feeding on the grass. I really didn't think too much about it, as I had already brought home two does and I did not want to shoot another one. I really wanted to take my first buck so I could tell everyone back at school."

With eyes fixed on the distant tree line, John Bryant noticed a dark form taking shape just steps outside of the food plot. The doe he'd been watching continued to feed without even looking up at the other presence materializing on the scene.

Just then, another deer stepped into the clearing. John Bryant quickly noticed this new deer carried antlers. He remembered seeing the pictures in the deer magazines and knew this was the real thing.

"Whispering in a low, but nervously broken tone, John Bryant tugged at my coat, trying to dislodge the lump in his throat," recalls the young hunter's dad. "'Dad, it's a buck, it's a buck!'

John Bryant exclaimed. The funny part is my eyes are so bad at a long distance that I could not tell very well how big the buck was. I used my binoculars, trying to study the rack. I was sure it had at least 6 points, so I knew it was a legal buck that the landowner would approve of. I told John Bryant to get his gun up and ready," Jeb recalls.

John Bryant got his rifle to the ready, and put the V-notch in the open sight on the deer's shoulder. At the first shot the buck did nothing. Jeb helped John Bryant cycle the bolt for three more shots. Finally, the buck took a half-step forward and collapsed. John Bryant and Jeb later determined that two of the 80-yard shots had taken out the heart, lungs and shoulder.

"When we reached the buck, we both were speechless," Jeb said. "I counted 15 points, with one point kind of hanging down. Later, I learned that meant nontypical. We had the buck scored and it came out to 184$^{0}/_{8}$ inches, making it a trophy buck in the state's own record-buck program."

The big nontypical sported main beams measuring 26 and 27 inches, and a 22-inch inside spread.

All in all, you would have to agree that John Bryant's 15-point is quite a first buck for a 7-year-old, or any deer hunter for that matter. And after bagging his first buck, John Bryant certainly had a story to tell all the kids back at school.

— *John J. Woods*
Clinton, Miss.

Hunt for Giant 11-Pointer Lasted Just Minutes

Jason Hastings of North Bangor, N.Y., had scarcely climbed into his stand before this 160-class 11-pointer appeared chasing a doe. The buck sported four tines that were more than a foot long.

Jason Hastings, of North Bangor, N.Y., has been studying deer ever since he was old enough to walk in the woods with his father. This early training eventually paid off handsomely for Hastings, helping him tag several bucks through the years with bow, rifle and muzzleloader. He arrowed his first buck, a 7-pointer, when he was 14, and until last year his biggest buck was also a bow-kill — a 10-point that scored 137 inches.

Last fall, however, he killed a Franklin County giant that was not only his best buck ever, but it could be New York's largest gun-kill in 2004.

"My father, my friend Adam Southworth and I spend our summers determining the quality of bucks in the neighborhood by riding the back roads looking for deer in the evening and by maintaining several deer cams we have positioned on our hunting grounds," Hastings said. "We also tend several food plots where we grow alfalfa, white clover and

Imperial clover. Taking care of those food plots is a full-time job! Even with all this work, however, I never saw the buck I shot in the fall of 2004 during the summer months.

"The early deer season was slow, but on Nov. 14, I walked across the road from my house about 3 p.m., and climbed into a tree stand overlooking one of our food plots. I had no sooner shut the door when I noticed a doe cross one of the shooting lanes with a buck hot on her heels. Even at 150 yards, I could tell it was a shooter buck, so I immediately pulled up my 7 mm, found him in my scope and squeezed off a shot. The bullet hit a bit high in the shoulder, but the buck only went 65 yards or so before collapsing."

The 11-pointer dressed out at 235 pounds and was estimated to be $8^1/_2$ years old. The rack sported a $24^4/_8$-inch outside spread, a $20^1/_2$-inch inside spread and G-2s and G-3s in excess of a foot in length, bringing the total score to $167^4/_8$ inches.

Hastings was in the right place at the right time, but more importantly, he knew what to do when the shot opportunity presented itself!

— Bill Vaznis

New Hampshire Bow-Hunter Scores Grand Slam

There are three state, one regional and three national record-keeping organizations that record record white-tailed deer from New England. Taking a buck big enough to qualify for any of the organizations is an honor. Last fall Scott Chevalier arrowed a buck that made not one, two or three, but four whitetail record books. In fact, his Rockingham County, N.H., buck was the region's best archery buck for 2004!

Chevalier, of East Kingston, N.H., has been chasing deer since he was a kid. His mentor, Denny Plant, taught Chevalier how to interpret deer sign correctly. Over the years, Plant's lessons sunk in, and Chevalier began to rack up plenty of kills with bow and gun, including a 6-pointer with a 23-inch spread he killed early in his career. But he had no idea his best bow-kill would turn out to be such an impressive deer.

"I scout for deer year-round," Chevalier said, "and I keep tabs on bucks all summer by riding the back roads and glassing open fields. I also practice with my bow regularly, shooting foam deer targets from ground level, as well as from a tree stand, and up to just recently I also enjoyed sharpening my shooting skills at a video range.

"I never saw a big buck last summer (summer of 2004), although a local farmer kept telling me a whopper of a buck was entering one of his open fields almost every evening. I checked out his story a couple of times, but never saw the buck. I could only surmise that the buck wasn't really all that big, or it didn't exist at all.

"When the bow-season opened, I hunted a week or so elsewhere, but then one evening I set up a stand at the back of that farmer's field. A small buck came through, but I couldn't get a shot at him.

"The next evening I moved the stand, and almost without warning this big buck came out of a nearby swamp and sauntered past my stand. I remember Denny Plant always telling me not to look at the rack, so I concentrated on making a good shot as the buck stood quartering away from me at about 20 yards.

"I drew my bow, held steady and then released. The shot felt good, but I couldn't find the buck that evening. I came back the next morning with several friends, but we searched for four or five hours and could not find him

Scott Chevalier arrowed this 13-pointer early in the 2004 New Hampshire archery season. He couldn't find the buck right away, but a tip from another hunter helped him find the deer 200 yards away in a puddle.

anywhere. I was heartsick. I knew I had a good hit, but now all I could do was second-guess myself.

"Then my parents told me another hunter had told them he had found a big buck half-submerged in a puddle of water, and thought it could very well be the buck I had lost. Sure enough, it was my buck! The arrow had entered the buck behind the last rib and exited between the shoulder and the first rib on the opposite side. The buck had traveled 200 to 250 yards before expiring!"

The buck later dressed out 190 pounds, and was estimated to be $4^1/_2$ or $5^1/_2$ years old. After waiting the required 60-day drying period, Chevalier got the surprise of his life. The 13-point typical rack grossed 183 even, and netted $175^4/_8$ inches, qualifying it for the Northeast Big Buck Club, the New Hampshire Antler and Skull Trophy Club, the Pope and Young Club and the Boone and Crockett Club — a Northeast grand slam!

— *Bill Vaznis*

Michigan Girl's First Hunt is Good Luck for Dad

I love bow-hunting, and for the last 10 years I've been in the woods every weekend during the fall until gun season. I've taken 10 bucks over those years, and with the exception of two average 8-pointers, they were mostly small.

My wife and 8-year-old daughter, Cortney, know that I really love bow-hunting, but probably don't realize how much I think about it when fall gets here. But last fall, I decided that Cortney was growing up very quickly, so I volunteered to coach her soccer team. I thought this would be a good chance to do something with her. I knew that from September through October I would be coaching soccer every Saturday. This meant I would not be able to make my weekend hunting trips to my dad's place, where I had normally hunted during October. I knew it would be hard to listen to the guys at work and my dad talk about being in the woods, but I wanted Cortney to know that coaching her soccer team was just as important to me.

It was the fourth day of the early bow season, and I hadn't even thought about going hunting when Cortney asked if I would take her hunting that afternoon. She had asked a couple of times the previous season, but we never went. This time I followed through on the request and grabbed two tree stands and a climbing stick, and we took off for the woods behind my house.

I had only hunted in this woodland a few times the previous years and never really thought that it would hold many deer. We found two potential spots, and I let her pick the spot

we'd hunt. Cortney surprised me when she picked the spot that was the harder to get to, but I hung the two stands facing opposite directions in the same tree. We were about 200 yards from our house, but it was a tough walk for an 8-year-old, because half of it was through a swamp with numerous fallen trees.

We got back to the house and drove to buy a hunting license. We returned home at 5 p.m. I quickly pinned up an old set of hunting clothes for Cortney and we had dinner. We were dressed in full camo by 6:10. As I took my bow out of the case, I noticed that the sight had come loose and I had to quickly tighten the two screws. I took one shot at the target in my back yard to confirm my accuracy, and we began walking to our stand.

Cortney had never been hunting before, let alone been in a tree stand, so we took our time to slowly climb up into the two stands. Once I had Cortney's safety harness secured, she asked for her camouflage facemask and book. She was a little nervous getting up the tree, but was in her glory once she was secured. It was now around 6:40, and we had about 50 minutes of hunting time left. I had hunted this area the previous year and was pretty sure that if we saw any deer, they would come from the northwest, which was the direction I was facing. I didn't give Cortney any instructions before the hunt, but I told her while we were sitting in the tree that if she felt my hand touch her shoulder, she should assume that I saw a deer and should slowly turn and look in the direction I'm looking.

Todd Kovacic was looking for ways to spend more time with his daughter, Cortney, so when she asked to go hunting, he jumped at the chance. During Cortney's first hunt, she spotted this 8-pointer and tapped her father on the shoulder. Minutes later, they both stood over Todd's most memorable buck.

We were 10 minutes into our hunt when I noticed Cortney was picking leaves off a branch and seeing how far she could throw them. I decided to let the fun go on because I thought the chances of seeing a deer were slim because we had made a lot of noise getting into the stand.

The minutes ticked by quickly as I thought about how cool it was to be sitting in a tree stand next to my daughter, sharing something that I love so much. I wasn't even thinking about seeing a deer, let alone getting a shot.

About 10 minutes before I was going to pack up, I felt Cortney's hand on my shoulder. Cortney was reading her book, when out of the corner of her eye she spotted what she thought was a branch moving back and forth. She continued to stare at the branch and all of a sudden this huge buck came out of nowhere and was standing right in front of her. Her first thought was that her book cover had bright colors on it and she didn't want the buck to see it, so she slowly slid it down the front of her hunting jacket and slipped it into the front pocket. The buck looked up in her direction, just as she was putting the book into her pocket, and she closed her eyes so he wouldn't see her. Remember, that this is the first time she had gone hunting!

She opened her eyes slowly to make sure he wasn't looking anymore, and decided it was time to let me know this buck was in front of her. She felt behind her for the tree and started to slide her hand and arm around the tree, keeping her arm right next to it because she thought if the buck looked up, he would just think her arm was part of the tree. She never took her eyes off the buck the whole time.

She finally felt my shoulder and tightened her hand around it to get my attention. Out of the corner of her eye, she saw me stand up. Cortney knew I had my bow pointed at the buck, and she hoped she wasn't in the way.

The buck started to walk right in front of Cortney, then stopped. She could see me drawing my bow, then she heard a noise and the buck jumped straight up in the air. When the buck came down he slipped a few times, then bolted.

Cortney asked me right away if I'd gotten him. I told her I wasn't sure, and explained that in a few minutes, I'd climb down to see if I could find my arrow or any blood. I didn't see my arrow, but there was good blood after the buck's first jump. I climbed back up to the tree stands and told Cortney that we had hit him hard and we were going to wait a little bit to make sure he was dead. Cortney then extended her hand to congratulate

me. I will never forget that moment. We waited about 15 minutes, while talking about the events that had just taken place, then slowly made our way down the tree. Cortney was a little nervous climbing down, but I was basically bear-hugging her the whole way down the tree.

It was getting pretty dark now, and I was trying to decide if I should take Cortney back to the house and come back to look for the deer, or start to look with her right away. I decided to follow the buck's trail for 15 to 20 yards to decide how well I had hit him.

The blood trail was very easy to follow and I knew I had hit him hard, so we continued. I would walk ahead of Cortney about 5 yards, then motion for her to stand at the spot of sign I had just found. The buck made a 90-degree turn at 30 yards, and within 20 yards, my flashlight caught the white belly of the deer. I called Cortney over to me and we walked up to the buck. I touched his rear end to make sure he had expired.

I couldn't believe what a great buck I had just harvested! And the best part was my daughter was sitting right next to me and not only witnessed the experience, but was actually responsible for the hunting adventure! The buck was a very symmetrical 8-pointer with a $17\frac{1}{2}$-inch inside spread. I was so thankful for this father-daughter hunting experience. The buck will be on the wall for a long time for both of us to reminisce over. I may end up harvesting a bigger buck, but never a more memorable one. Thanks, Cortney, for wanting to go hunting with dad!

— *Todd Kovacic*
Romeo, Mich.

Only Maine Buck Sighting is a Big Buck Sighting

Pennsylvania hunter Gary Gettig hunts in Maine every other year, from his uncle's cabin near Newport. During odd years, Gettig's uncle and his gang hunt in Pennsylvania with Gettig. It is a good strategy, as Gettig has tagged three good 8-pointers in Maine, including a whopper that qualified for the Maine Antler and Skull Trophy Club's (MASTC) 200-pound roster.

Gary Gettig traveled to Maine to hunt big bucks with his uncle, but after a week of hunting, no one had seen a buck. Gettig made up for the uneventful season when he dropped this 166-inch 12-pointer.

Last fall Gettig hunted trophy bucks in Maine, but the action was slow. The hunting party saw only three does all week, and there was no word about a big buck haunting the area. Things looked grim.

"I had a hunch on Nov. 10," Gettig said, "so I decided to hunt by myself that afternoon by still-hunting along an old logging road that snaked its way back to camp. I was familiar with the area, and thought maybe I would stand a chance of at least seeing a deer. As it turned out, I was right about seeing a deer that afternoon — a buck actually. What I couldn't foresee was the size of the deer I would come across.

"I walked slowly and stopped often, keeping my eyes and ears open for any sign of a deer. I slid in next to some rocks, and looked deep into the forest. Suddenly, I glimpsed a deer a couple hundred yards distant, working its way in my direction. I soon realized it was a buck, and the closer it got, the more I realized it had a pretty good rack. I was astonished!

"I turned and faced the deer now as it zigzagged through the ferns. When it stopped, I shouldered my .270 and found him in my scope. When I was steady, I squeezed off a shot, hitting the 12-point buck in the neck. He traveled less than 50 yards before expiring.

"The buck later dressed out at 192^1/$_2$ pounds, and tooth analysis revealed he was 7^1/$_2$ years of age. He green scored 166^0/$_8$, and I hope to have Al Wentworth from MASTC put a final tape on him later this year."

— *Bill Vaznis*

Wisconsin Man's First Buck Wins Big-Buck Pool

I sat in my blind overlooking a black spruce bog, thinking of the history and tradition of the land I was hunting, and of past hunters and the deer they hunted. To my right I heard movement and spotted a deer moving through the thick spruces. A buck moved across a well-traversed deer path, his head down and antlers extending out in front of him. I adjusted my position and prepared for a shot, just waiting for the buck to appear in the open ...

This was Day 2 of Wisconsin's nine-day gun-deer season. It was my fifth deer season, and I was part of a group of six friends hunting together in northwest Wisconsin. Some of us had hunted together for several years, while others were hunting the North Woods for the first time. We all, however, were friends and avid hunters.

Although my anticipation of the hunt is a year-long affair, my preparation really began the previous weekend. My friend, Andy, and I made our way north for some duck hunting and deer scouting. The weather was not conducive to duck hunting, so we spent the majority of the weekend scouting for deer and building blinds.

My friend, Ryan, his wife Jen, and I had hunted these woods for the last few years and had previously built some blinds from fallen logs and other debris from the forest floor. This year three other friends were joining us, and we would need to find more hunting spots.

Ryan, a local resident, hunted the area all fall and picked out several spots that appeared promising.

That weekend we spent a great deal of time in the woods. We fixed up several existing blinds and built some new ones. The blinds were constructed on the ground, built around trees overlooking promising areas. Each blind was constructed with materials from the immediate area. Logs were stacked in a cabin-like fashion, and the gaps were filled with branches and leaves. Each blind was big enough to fit a chair, some gear and a hunter, and we equipped each with a shooting rail.

Although we were confident in each blind's location, one blind seemed most likely to produce deer sightings. It was difficult to get to, and we knew no other hunters would venture to this location. Getting to it meant walking more than 1 mile through the forest, or coming across a lake by canoe. This was followed by crossing a swampy area with waders.

The "Black Spruce Blind" was situated on a floating bog in the middle of a black spruce forest. Although the black spruce in the area were small, the slow-growing evergreens were several decades old and served as thick cover. The soft ground was covered with swamp grasses, various mosses and pitcher plants. Each step had to be carefully placed in order to avoid sinking into the bog up to one's waist. The swamp grass revealed dozens of heavily beaten deer paths crisscrossing the bog, signifying an area heavily used by passing deer.

The blind itself was built from black spruce boughs positioned around a patch of thick spruces. A plastic chair was situated in the middle of the blind in several inches of standing water overlooking the most open portion of the bog.

Andy Lecker of Oshkosh, Wis., once helped a pair of North Woods hunters drag a heavy buck out of a Wisconsin forest. At the time, he imagined how it would feel to drag his own big buck from the woods. He found out on Day 2 of Wisconsin's 2004 gun-season when he spied this 11-pointer slipping through the spruces.

With the blinds established, Andy and I returned home, awaiting our return the following Friday. Those five days were spent preparing for the upcoming hunt. Food and gear where prepared and packed, rifles were sighted in, and the truck was loaded. By Friday, everything was ready for the journey back up north.

By 3 p.m. Friday I was parked outside of Andy's house. We stowed his gear in the back of the truck and we were on our way.

Our next stop was an hour to the northwest where we would pick up Joe. Once Joe and his gear were on board, we began the last four-hour leg of our journey.

Traffic was heavy as it always is the Friday before opening weekend, and the weather was rainy and cold. It rained the entire ride, adding an extra hour to our trip. By the time we reached our destination, it was late.

When we finally arrived we were tired from the long drive, but excited because opening morning was only hours away. We hauled our gear into Ryan's place and greeted the rest of the group. We then gathered around a large aerial photo of our hunting grounds. There were several minutes of excited chatter as last-minute plans were set in place. Once our plans were complete, we packed our gear and lunches and were off to bed.

Although it was late, it was difficult to fall asleep with all of the excitement of the upcoming hunt.

Despite the lack of sleep, everyone was up in a flash at the beeping of the alarm at 4 a.m. We had to be up extra early because it would take some time to get to our blinds and get situated before shooting hours. We ate breakfast, gathered our things, filled thermoses with hot chocolate and piled into the trucks. Opening morning was here.

Andy and I would drive to a nearby farm where we would walk more than a mile to our blinds while the rest of the group would launch canoes and paddle in. "Good lucks" were exchanged as we split into two groups and left camp. As we left we could see lights in several other camps and a few trucks making their way toward the woods.

Within minutes, Andy and I had parked and were walking into the forest. It was completely dark with the overcast sky and quite cold. After a 20-minute walk I found my blind. I stowed my gear and got situated. It was still dark and the woods were quiet. I leaned my head back against a tree and dozed off a little. Shooting hours weren't for another 40 minutes.

By the time the sun was creeping up and the woods were beginning to become visible I was awake and alert. Soon I began to hear shooting in the distance. My 7 mm bolt-action rifle was situated on my shooting rail, and I was ready.

Typically we sit in our blinds the entire day opening day, but this year we had planned to make some small drives late in the morning. Shortly before 11 a.m. I spoke with Ryan on the radio. He indicated that Jen, who

was sitting about 200 yards to the south of him, had shot a buck fawn. He told me to begin my portion of the drive. We were unable to make contact with Joe, but he had prior instructions to begin his portion of the drive, picking up Andy in the process.

This drive involved walking a low, swampy area. My portion of the drive was much shorter than Andy and Joe's, and I arrived at Ryan's blind several minutes ahead of them. I joined Ryan in the blind and began to watch the edge of the swamp, hoping a deer would emerge ahead of Andy and Joe. After a short sit, I heard a noise, then a doe and a fawn emerged from the swamp. I nudged Ryan and we waited for a shot. I didn't have a clear shot, but Ryan did, and his rifle rang out. Both deer bolted, and I took a quick shot as well. The doe ran about 70 yards before going down. Ryan's shot had found its mark. Andy and Joe joined us shortly after. We were all excited about the drive's success.

I then made my way back to my blind where I remained the rest of the afternoon. I spotted only one deer on the run, well out of range.

When shooting hours ended, I met Andy, and we made our way out of the woods. He had also seen only one deer off in the distance.

We met the rest of the group back at camp. Nick had harvested a doe — his first deer. Opening day was a success.

We hung the three deer from the buck pole and headed inside. We all showered and warmed up. The long day had taken its toll on us, and we were tired and hungry.

It felt good to eat a hot meal and

relax, and to know three deer already hung outside.

Several phone calls were made to other family members and friends, and stories were exchanged. We discussed the day's hunt and planned our strategy for the morning. Once again our gear was organized and lunches packed, then we went to bed early. Day 2 would be another long, exciting day.

Morning came early and we were all up and ready to go quickly. Jen would not be joining us today, but the rest of us headed to the farm together. We walked deep into the woods, separating to go to our own blinds. Joe would hunt out of the Black Spruce Blind, Andy and Ryan headed toward Ryan's blind and Nick and I returned to the area of my blind. I situated Nick in a blind about 250 yards from my own.

Today's plan was to remain in our blinds till mid-morning, then make some drives. Throughout the morning I heard several shots and saw a lot of wildlife, but no deer.

I met up with Nick and we repeated Andy and Joe's drive from the previous day. We heard several close shots during the 45-minute drive and thought maybe Andy had taken a shot, but when we arrived at Andy's location, we learned he hadn't shot. There was, however, an adult doe already field dressed near his blind. Andy explained that Joe had shot the deer, and that Ryan was at the Black Spruce Blind assisting Joe with some gear.

A few minutes later I saw Joe and Ryan approaching. They were not hauling gear, but dragging another deer, and this deer had antlers. Joe had shot two deer out of the Black Spruce Blind; the first an adult doe, and the second a nice 8-point buck! We all were excited for Joe. It is rare to see a nice buck during the gun-deer season in the North Woods, let alone harvest one. This was turning out to be one of the most successful hunts I had ever been a part of.

Before the weekend started, we each threw a dollar in the buck pool. At the end of the weekend, whoever harvested the largest buck would win $6 and bragging rights. We joked about the pool all weekend, but were all sure that Joe would be the winner. None of us expected to harvest a big buck, and we were certain no one would see a bigger buck than Joe's.

It was now early afternoon. We spent the next hour dragging the deer out of the woods and getting them back to camp. After a quick meal, Nick and Joe remained at camp, while Ryan, Andy and I returned to the woods.

I decided I was no longer going to sit in my blind. In two years of hunting there, I hadn't had any luck and was becoming discouraged. The three of us made our hike back into the woods. This time I would sit in the Black Spruce Blind.

I made my way across the swampy area onto the bog and found the blind. I situated myself and prepared for the evening hunt.

Darkness was fast approaching. Within the next hour, the season would close for the day, and another opening weekend would be gone. I sat in my blind, staying quiet and still. If I looked hard to the east I could see Andy seated in his blind, and I knew Ryan was in his, several hundred yards to the north. The evening was breezy and cold; a perfect evening for hunting. While I looked out over the area in front of me I was in awe at the deer trails crisscrossing the bog. I wondered if other people had hunted this area in the past, and what they saw.

These thoughts ran through my head as dusk settled in. Then, somewhere off to my right I heard movement. At first I wasn't sure if it was the wind or something else. I focused on the thick black spruce growth, hoping to see something. As I peered into the thick growth, I spotted a deer moving down one of the more heavily traveled deer paths. The deer had its head down and I caught a glimpse of a large set of antlers protruding out from the deer's head. As the deer disappeared behind the brush, I wondered if I had really seen antlers or if my mind had been playing tricks on me.

I didn't have time to sit and wonder. I had to get myself situated to take a shot. The deer had been directly to my right, and being a right-handed shooter, I needed to get turned in order to take a shot if one presented itself. I turned while the deer remained behind the thick growth, hoping it wouldn't see or hear me. Once I was situated, I waited for the deer to come into an opening where I could shoot.

Seconds ticked by, and the deer did not emerge. A thousand thoughts ran through my head. Did the deer hear me and bolt? Did it turn down a different path and walk away? Just then, I noticed some white in a small opening I had not seen before. It was too far away to see without magnification, but when I raised my scope I could see the white face of a deer looking at me. I couldn't see antlers,

and I wondered if this was the same buck.

This area had a limited number of bonus tags available, and I was fortunate enough to have one. This left me the option of taking a buck and a doe. I decided to shoot. I knew that my only available shot was a head-shot and if I missed, I would leave the animal unharmed. The deer had seen me and I knew that it would not continue down the path toward the opening. It was now or never.

I put the crosshairs of my 3x9 scope right between the eyes and squeezed the trigger. My bolt-action rifle thundered, and at the sound of the shot, the animal disappeared.

I sat for several seconds in silence. Did I hit the deer? Was it the same buck I thought I saw? After a few moments I was able to collect myself. I ejected the spent shell and racked another round into the chamber. Andy and Ryan were both on the radio. I told them I had taken a shot and was on my way to check on the deer. I knew that if I'd hit the animal it would be right where I had shot it. I made my way slowly and carefully toward the spot where I had last seen the deer.

As I closed in on the deer's last location, I spotted the body of a large deer. Although I could not see its head, I knew I had shot a big buck by the sheer size of the body. As the buck's head came into view, I realized I had shot a trophy. I quickly counted 11 points; 5 points on one side 6 on the other. My shot had been true. However, my shot did not hit the deer exactly where I aimed. My shot struck the buck in the left eye, dropping him where he stood.

I stared at the animal for several

moments. I had not expected to see any big bucks, let alone harvest one. The feeling was one I will never forget. This was not just my biggest buck, but it was also my first. I continued to look at the animal. He was a mature buck — a $3^1/_2$-year-old with dark gray and brown hair on his face and neck. His neck was large and swollen. He was definitely still in rut. I now assume he must have been tracking a doe that most likely wandered down that same path earlier in the day.

Andy and Ryan were still on their radios, and I stammered that I had just won the buck pool. Both were excited, and Ryan began to make his way to me. While I waited for Ryan, I tagged and gutted the buck. I also gathered up my gear and began dragging the deer. Ryan soon arrived and was excited to see the buck. Together, we dragged the deer across the swamp to the higher uplands where Andy waited for us. Andy also expressed his excitement and congratulations on my good fortune.

Shooting hours were now coming to a close, and the woods were quickly becoming dark. We decided Ryan would haul as much gear as he could handle back to our trucks and recruit Joe to help with the drag. Andy and I began dragging the buck. It was slow going, due the buck's large size, the terrain and the gear Andy and I still carried. We managed to get the buck about a quarter-mile before we decided to walk our gear out of the woods and come back for the deer. We left the buck where we knew we could find it and made our way back. We left our gear at the trucks and returned to the buck.

The woods were now dark and quiet. We hoped Ryan and Joe would soon be back to help. We were getting tired and knew Ryan would know the best route to drag the deer out of the woods.

Joe and Ryan soon were back to help us. We took a short break while I filled Joe in on the story of my buck. Although he had now lost the $6 buck pool, Joe was excited about the deer.

As we took turns dragging the deer out of the woods, I recalled an experience I'd had a couple seasons ago. Ryan and I hunted Day 2 of opening weekend and were leaving the woods at the close of the day. As we exited the woods, we came across two hunters dragging a nice 9-point buck. Ryan and I helped the older hunters drag the deer the rest of the way. It was a nice North Woods buck with a wide, dark rack and dark-colored neck and face. I remember thinking how privileged I would be to harvest a buck like that. I now had that honor. It was extra special to harvest a buck in Wisconsin's North Woods with this group of hunters. We worked hard, hunted the way true hunters did, and our efforts paid off. This experience was one I would never forget.

The following day we hunted most of the day before journeying home. Every hunter except Andy harvested a deer over the opening weekend. Andy harvested a nice buck several days later in central Wisconsin.

As we traveled home, I knew I would hunt several more times in areas near my home, but I already missed the North Woods, and looked forward to returning next deer season.

— Andy Lecker
Oshkosh, Wis.

Rhode Island Man's Best Buck Comes at Age 94

Unlike with organized sports such as baseball and football, deer hunters generally get better with age. Just ask 94-year-old William Goodhue. While hunting with his cross-bow, Goodhue nailed a trophy buck on his 20-acre property in 2004, the likes of which few other Rhode Island residents have ever seen.

"I've been an outdoors-man all my life," Goodhue explained, "taking my first buck in Massachusetts when I was only 16 years old. And except for a 13-year hiatus I took while rais-ing my family, I've bagged one or two deer every year since. Indeed, I've got racks from Maine, New Hampshire, Vermont and New York, and there is a solid hunt-ing story behind each one of them.

William Goodhue has hunted deer for decades, but he killed his biggest buck (so far) at age 94. He shot this 9½-year-old 10-pointer on the 20 acres he owns surrounding his house.

"I used to hunt with a bow, but I can't pull a bow back anymore. This past fall, however, the state opened up a crossbow season. This got me thinking about deer hunting when the leaves are yellow and crimson again, so I bought a license and then a crossbow. I practiced in my back yard until I got pretty good with it.

"I own about 20 acres of woods around my home, but I can't walk it like I used to. I now get around the property on a camouflaged golf cart, which suits me just fine. This enables me to scout out the surrounding land for deer and deer sign a little more easily.

"One afternoon while pulling into my driveway, I saw several does in the woods next to the house. I see deer in this 200-yard strip all the time. I quickly grabbed my crossbow, and slowly walked back up the driveway to where I'd just seen the does. The woods here are about 150 yards wide, with an open field on the far side. There is a faint trail that enters the woods from my driveway, so I sneaked in a ways and stood next to a big tree. I guess I kicked those does out in the process. Suddenly, I saw this big set of antlers following those does. He wasn't in any kind of a hurry, so when he got about 50 or 60 feet away, I took aim and shot. The bolt entered the buck right behind the shoulder and exited through his liver.

"The buck took off. It was an easy shot and I knew I hit him, but I looked until dark and couldn't find him. The next morning my neighbors and my 8-year-old grandson, Christopher, helped me with the search. It was Christopher who first spotted the rack about 9:00, stuck in a brush pile about 300 yards away from where I had shot.

"Now I've shot some big deer in my day, but nothing like this one. I was told he was $9^1/_2$ years old, which is very old for a buck living in the wild. He only dressed out at 195 pounds, but he was quite gaunt from the rigors of the rut. His most impressive feature, however, was the inside spread of this 160-class 10-pointer. It measured 22 inches!"

You would think that after tagging a buck like that, that Goodhue would relax and take it easy. But no, the season was still open! Two weeks later, he nailed another deer on his property — a big doe, which proves that once the deer hunting bug bites, you have the fever for life. Just ask Goodhue; he can't wait for this fall!

— *Bill Vaznis*

New York Hunter Makes Up for Lost Hunting Time

It's been said that if a youngster doesn't get the urge to hunt by the time he reaches high school, he may never hunt. That was almost the case with James Marinaccio of Grand Island, N.Y. He grew up in the city, and none of his friends hunted. But he married into a family of outdoorsmen who tutored him in woodsmanship and helped him kill his first deer when he was 27. Since then he has tagged seven or eight nice bucks, three of which would qualify for the Pope and Young Club if he had them scored.

Last fall, however, he tagged a buck that begged to be tallied; a buck he had never seen before — or one even remotely like it for that matter!

"Nov. 14 dawned a perfect day," Marinaccio said. "It was the peak of the rut, and it was cold; maybe 18 degrees, and calm. We finally caught a day with no wind, and I was excited as could be. I climbed into my stand about 9:00 in the morning, and stayed alert. About two hours later I saw a buck circling me in the hardwoods about 150 yards out.

"I could tell right away he was a good buck, so I started giving him the one-two punch by using my grunt tube and my doe-in-heat call, one after another. At first the buck seemed to ignore my renditions, and continued circling. I kept calling, however, in hopes he would eventually turn and come in my direction.

"I heard a noise off in another direction, and turned toward it. When I looked back, the buck was coming closer, obviously looking around for 'other deer.' I must have hit the right pitch because he suddenly turned and walked right toward me, stopping dead in his tracks about 30 yards out. He then raised his head and looked straight up the tree at me, and froze. He saw something he didn't like, and I was sure he was going to bolt. I

James Marinaccio didn't take up hunting until he was in his 20s, but he has made up for lost time. The pinnacle of his hunting career so far was this 180-class 16-point buck that he killed in 2004.

knew the buck wasn't going to stick around much longer, so I brought my bow to full draw, took careful aim and released. It looked like a good hit. The arrow struck dead center, penetrating right up to the fletchings. The buck turned, and high-tailed back into the woods.

"I got down and got my brother-in-law, but I think we went after him a bit too soon. We could see blood everywhere, like a red carpet. We found him lying down, but still very much alive about 150 yards away. He must have sensed our presence because he got up and walked another 100 yards before expiring."

The estimated dressed weight of the 16-point nontypical was 225 pounds, and the buck was thought to be $5\frac{1}{2}$ or $6\frac{1}{2}$ years old. The rack had 14 points with two $1\frac{1}{2}$-inch stickers on the left main beam, and a 20-inch inside spread. The net score of $186\frac{6}{8}$ inches should stand as New York's best archery nontypical for 2004.

— *Bill Vaznis*

Luck Doesn't Run Out, But Monster Buck Does

You never know when a big buck is going to step into your life. You can read deer sign, read topo maps and read the wind, but when it comes right down to it, luck is often the determining factor in a hunt. Take Rob Smith's 2004 hunting season, for example.

Smith, of Erin, N.Y., caught a glimpse of a tall-tined monster during bow-season before it disappeared into the woods. He hunted the rest of the bow-season and most of the regular firearms season and didn't see the Steuben County buck again.

Then, on the last Wednesday of the gun-season, Smith and his brother-in-law, Burdett Madigan, decided to hunt the last few hours of the day by putting on a short drive in the same area where Smith had seen the buck. Madigan entered a small woodlot, and out popped the giant buck!

As it bolted across an open field, Smith fired two shots from his bolt-action 12-gauge. The second sabot struck the buck in the spine, dropping him in his tracks. He and Madigan had not been hunting more

Rob Smith spotted this tall-tined 11-pointer while he was bow-hunting, but didn't see it again until it ran out of a woodlot during firearms season. He dropped the bruiser with a 12-gauge slug.

than 20 minutes!

The tall-tined 11-pointer had an $18\frac{1}{2}$-inch spread and was estimated to be $4\frac{1}{2}$ or $5\frac{1}{2}$ years old. It had a lot of loose skin indicating it had been rutting hard and had lost a lot of weight. In fact, the buck only dressed out at 160 pounds. But age and dressed weight don't make the record book. The 11-pointer's antlers scored 161 even.

When asked how he felt about his best buck ever, he simply replied, "I'd rather be lucky then good."

— Bill Vaznis

An avid bow-hunter, Doug May hadn't gun-hunted for years. But when he saw this 200-class buck out his window as he prepared for his bow-hunt, he reached for his dad's old 16-gauge and put on the stalk of his life.

Man Spots Huge Buck While Getting Into Shower

It was the morning of Nov. 30, 2004 — squarely in the middle of Ohio's gun season — and I was getting ready to shower and head to an area farm for a few hours of crossbow hunting. I thought that by now maybe the gunners had gone south and I could enjoy some late-rut action with the big 12-point buck I'd seen earlier in the year.

With my shower water running, I glanced out the bathroom window and noticed a loosely spaced herd of deer near the rear of our distant hayfield. One of the deer was very large. I yelled for my wife, Jen, to join me, and she came running with binoculars in hand. Through the binoculars, we realized that we were looking at the largest deer we had ever seen. I gathered my children at the window to watch the amazing display that was playing out before us. There were four bucks trailing one very small doe. We passed the binoculars back and forth, each of us in awe of the big buck next to the doe.

Twenty minutes had passed since I'd first spotted the big buck out the window, and I still had no inclination of hunting the deer in our field. That was, until my 10-year-old daughter, Morgan, asked, "Daddy, aren't you gonna get him?"

I was surprised by her question, and paused a moment to ponder my answer. I responded, "Morgan, I'm not a gun-hunter, and it's gun season." I explained that I could not get within reasonable bow or crossbow range in the open field.

Morgan didn't hesitate to shoot back, "I think it's time you started gun-hunting, Daddy!"

My wife and 7-year-old son, Austin, agreed, and that was all the coaxing I needed! "Are you sure it won't bother you if I kill the deer?" I asked my daughter. "Go get him, Daddy!" was her enthusiastic reply.

In Ohio, a deer tag isn't weapon-specific. I hadn't used a gun for a few years and didn't know if I could even find my 12-gauge. My dad had recently gifted me his Ithaca "Sweet Sixteen," and I knew exactly where *that* was. My wife and children scoured the house for the blaze orange vest, hat and gloves that I told them I needed. I met my wife and children in the kitchen and they quickly dressed me in the blaze-orange articles I had asked for. I gave my wife a kiss and slipped out the back door of the house.

As I reached the field, I could still see the big buck, but he was heading for the next field. In the distance, I could faintly see a few orange "dots" that must have been other gun-hunters in the adjoining woods and fields. My 9-acre field has a gentle swale in the middle and is edged by a field of over-grown goldenrod and brush.

The wind was perfect — right in my face — and I figured I could sneak along the edge of the field down into the swale, and about the time I crested the top of the draw, I'd be close enough for a shot. As I crept along the edge of the golden-rod in a crouch, the smaller bucks became edgy and trotted off. I kept

Doug May shot this 17-pointer with a bead-sighted 16-gauge shotgun in a field behind his house as his family watched from inside the house. He dropped the deer from nearly 100 yards with a single shot.

moving, hoping that the retreating deer hadn't spooked the doe and big buck that were just ahead and still out of view.

As I got closer to the top of the draw, I had to crawl on my knees to keep my body from being silhouetted against the field. My heart began to beat faster as I realized the "moment of truth" was near. Would I raise my head, only to see that the pair of deer had sensed my approach and high-tailed it out of the field, or would I be laying my eyes and my shotgun

bead on the biggest deer I had ever seen?

I eased my head over the short alfalfa, and almost like a dream, the buck and doe stood nearly in the same spot where they had been for the past half-hour. The bad news was I had greatly underestimated my distance from the pair, of whitetails, and after a painstaking "stalk," I was still nearly 100 yards from them.

I slowly shouldered the shotgun and looked down the barrel. The doe was directly in front of the big buck, completely blocking the buck's vital area. I attempted to grunt at the big deer, thinking he would move enough to allow a shot. Instead of moving and giving me a shot, he was now staring in my direction on full alert with his front leg raised, as if ready to stomp or run. I realized that I had to take a shot without further delay, or the two deer would be off my property and headed toward the group of orange dots in the distance. I carefully placed the bead of the shotgun on the forehead of the big buck and could not believe how big the tiny bead appeared on the distant target. I took a deep breath, raised the bead a few inches, and squeezed the trigger.

As most any hunter can attest, I can't remember hearing the shot go off. I moved my face away from the gun and saw one deer running away — the doe. I popped up on my knees and looked around frantically, until I spotted the distinct outline of the tall, heavy antlers sticking up above the hay. I nearly yelled out loud as I stood up and saw the behemoth down on his side.

Before I started toward the buck, I turned back toward the house and saw my children and my wife running through the alfalfa field in their pajamas! That sight made me chuckle, and helped settle me down. I consciously stepped slowly forward at a normal pace, but soon found myself running toward the big deer. I could hardly believe my eyes as they focused on the biggest set of antlers I'd ever seen, and on a deer

with a body that was equally as impressive.

My daughter was out of breath as she approached, but managed to ask, "How many points, Daddy?" I hadn't even counted them yet! Morgan didn't waste any time grabbing the thick rack and began counting out loud, touching each tine as she went. "Seventeen, Daddy!" I gathered the family around the fallen monarch and explained the significance of what they had just witnessed. We took a moment for a group hug and to share an unforgettable moment together just staring at the beautiful buck.

The next few hours were like a dream, except for the nightmare half-hour of trying to get the deer into my pickup truck! I changed clothes while the others got dressed and we drove to the check station and then to the taxidermist to get a rough idea of how the deer might score. We did a cursory taping of the rack and came up with more than 200 inches of antlers! At the butcher's, we hung the deer and found that he weighed more than 215 pounds dressed, with an estimated live weight of nearly 300 pounds!

Taking a trophy buck is a once-in-a-lifetime opportunity. Achieving the feat on your own property is even better. But the experience of having my family with me, watching the drama of the entire hunt unfold, was a wonderful experience that ranks at the very top of my hunting memories.

— *Doug May*
Massillon, Ohio

Michigan Brothers Tag Buck "Pheasant-Style"

Jerry Lambert (left) and Joe Lambert hunted this Michigan 10-pointer like a pheasant. The brothers inched through a grassy field to roust him from his bed.

Orange-vested and toting loaded shotguns, my brother Joe and I are standing at the south property line of a 50-acre grass field. This parcel is like a little piece of Iowa in southern Michigan. Cackling rooster pheasants are heard virtually every outing. It's excellent pheasant habitat — a rarity in our state.

Although there are plenty of birds, they are not our quarry today. It is high noon, the day after Thanksgiving. Counting this day, there are three days left in the firearms deer season. Joe and I both know that deer like to bed in this tall-grass field, and conditions are perfect for a two-man still-hunt.

A strong wind blows out of the northwest, accompanied by a misty rain. Our hopes are to flush a buck much like you would roust a rooster pheasant. It is late into the deer season, so pushing deer off of our property isn't much of a concern.

Joe walks a mowed lane to my left, while I act like a dog and zigzag my way through the grass. We move very slowly so that a buck won't hear us and flush wild, way out in front of us. The wind and rain help cover any noises we make.

Joe stays slightly ahead of me, "pushing" the cover with his scent. Joe takes a step or two and stops and then I take a step or two. My chest tightens with anticipation, knowing that at any second a big buck could jump up from under my feet.

After covering about 150 yards in an hour, we have only 50 yards to go to complete this section of the field. I'm thinking that most people would probably give up at this point, with such a little strip of grass remaining. But I'm also hoping that Joe remains patient and alert, because I am moving very slowly, standing for minutes at a time.

Luckily, Joe and I are on the same page, and we both turn it up a notch and go into stealth mode. It helps that we both know that my brother Jeff and I jumped a wide 8-point here last year as we made our way to our tree stands. Even if he's not still around, we know that another big buck could move in and take his place as they so often do.

After a very long pause, I take a step and it happens. A deer suddenly bolts from a small patch of dogwoods. He runs toward Joe until he sees Joe and then turns south. Hearing him in the dogwoods, I have my gun up and ready. As soon as he comes into view, I identify him as a shooter, find him in my scope and pull the trigger. Seeing that he is still up and running, I shoot a second time. Joe then shoots and the buck goes down. "I got him, I got him," Joe yells.

We run 50 yards to where we think he is. Joe and I arrive at the spot at the same time and anxiously scan the grass. Joe immediately finds blood. Cautiously moving forward, we find him after just a couple of steps.

"We did it, we got a big one!" I yell. Joe is equally excited and bends over and counts the points out loud. It's a 10-pointer.

Joe calls Jeff on his cell phone and reports the news. Jeff asks who shot it. At this point we aren't sure and don't care. We are two very excited hunters. Our plan has worked perfectly.

Once we get off the phone, we decide to do the detective work. I tell Joe that I think that I hit the buck with my first shot because I had a good sight picture and it felt good. It was the same feeling you get when shooting free throws and you know it's good right from the release.

Sure enough, there is a very obvious blood trail that went back to the dogwoods. We then find the sabot slug hole on the deer's left side. The shot went through the heart and one lung. We discovered that Joe's shot hit the buck's right antler, which caused him to go down.

If you have a large grass field, try the two-man still-hunt. We're glad we did.

— *Jerry Lambert*
Kalamazoo, Mich.

Trip to Dixie Yields Bucks, Hogs and Memories

Susan Dillman booked a deer hunt in South Carolina and wasn't disappointed. She shot these two pigs and a 9-point buck all in the same day!

My husband, James, and I went on a three-day hunting trip Oct. 25-27, 2004, to the Deerfield Plantation in St. George, S.C.

The first day, I didn't see anything in the morning, but in the afternoon I saw seven turkeys. That afternoon was unusually warm. I was overheated and became ill that evening. I was worried that I wouldn't get to go hunting the next day. Boy, am I glad I felt better the next morning!

The second day would be very successful. My guide, Lee, got me settled into my stand at 5:45 a.m., and after just 15 minutes, I started to hear noises. I heard heavy foot-steps, then I heard a wild pig chomping corn. Finally, around 7 a.m., it was light enough to look

through the scope on my .308, and I saw the pig. POW! I shot my first Southern pig! I dropped him in his tracks.

Around 8 a.m., I took my second pig. I got on my walkie-talkie and told my husband the story. He told me to quit shooting pigs, but if I saw a buck, shoot it. Little did he know I was about to do just that.

I was actually fooling around with my binoculars when I first saw him. Something told me to look over my left shoulder. When I did, a buck caught my attention. When he came into an opening, he started to walk away from me. I prayed that he would turn so I could get a shot. He finally started to quarter to the right. I didn't

Susan Dillman's hunt just kept getting better. On the last day of her hunt, she connected with this 10-pointer.

hesitate. POW! The buck actually ran toward me. I knew I'd hit him because I saw blood on his right side. When I shot, I really didn't concentrate on how big he was.

When Lee came to pick me up, we couldn't find him. The brush was so thick. Thank goodness the buck had left a blood trail. My guide and another guide got "Slow Joe" to track him. Slow Joe is a beagle worth his weight in gold. He found my trophy!

When we brought the buck back to camp, I found out that it was a beautiful 9-point with a 16½-inch inside spread. He weighed 150 pounds. It was my best buck! But what I didn't realize is the best part of the hunt was yet to come.

On the last day of the hunt, we all got to go into the trophy area. I prayed to God that I would at least see something, and boy would I!

That morning, I only saw a spike buck. Late that afternoon is when the action started.

First, I saw a doe with a 6-point hot on her trail. I couldn't shoot because in the trophy area, it had to be 8 points or more with a 14-inch minimum inside spread. Even though I couldn't shoot, I did enjoy watching the rut in action.

Later, around 6 p.m., four does came out to eat some corn. A spike buck eating with them jerked his head up toward the woods. To my amazement, out walked what I would call "Big Daddy." I had to try to count points because I needed 8 points to shoot. I counted

8, so I waited for a shooting opportunity.

The buck started to follow a doe. He trotted behind her a short distance, then started to walk away like my other buck did. He stopped at one point to check out the other does. I was again praying he would turn. My prayers were answered again! As he started to quarter to the right, I took aim. POW! The buck dropped, but started to crawl into the woods. I was stunned. I was scared that I would lose that buck.

When Lee came to pick me up, he couldn't find the buck in the brush. I was beside myself. We didn't even have a blood trail this time. Again, we called upon Slow Joe's skills to pick up the buck's scent. I waited back at camp for what seemed a lifetime! An hour later, the guides were back with a huge 10-point with a 15-inch inside spread. The picture doesn't do it justice! The left brow tine had two kickers to give it character.

Everyone was so happy for me, after I harvested two pigs and a 9-point the day before and now a 10-point. Wow! I couldn't ask for a better hunt! My husband didn't harvest anything, but he was very supportive of my success. And to top it off, I was the only woman in camp, and I harvested the most game. I felt on top of the world. What made the experience even sweeter was how every person at Deerfield made me feel. They made me feel like their best friend; like family. What more could you ask for!

— *Susan A. Dillman*
Gettysburg, Pa.

Adirondack Hunter Bags Monster Despite Illness

George Davidson has been deer hunting with the same rifle since he was 21 years old. Now 58, Davidson has tagged more than 40 bucks with his Remington Model 742 Woodsmaster, including a 10-pointer that scores in the low 130s and several others that now adorn his living room wall. Topped with a Leupold 4X scope and tip-off mounts, Davidson's .308 has proven deadly. "Why would I want a new gun when this one has done all that I have ever asked it to do?" Davidson said.

Davidson started tagging along on his father's hunts when he was 8 years old. He killed his first deer, a button buck, when he was 16, and at 18 he tagged a spike-horn. There haven't been many years since that he hasn't tagged at least one deer with a bow, shotgun, rifle or muzzleloader. Last fall, however, he bagged his best buck ever with his favorite rifle: his .308 Remington.

"For the last 25 years or so we have taken 10 days off and headed deep into the Adirondacks to hunt wilderness bucks from a tent camp," Davidson said. "There is a certain lure to the big woods that you cannot get anyplace else. You are not surrounded by roads, and you can wander over the next ridge without fear of bumping into another hunter. Now, we do not see as many deer as those hunters who prowl active farmland do, but when we do come across a buck in the mountains, it is usually a keeper.

"Last fall my brother-in-law Bill Vogt, my brother Charles, my son Nicholas and his buddy David Michaelson got three or four miles off the beaten path and hunted 10 days from a tent, tagging three bucks for our efforts.

"I was sick for most of the hunt with a sinus infection. Nonetheless, I hunted every day, despite the coughing and sneezing. One afternoon after being in place for only 10 minutes or so, I spied a buck walking in my direction about 100 yards out. I couldn't get a shot through all the brush, but experience told me

George Davidson had a sinus infection during most of his annual 10-day hunt in the Adirondacks, but he didn't let his illness keep him out of the woods. His reward was this 160-class 9-pointer.

he was coming my way. I kept my cool. At 75 yards I found a hole and shot once. The buck dropped behind a blowdown, but when I approached he tried to stand up, so I shot again. That's when I realized how big he was! His rack was outside his ears!"

Davidson's Hamilton County buck was estimated to dress out around 185 to 195 pounds. A taxidermist later gauged the age of the 9-point buck at $4^1/_2$ years. The rack was most impressive. The greatest spread was $25^3/_8$ inches, and the inside spread was $23^1/_8$ inches. It had good mass with 5-inch bases and long main beams of $27^6/_8$ and $27^1/_8$ inches. If it weren't for a $3^1/_2$-inch nub on one side, Davidson's buck would have grossed $170^7/_8$ inches. The net score of $164^5/_8$ inches made it one of the best bucks ever bagged in Hamilton County.

And to think Davidson was so sick that day that he almost stayed in bed instead of going hunting. Now, *that's* dedication!

— *Bill Vaznis*

Hunters Outsmart Buck After Nearly a Decade

A group of Massachusetts hunters finally outsmarted this elusive, well-known buck. The 160-class 9-pointer survived in a suburban area for nearly a decade.

Big bucks don't get big by being stupid. They learn at a very early age that to survive to a ripe old age, they must avoid all predators, especially man. In some instances, bucks simply go nocturnal, while in other cases bucks stay out of sight by fleeing to the most remote regions available.

However, one Massachusetts buck took a different route and beat the odds for many years. He learned to live in close proximity to man and in plain sight. And in so doing, the 9-pointer lived for nearly a decade.

"This buck lived his entire life in and around a moderately settled area in Middlesex County, Mass.," said Wayne Tuttle, a highway worker for the town of Groton. "He was seen regularly in and out of deer season, and in fact, liked to bed right under people's noses. It was not uncommon, for example, to find him laid up in someone's back yard, close to local businesses or even in the middle of a large open lot in plain view for all to see.

"On some days there would be several vehicles pulled off to the side of the road with onlookers ogling over his rack. He might have looked like an easy target, but the fact of the matter was it was difficult in most cases to get a legal shot at him, and even if you could put the sneak on him there was always a solid escape route nearby which made him all that more difficult to hunt."

However, time ran out for the buck last year on the last day of the muzzleloader season. Tuttle, Peter McGreggor, Troy Conley and a few other friends had put on a couple of slow pushes that morning without much luck.

"McGreggor, who had missed an opportunity at the big buck the previous week, had to leave early to go to work while the rest of the group continued with the hunt," explained Tuttle. "Soon, Conley's cell phone rang. It was McGreggor, telling him he saw the big buck bedded in a swamp as he was driving to work.

"We knew where the swamp was, but not exactly where the buck was bedded. We decided to go look for him anyways. After all, it was the last day of the season.

"As luck would have it, we found the buck, but he was bedded on posted property. I knocked on the door and got permission to go after the buck. Conley and I decided to put a pincers movement on him. I would take a stand along a probable escape route while Conley would try to sneak up on the deer. We really didn't care who got the deer. We hunt together as a team for the pure fun of the hunt.

"When Conley got close, the buck got nervous and started to rise out of his bed. Conley thought the buck was about to bolt, and in anticipation of such a move aimed high. As it turned out, the buck was probably just going to slowly skulk off, and Conley fired over the buck's back.

"The buck took off running now, crossing in of front me. The swale grass was so tall, however, that I couldn't get a clean shot at him. I waited and when the buck jumped a brook, I got a 75- to 100-yard quartering-away opportunity. I found him in my scope and squeezed off a shot. The bullet hit him behind the left front shoulder about a foot back and lodged in his neck. He only went 75 yards before collapsing in a heap."

The 9-point typical with four small stickers dressed out at 203 pounds. The Northeast Big Buck Club scored the buck at 165$^{1}/_{8}$ inches — not bad for a last-day buck!

It was difficult to age the buck because there was plenty of tooth wear. The buck was also missing two front teeth on his lower jaw. It is believed the buck was 8$^{1}/_{2}$ or 9$^{1}/_{2}$ years old.

— *Bill Vaznis*

Massachusetts Hunter's First Buck Scored 162

Our first buck with a bow is a memorable event. It doesn't matter if it's a spike or a wide-racked 8-pointer, that buck will live in our minds forever.

So it should come as no surprise that when Christopher "Tigger" Talbot arrowed his first buck after tagging several does, he, too, would be ecstatic! But his first bow buck was no average deer; it was a whopper that made the record books!

"I knew a big deer was in the area," Talbot said. "I found a logging road that ran along the base of a steep ridge during the spring turkey season that was littered with big rubs. I returned in September and laid down 10 mock scrapes along that road, doctoring each scrape. They were hit almost immediately, but I kept them fresh and did not hunt over them until early November when I knew the rut was in high gear.

"Finally, on Nov. 10, I set up a tree stand in the morning, and hunted from it that evening. I had a doe come in that rubbed her head against the tree I was sitting in. Later, 10 or 11 more does showed up. Then, just before dark, I heard a buck grunting as he came toward me. I came to full draw when he stepped behind a jack pine, but I couldn't see through my peep sight. It had somehow twisted to the point that made it useless. Unable to shoot, I was stuck in my tree stand for some time before I could exit the scene without spooking all the deer away. Even then I could hear that buck chasing does around. The rut was indeed in high gear!

"I climbed back into the stand before first light the next morning. A doe came wandering in, and for practice I decided to draw on her. Much to my surprise, I still couldn't see through my peep sight! I thought all it needed was a simple twist to get it to re-align, but I was wrong. After the hunt, I took my bow to a sport shop. Thankfully, they had me back in the woods in no time.

"I couldn't hunt that evening because it was my girlfriend's birthday. The next morning the weather was absolutely miserable, with high winds, sleet and heavy rain. I went to my parents' house and the weather forecast was for more of the same, with snow later on in the morning. I was dejected, as it was the last morning I could bow-hunt before traveling to Vermont for the rifle opener.

"Despite the inclement weather, I eventually decided to bow-hunt that stand one more time. I attached a drag rag to my boot and hoofed it to my stand, jumping a deer en route. By 8:00 it turned to snow, freezing me in my stand. I was doing deep knee bends to increase blood circulation when I saw a deer 45 yards away, working its way toward me. The closer it got, the more I realized it was a good buck. I grabbed my bow, and when he stepped into my one and only shooting lane, I brought my bow to full draw, aimed and sent an arrow toward him. The arrow went clean through the buck as he stood broadside 20 yards away.

"The buck kicked like a mule

Christopher Talbot almost didn't go bow-hunting when he saw that it was windy, with rain, sleet and snow. But it was his last chance to bow-hunt before going rifle hunting, so he endured the elements. After he bagged this 160-class buck, which weighed 250 pounds field dressed, the weather didn't seem so unbearable.

deer and ran off into the woods. I soon heard a deep guttural grunt. I started to shake then and had to put my head between my knees to help me calm down.

"I waited about 10 minutes before picking up my arrow, which was covered in blood, and started trailing the deer. It was an easy trail to follow, as there was blood everywhere on the fresh snow. He ran only 65 yards or so before expiring.

"I didn't realize how big the rack was until I picked up his head, and I didn't realize how heavy he was until after I field dressed him. In fact, he was so heavy I couldn't drag him out myself. I had to enlist my hunting partner Dane Stolgitis for help.

The Hampshire County, Mass., buck later tipped the scales at 250 pounds dressed, and was estimated to be $4^1/_2$ or $5^1/_2$ years old. The Northeast Big Buck Club scored him at $162^2/_8$ inches.

And to think "Tigger" almost didn't hunt that morning!

— *Bill Vaznis*

Marine and Brother Score a Pair of Bruisers

Lance Golomski, left, and his brother Brad Kealiher experienced a highly successful 2003 Wisconsin gun season. Lance shot his 14-pointer on opening day, and Brad — a Marine who had just gotten home from Kuwait — shot his 10-pointer with 15 minutes to go on the last day of the gun season.

Lance Golomski and his brother Brad Kealiher connected in a big way during the 2003 Wisconsin deer season. Lance (left) shot his buck opening day at 1:30 p.m., while Brad shot his buck on a drive the last day of the season, 15 minutes before closing time. Lance's buck had 14 points with a 15-inch spread, while Brad's buck had 10 points and a 16-inch spread.

Brad, a U.S. Marine, had just come home from Kuwait, and wasn't sure if he'd be able to make the 2003 Wisconsin gun-deer hunt. It wasn't until three days before

opening morning that his leave was approved. The next day he was on a plane from San Diego to Wisconsin in anticipation of the big annual tradition.

After a mid-afternoon rattling sequence on opening day, Lance's buck appeared behind a smaller buck. Lance saw the two bucks come through a small opening more than 150 yards away before they disappeared into the thick swamp again. After 10 minutes, the smaller buck came out of the swamp into the hardwoods while the larger buck waited. A few minutes later, the larger buck wandered out of the swamp to see what the commotion was about. Lance stopped him in an opening with a quiet grunt and shot. The buck ran only 30 yards before falling.

Brad wasn't successful until the last drive of the last day. He was a driver on the last drive of the year, and in the middle of the drive, he was already accepting the fact that he wasn't going to get a deer after all the work he went through to get home for gun season. Then, out of the corner of his eye, he saw a buck trying to backtrack through the drivers. Brad zeroed in on him and three shots later, the buck was down.

The two brothers have shot nice bucks before, but never in the same season. It all came together in a season that neither will ever forget.

— *Lance Golomski*
Plover, Wis.

Connecticut Archer Arrows Giant With Ol' Trusty

Stephen Kiback III's family poses with the 16-point nontypical he killed with the same bow he's used for more than a decade. The buck grossed 181⅛ inches.

One of the secrets to success is knowing your equipment. When the moment of truth suddenly presents itself and time is of the essence, the last thing you want is to be caught fumbling around looking for the right pin on your bow.

Stephen Kiback III, is very familiar with his bow, because he's been shooting the same one since 1993. This familiarity with his equipment paid off last fall when he arrowed the biggest buck of his life on state-owned property in Connecticut with his 73-pound Jennings Machine Extreme XLR.

"My draw length is only 25¼ inches," Kiback said, "but I've tagged at least two deer every year since I've owned that bow, and most of those were bucks, and a couple of those dressed out at over 200 pounds!

"I did not know that the buck was in my hunting area before I killed it, but I learned after I tagged the buck that other hunters had found his sheds in the same area and were hunting the same Middlesex County state land as I was.

"I had a stand set 15 feet off the ground overlooking a prime feeding area — a stand of white oaks. The deer were in there feeding regularly, and I thought it would only be a matter of time before I got a shot.

"The first time I climbed on board four does came in to feed, but none of them presented me with a shot. The second time I arrowed a 110-pound doe at 30 yards. I knew the area was hot, and I couldn't wait to get back to that stand.

"My third opportunity in that stand came when I got off work around 8:00 in the morning. I rushed over to the property and was in my stand by 8:45. I must have dozed off because when I woke up an hour or so later I saw this buck with massive antlers standing 30 yards away in the mountain laurel, feeding on acorns.

"He was facing me head-on. I had no shot, but I stood up and prepared myself in hopes he would soon give me a crack at him. Five or six minutes later (it felt like hours) the buck stepped into the clear, giving me a clean 22-yard shot. I finally came to full draw and sent my arrow, taking out one lung.

"I waited for about an hour before picking up the blood trail. There was blood everywhere and the trail was easy to follow. In fact, I walked right up on him, but when I realized just how big he was, I tagged him and went back to my vehicle to dump off my gear. I knew it was going to be a tough drag.

"Then more good luck came my way. Two game wardens showed up and offered to take their 4x4 right to the buck, which they did. They took lots of photos and seemed as excited as I was about the deer. They wanted to show other deer hunters that Connecticut has got some big bucks, too! They were both very helpful and very friendly. I was glad they showed up."

Those two game wardens were right. Kiback's 16-point nontypical buck was truly impressive. It field dressed at 183 pounds, and was estimated to be 4½ or 5½ years old. When scored by the Northeast Big Buck Club it grossed 181⁴⁄₈ inches, making it one of the best bucks to ever come out of the Constitution State.

It doesn't look like Kiback will be selling his trusty old bow anytime soon.

— *Bill Vaznis*

Indiana Man Slips in on 300-Pound Monarch

I hunted whitetails for the first time in 2004. It was also the first time I hunted with a muzzleloader. I ended up shooting the biggest buck of my life so far.

I was hunting on Dec. 4 in Vermillion County, Ind., when I spotted him going down into a hollow toward a creek at about 11 a.m. I watched him disappear over the end of the hill I was on.

I sat for about a half-hour, then slowly and quietly moved down to where I first saw him sneaking along. When I got to that spot, I stayed for about 45 minutes, looking and listening. I spotted some movement in the bottom of the hollow, but it was a small flock of turkeys. I thought to myself it must be pretty safe down there for the buck if the turkeys were moving as slowly as they were. So I decided to move down off the end of the hill into the deep hollow after the turkeys left.

Moving as slowly and quietly as possible, I arrived at the bottom of the hollow, with a 40-foot-high hill on both sides of me. The hill on my right side came to an end at the creek, so when I reached that point, I stopped and looked for a bit. A noise to my left got my attention, but I saw nothing. Then another noise to my right got my attention. When I turned my head slowly to the right, I saw the monster buck stand up next to the creek on a little peninsula almost completely covered in brush. The buck was looking back toward the first noise I had heard, but he wasn't too worried. I was in disbelief that I

Mike Biggs spotted this buck in a hollow while muzzleloader hunting. After the buck disappeared, Biggs stalked to within 40 yards of the 300-pound monster.

could stalk to within 40 yards of this buck.

I aimed my muzzleloader, said a little prayer and pulled the trigger. When the smoke cleared, all I could see was this monster lying right where he had stood. I think I dumped everything possible out of my backpack in a rush to get my muzzleloader reloaded, but he was down for good.

Then the work began. Just about every way out of there was straight up, except down the creek. I called another person in my hunting party to help me. It took about two hours to get the buck back to a road.

The buck weighed 322 pounds dressed, and his neck circumference was 29 inches. He was scored as a typical 10-point with seven sticker points for a total of 17 points. He had a gross score of $171^{6}/_{8}$ inches.

— *Mike Biggs*
Cayuga, Ind.

Patriotic Shorts and a Buckeye Dupe Monarch

It was a gray November day as I stood in front of the old-time bow-hunter. He told me to hold out my hand and close my eyes. When I did so, he placed a small object in my hand and whispered these words to me: "Robert, may you bag the biggest buck of your life this hunting season."

At that moment, I felt a strange sensation as the sun broke free of the cloud-covered sky and washed my face. The odd feeling coursed through my body, and I knew right then that something special was happening. I opened my eyes and there laid a buckeye — a nutlike seed the size of a half-dollar. As I gazed into the old man's weathered face, I knew this was the most magical moment I had ever felt. The man told me to carry it with me every time I went into the woods and the buckeye would work its magic. I thanked the wise, kind-hearted bowman and gently stuck the buckeye into the pocket of my hunting pants.

A few days later, in the dark of early morning, I was cradled 25 feet up within the huge limbs of a giant white oak. My bow was lying across my lap with an arrow nocked and ready.

The ancient tree stood in the southwest corner of a picked bean-field. The narrow, 100-yard-wide field ran along the top of a ridge for more than a mile. Numerous oak-wooded hogbacks and thickly covered draws sloped down off the ridgetop field. The thickets provided excellent bedding spots for doe groups, and the ridge was a perfect place for a rutting buck to look them over. Thus, the huge oak I was in became a strategic place to try to ambush one of these ridge-running stags. With the aid of my binoculars, the majestic oak became a good vantage point to observe the way bucks scoured the area for hot does.

As I sat patiently in my comfortable tree stand, a small glow of light began to appear on the eastern horizon. A new hunting day was about to unfold, and with my buckeye safely tucked in my pants, my anticipation was running high.

Already I could see shadows of deer feeding on tender new bean shoots. The original soybean crop had been picked much earlier, and the deer found the delectable new shoots of the leftover beans much to their liking.

As the rising sun lit up the landscape, I identified a tall-antlered buck in hot pursuit of an unwilling doe. With my binoculars I watched him about 300 yards away, chasing does in and out of the field, in and out of the thickets and always well out of bow-range. As I observed the big boy, I noted a particular spot that the buck traveled past whenever he searched for a new doe. I watched him for more than an hour, and he never stopped searching the ridge for a willing doe.

About the time I decided to climb down and head over to the buck's favorite draw to set up an ambush there, he found a doe to his liking. I watched the two deer head down into a timbered draw to

Using good luck, trickery or maybe divine intervention, Robert Law arrowed this dandy Michigan buck. And he wouldn't trade all the buckeyes or patriotic drawers in the world for the experience.

bed down for the day. I waited an hour in case the happy couple popped out again, formulating a plan as I sat.

I needed some help to execute my strategy, so I climbed down and headed back to camp. Once there I told my brother, Gary, my long-time hunting partner, what I had seen. I told him that I'd formulated a game plan, but I needed his help.

"No problem, brother, I will help you," he replied.

I told him I knew where the buck and doe would probably pop

back out into the beanfield that afternoon to feed. At that spot stood a big oak tree where I intended to set up an ambush. Hopefully, I would get a shot at the buck as he followed his girlfriend out to the beanfield.

There was one problem. On the other side of the draw was a cornfield. If the pair of deer decided to have corn for dinner, they would not be coming to my ambush point along the picked beanfield.

To make sure they didn't go to the cornfield, I wanted Gary to drive down the gravel road that ran along the edge of the cornfield about 300 yards from the bedded pair. There, I wanted him to place some articles of dirty clothing on the telephone poles every 100 yards. The wind was blowing from the south that day, and I figured the wind would blow enough human scent from the clothing toward the bedded deer that when they got up to feed for the evening, they would smell the human odor and stay away from the cornfield. Instead, they would probably head for the beanfield, where I would be set up in my ambush tree waiting for them. With the wind blowing from the bedded deer to me, the two deer would have no idea I was there.

As we discussed the plan, we tried to decide which articles of clothing to use. I wanted something that reeked of human odor and suggested some of our dirty socks.

"How about some dirty drawers?" my brother suggested.

"Heck, I want to push the deer into the beanfield next door, not scare them to the next county!" I replied.

But we eventually agreed upon the dirty drawers. It was Veteran's Day, so my brother came up with a red and blue pair, and I found a white pair. We were being as patriotic as we could.

Early that afternoon I reached the oak tree and quickly set up a tree stand. The tree was 25 yards from the spot where I had watched the buck travel past three times that morning. My brother did his job, and the dirty drawers were hung.

At around 3:30 p.m., I saw the doe pop out into the beanfield about 60 yards away. As I watched her, she kept throwing her nose into the air, smelling something wafting on the wind. She seemed to have a disgusted look on her face! It had to be the aroma from the flag-waving pairs of dirty drawers!

A few seconds later, out popped her grinning stud muffin. That was when I first got a good look at the tall rack. Man, oh man, what a sight! I threw the binoculars up and almost fell out of the tree as I focused in on the buck's impressive headgear. His thick, knurly rack had points sticking out everywhere! What a beautiful sight — truly a bow-hunter's dream buck!

I took a deep breath and tried to think of a way to entice the pair my way. Should I grunt or bleat? I chose to wait them out because I figured if they couldn't see the deer making the call, it would probably spook them.

Within a few minutes, the doe started walking down the beanfield edge away from me, taking her stud muffin with her. I should have called, but I was too shocked to see them walking away.

Within a couple of minutes they disappeared. Even though it truly was a blessing just to have seen such a beautiful sight, I am a bow-hunter, after all, and my spirits sank as the deer went out of sight. I knew better than to give up, though, because there was still an hour of daylight left, and during the rut, anything can happen. I pulled the buckeye out of my pocket and turned it over a few times in my hand and whispered a small prayer.

Five minutes hadn't gone by since the pair disappeared when I heard the crunching of dried leaves. I threw the binoculars up and searched for the source of the noise. I was hoping and hoping it was the bruiser buck. Soon, I saw a patch of brown in the lenses, then I saw the sunlight glinting off the antlers of a huge rack. It was Mr. Big! He was a coming my way, and he was a coming fast!

The leaf crunching kept getting louder as the buck rapidly approached my tree. I let go of the binocs, grabbed my bow and got ready. Within seconds it became difficult to control my breathing. The excitement within me was like hot lava in a volcano ready to explode. I tried to tame it by talking to myself. "Stay calm. Pick a spot. Stay calm. Hold steady. Don't blow this. You can do it!"

After what seemed like hours but actually was only a few seconds, the buck closed the distance and now was only 20 yards away and walking steadily around the oak tree I was standing in. I drew back the arrow and anchored at the familiar spot on my face. The buck soon materialized in a clear opening between the limbs of the white oak. I made a "baa" sound with my voice and the buck quickly stopped to search for the source of the sound.

That point was when it was the hardest for me not to come unglued! It would have been so much easier to just let the arrow sail over his head to get rid of the volcanic stress of the moment.

Luckily, predator instincts, years of bow practice or the Lord above put me on autopilot. I effortlessly lifted the bow and put the sight pin on a spot on the buck's chest. I did a quick three-second count, held steady and finally let the string go from my fingers. Whack! I heard the arrow hit the buck hard in the chest. Within seconds the buck was on a death run, and just as quickly the buck crashed to the ground.

Holy mackerel, I did it! I felt so high; there is no drug on this earth that can give me the feeling I was enjoying at that moment! I quickly sat back down because suddenly my legs felt like rubber hoses. I savored the moment and reflected on what had just happened. One question baffled me though: Why did the buck leave his girlfriend and head directly toward my tree? It was like I was reeling him in to the tree.

I know I did a few things right to put myself at the right spot at the right time, but the way the buck left the doe and came directly to the very tree I stood in seemed somewhat mystical.

A few minutes later I slowly climbed down and walked over to the buck and held his heavy antlers in my hands. I felt sad and ecstatic at the same time. I then looked up into the sky and thanked our Lord in heaven for giving me such an opportunity. I pulled out the magical buckeye, rolled it over a few times in my hand, then I gave it a big ol' lip smack! Man, oh man, what a buck!

— *Robert Law*
Royal Oak, Mich.

Lost Hunting Area is Blessing for Illinois Brothers

In 2004, Wayne Hadley and his brothers experienced something that's becoming more common across whitetail country. After 30 years of hunting on the same property, land use changed, and the Hadleys had to find a new place to hunt.

But like the old saying goes, sometimes when a door closes, a window opens.

One of Wayne's brothers had done some drywalling for a farmer in Macoupin County, Ill. The farmer is a very generous man, and asked if the Hadleys would like to hunt his 320 acres.

Would they!

On Oct. 29, the Hadleys went to the farm to bow-hunt it for the first time.

Wayne has had back surgery three times, and therefore, doesn't hunt from a tree stand. A lot of people laugh at him as he carries his 5-gallon bucket to bow-hunt from, but he's killed bucks while sitting on it before.

Hadley was making his way across a plowed soybean field, heading for a finger of oak woods. He'd seen a lot of rubs and other deer sign there, so he planned to sit at the edge of the timber.

Before he could even get situated, he noticed deer crashing through the trees. Two does were on a mad scramble, heading right for him. Hadley, who was still just inside the open field, dropped to his knees and got ready to shoot one of the does, which were now standing about 15-18 yards away. However, his bow got hung up on his bucket, which he had slung around his shoulders, and he couldn't get to full draw. He fumbled with the bucket and got it off his shoulders, but now it got hung up on his knife! Meanwhile, the does just stood and watched.

Finally, Hadley got everything untangled. But now, instead of watching him, the does were watching their back trail. It didn't take long to figure out why.

Hadley heard loud crashing coming toward him, and suddenly, all he could see were antlers coming right for him. Hadley stood up, but the buck continued on its course, because the does were now behind and to the side of Hadley.

Hadley began to worry if the buck would ever stop. He tried grunting with his mouth, and finally the buck stopped 25 yards away. To say Hadley was excited would be a gross understatement, but he gathered his wits, concentrated on the buck and shot. The buck bounded away, Hadley sat on his bucket to calm his nerves and thank God, and the does continued to stand around!

Finally, the does left, and after 20 minutes or so, Hadley took up the buck's trail, which was very easy to follow. Although the buck traveled a long ways, it wasn't hard to find.

It wasn't until he recovered the buck that Hadley got a good look at the rack. He knew that the deer's body was absolutely huge, but he assumed the buck was maybe an 8- or 10-pointer. Instead, the buck carried 14 scorable points, including a $6\frac{1}{2}$-inch tine coming up from the center of the skull. Although the rack was narrow, the mass was incredible.

After losing their hunting area, Wayne Hadley and his brothers obtained permission to hunt a 320-acre farm. Hadley arrowed this 150-class nontypical while bow-hunting from the ground during his first hunt at the new location.

The right base measured $10^3/_4$ inches in circumference, while the left base taped out at $10^1/_4$ inches. Hadley's brother, who has been a taxidermist for 30 years, had never seen bases of that size. The unusual rack from Hadley's "unicorn" buck had other amazing features as well. The back of the brow tine still had shards of velvet, which apparently the buck was unable to rub off. Also, the main beams were only $1^1/_4$ inches from touching. The buck netted $158^4/_8$ inches as a nontypical.

But amazing as the rack is, the buck's body size was even more impressive. Hadley and his three brothers, all of whom weigh more than 200 pounds, were unable to lift the deer. In fact, the massive buck snapped a $5/_{16}$-inch cable on a winch, and when the buck was finally lifted up onto an ATV, the rear rack "folded up like an accordion."

The farmer had to move the deer with his tractor. The incredible buck dressed out at 248 pounds, and may be the heaviest deer ever killed in the county.

Although the way Hadley killed this incredible buck may sound crazy — bow-hunting from a bucket — he killed a 9-pointer three years earlier almost the exact same way.

Although Hadley's buck is the talk of the family, a deer with a similar-sized body, but with a larger rack, was spotted on the farm, and the Hadleys have hopes of getting a crack at it this year, if the farmer lets them hunt his land again. His price for hunting privileges last year? One photo of Hadley's buck!

— *Joe Shead*

Hunters Doggedly Track Down, Ambush 8-Pointer

Deacon Crocker, along with his friends Roger and A.J., doggedly pursued an 8-point Massachusetts buck that suffered a superficial wound from Roger's arrow. The trio tracked the deer for several hours through swamps and across driveways. Deacon finally arrowed the buck from a distance of 4 feet while wearing nothing but bluejeans and a white tank top!

We've all seen the picture of the heron eating a frog. Although it's in a dire situation, the frog isn't about to be eaten without a fight, and it tries to choke the heron and escape. The picture is accompanied by the phrase, "Never give up."

I have found this advice to be extremely helpful in tough situations throughout my life. Although I've still lost some battles, trying my hardest has at least always left me with my pride and a sense of accomplishment. I've always believed that you should get back

what you put into something, and what you deserve eventually will find a way to catch up to you. Living my life this way has not only helped me as I grew up, but it has also proven to be one of my most successful bow-hunting strategies.

This hunting story begins on the evening before the last day of our bow-hunting season. My friend, A.J., and I had already had a pretty successful season, and with three good bucks between us, we were feeling confident for the upcoming firearms season. Don't get me wrong; we were still excited about the last day of bow-season and were eager to set foot in the woods the following morning. A much-needed cold snap had just moved in, and on my way home that night I had seen a good 10-point cross the road not far from my house. With the vision of this massive animal fresh in my mind, I was optimistic about the year's last bow-hunt.

A.J., my father and I would hunt one of our better spots in the morning. I had been seeing a lot of good bucks there, but the warm weather had greatly slowed down deer activity. I knew all we needed was a cold snap to increase deer movement, and here it was — better late than never. I suppose I should have known what would happen next.

On Friday nights, an all-too-familiar foe occasionally falls in our way of making it to our Saturday morning stands. The phone rang, and so it began: the teeth-clenching battle between our endless and extensive love for bow-hunting and our undeniable weakness for girls. My friends called and wanted A.J. and me to go out for the night. I wished I hadn't answered the phone, but I had, and now we were faced with a dilemma I didn't like. As usual, we convinced ourselves that we could go out and still make it to our stands before first light. After all, it was the last day. How could we miss it?

The following morning found me still in bed. The November sun glared through my window and into my eyes as if it were rubbing it in my face. We had blown it. We had chosen girls over a bow-hunt — a decision I'm still not comfortable admitting, but a lesson I will carry with me for many seasons to come. Ashamed, I went to wake A.J. He was already up, and he looked at me, grinning and shaking his head. That's all he had to do, I knew what he meant and I agreed.

"Want to go jump up some black ducks?" I asked. He just nodded his head and I went to make coffee.

The phone rang, and I was reluctant to answer it, with the consequences of last night's activities still so fresh in my mind. However, I knew my father had gone afield, and in hopes that it was him needing help tracking, I picked up the phone.

It was our friend, Roger. As he spoke of a heavy 8-pointer he had just arrowed, his voice sounded dejected and quiet. He told me the deer was standing broadside at 10 yards, but when he drew his bow, the buck turned and looked straight at him. Roger is a responsible hunter, and he grudgingly admitted that he had taken a shot that was less than perfect. The arrow ended up hitting the deer high in the rear, just below the spine. The arrow only penetrated a couple of inches and soon fell out. We both knew the hit was not lethal, but that went without saying. I could tell Roger didn't need to hear it.

A.J. and I offered to help Roger track it because we all knew we owed it to the animal. We waited several hours before picking up the blood trail.

Roger had seen the deer enter a small patch of woods surrounded by a saltwater marsh directly after the shot, so this is where we started our search.

With A.J. tracking the buck through the jungle of poison ivy and bull briers, Roger and I set up on what we hoped would be the receiving end of the push. It was a long shot, but when we wound an animal, we make every attempt to recover it.

Soon, the sound of cracking sticks and moving brush would produce nothing more than A.J. He stumbled out of the briers; he hadn't found a drop of blood. I was not surprised, but we were not ready to give up.

With the muddy conditions, we soon picked up the buck's tracks and followed them a ways. We managed to find a pin drop of blood where the buck had climbed onto a dike. Then we lost the track for a while.

After being on my hands and knees for a long time while searching for more blood, I stood up to stretch and rest my eyes. As I gazed across the marsh, I recalled a time when I was about 10 years old. I remembered tracking a heavy-racked 8-pointer that my father had hit in the shoulder blade while bow-hunting from the ground. We tracked that deer for three days for about 4 miles, and for all three days we had a blood trail. We tracked it through swamps and yards, across roads and a large marsh. On the fourth day it rained, and we never recovered the deer. However, it was then that my father taught me to never give up.

Roger waved me over to where he found evidence that the buck had jumped a creek. Sure enough, the deer had cleared a creek about 5 feet wide, and by no small margin. This only furthered my feeling that the deer would make it.

We picked up the track on the other side of the creek and followed them to where the buck had entered the woods. Here, the tracks were confirmed by a smear of blood on a sapling the buck had rubbed against as he pushed his way through.

The woods were almost impenetrable here, so we had to crawl for the next 40 yards. We found no blood in the woods, and there was no mud to show the buck's tracks. It appeared that we might lose the buck at this point, so we decided to split up and walk circles in three directions in an attempt to find more sign or the animal itself. I walked to the west and found nothing but a single large buck track, but by this time I was so far from the spot where we had lost the buck's trail that the track could have been made by any buck. There was only a slight chance that it was made by Roger's deer, but a slight chance is still a chance, so we followed it.

We followed this set of tracks through a swamp, over someone's yard and up onto someone's driveway. Then the tracks entered an oak grove that was thick with bull briers. At this point we had tracked the deer for nearly six hours, covering about a mile of ground and traveling through all different kinds of terrain. We had found a total of two smears of blood and the deer had shown no signs of fatigue or being seriously injured. The chances of us recovering the deer weren't looking good, but we agreed that the animal would be fine and collectively felt good about that. However, there was one more thing I wanted to try before we called off the search.

The woodlot that the deer entered was only about an acre and a half. To the north it was bordered by a large marsh; to the south a busy road. We stood to the east of the woodlot, and I knew of a small field on the west end. I suggested that I go around to the field while A.J. and Roger pushed through the woodlot. My thought was, if the deer was in there, he would most likely run through the field. The wind was right, so I set off. As I entered the field, my intentions were simply to get a look at the buck and to take note of his condition. However, I was still toting my bow.

By this time I had shed two layers of clothing and was left wearing a white tank top and blue-jeans. I found a tree on the northwest corner of the field and climbed in it. Here, I could see the marsh clearly. Feeling foolish in my attire, I laughed to myself as I nocked an arrow, thinking, "wouldn't it be funny if I actually got a crack at this brute?" Seconds later, a crack was exactly what I heard.

As I looked up, my heart fell to my feet. There he was, tail up, running straight at my tree. All I remember thinking was, "this can't really be happening!" I drew my bow nonetheless. As the deer approached my post, I gave him a quick grunt with my mouth, but he didn't hear it. I abruptly let out a louder one but got no response. My third grunt sounded more like an alarmed black duck, but it worked and the monster skidded to a stop directly underneath me. His antlers were a mere 2 feet from the bottom of my boots. I knew I had about a second before he was gone again, so I settled all three of my pins behind his shoulder and released. My arrow buried itself in a hurry because the buck was about 4 feet from my broadhead. He gave a kick and ran out into the marsh.

I don't think I took a breath as I watched him run down the woods line. He slowed to a stop, looked back over his shoulder and fell into some tall marsh grass. My screaming and yelling brought A.J. and Roger running from the woods. We had done it. All signs said to stop trying and go duck hunting, but we never gave up, and eventually, we got what we deserved. The big 8-point weighed 208 pounds dressed and had a wide rack with extraordinary mass.

Although this story had a very happy ending, I urge everyone to hunt responsibly. Only take clean shots that you are completely confident with, and please make every attempt to recover a wounded animal. We as hunters owe the animals we pursue the respect they deserve.

— *Deacon J. Crocker*
Massachusetts

Deer Season Deals Iowa Man a Pair of Eights

Kevin Muehlenkamp scouted this tall-tined 8-pointer before the 2004 Iowa bow season. The buck's tall, heavy rack scored in the 160s.

In hunting, as in poker, it helps to have good luck. And if you're skilled, you learn how to play what's been dealt to you. But let me start at the beginning.

My first encounter with a certain large 8-pointer was during the summer of 2004. I was watching several different bucks in the mornings and evenings in preparation for deer season. When I first saw the tall-tined buck, I only thought he had about a 14-inch spread. It turns out the rack's height and thickness were

deceiving, making the width seem smaller than it actually was.

I made at least 20 trips to this area that summer. Whenever I checked, the tall-tined 8-pointer was there. He had the same routine every morning and night.

At first I didn't really think a lot about the buck. I called my brother Mike (Pud) and told him what the buck looked like, and told him it would be a nice buck for our dad to shoot. Dad had shot one that looked similar to this buck almost 40 years

Kevin Muehlenkamp racked up another 8-pointer in 2004 during the gun season. This wide-racked buck scored in the high 140s.

ago, but my dad, David, did not draw a tag for Iowa this year.

Over the next several weeks, I made several calls to my dad and Pud, letting them know about the deer and where they were appearing. But now, after weeks of scouting and figuring out which stand looked the best, I wasn't able to hunt opening weekend of bow-season. I had promised my wife, Mary Ellen, that we would drive to Arkansas to visit her son and daughter, who were attending college there. Needless to

say I had nothing on my mind but hunting. I was so wrapped up in it at the time that I watched more hunting videos that weekend than I have ever watched in my life.

After our weekend in Arkansas, I returned to my hunting area the first chance I got. Of all the weeks I had to put up a tree stand, I didn't even have it done yet! I got off work early on Monday and drove as fast as I could to go set up my stand. I knew the 8-pointer's trail, so as quickly as I could, I put up the stand, changed

158

into my hunting clothes and got in the tree stand.

After about 20 minutes I started seeing deer — first a few does, then a few smaller bucks. A nice 10-pointer came out soon after, but he was too far for a good shot. I'm a firm believer in 20-yard shots. I don't have much time to practice, with my bow, so I don't shoot past 20 yards.

Soon after I spotted the 10-pointer, my luck started. I watched the 10-pointer look behind him, and then here came the 8-pointer. He started to walk away from me, but again luck turned my way. A truck on a road across the field I was sitting in made a rattling, rumbling noise and caused the buck to turn and come back my way. Just like that, I had my chance. I shot and he was gone.

I didn't know how well I'd hit the buck, so I decided to wait until the next morning before looking for it.

As you can imagine, I didn't get much sleep that night! I returned early the next morning and began my search. I found my arrow right away, and it didn't look good. There wasn't much blood. It looked like a brisket shot, with just a little fat.

I began to look anyway. After about 100 yards I found one speck of blood, hardly anything. I kept going and found a bed not 200 yards from my tree stand, but there was no sign of the buck. I kept going very slowly, looking and watching. I came over a little hill, and there he was looking at me, sitting like a statue. I hadn't bought my bow with me on the trail, so I starting slowly walking backwards, one step at a time, just as slowly as I had walked forward. I used my hat and the arrow that I had found on the trail as a marker to find

my way back to the place where I'd seen the bedded buck.

After getting my bow out of the truck, I slowly crept back to where I'd seen the deer. Sure enough, he was still there. I pulled up to shoot and away he ran.

I thought that was it; he was gone! But I kept up the pursuit and followed the blood trail he was leaving. About four hours later, I finally got my shot. He was lying down again. It looked like he thought he was invisible. It's hard to shoot a deer lying down, but I took the shot and connected.

At this time I didn't even realize how big he was or how perfect his antlers were. After getting him back to the truck, I took him to a friend who owns a sports shop. He told me it was the biggest 8-pointer he had ever seen! After having the buck scored, I couldn't believe my luck. It measured 163⁰/₈ inches and had only 1⁴/₈ inches of deductions.

Second 8-Pointer

My next card was dealt to me during shotgun season. I'd had many chances to scout out several old and new hunting areas. The problem is that in my hunting area, the herd is getting so large that it's tough to really know which stands are best. I've hunted this ground for more than 15 years. The hunting is fantastic, but sometimes the same scenery gets a little boring.

So during our short gun-season, I decided to take a chance and sit in a spot I had never sat in before. Again, I called Pud and told him where I was going to be sitting.

I told him I was going to do something I have never done before: I was going to sit all day, no matter what.

I took a portable chair, water, food, etc., and sat on the ground. I had never sat on the ground to hunt deer before.

The spot was perfect! Draws came from three different spots where deer could be pushed from other property owners, where the hunting pressure is heavy.

I got situated, making sure I was well hidden. Being on the ground was different for me, but I got used to it.

It was about 7:20 a.m., when I first saw the buck. It was the first deer I'd seen that morning. At first I thought he was just a small $2^1/2$-year-old. He didn't look like much from the side, and that's all I could see of him till he looked my way. I about choked on my doughnut when I saw how wide he was! As I got up, the chair fell over. I leaned up against a tree and shot, and the wide 8-pointer took off.

I watched him for a few seconds, then he went down. I gave him a few minutes to make sure he couldn't get back up. I checked him out with my binoculars and he wasn't breathing. The time was 8 a.m.

The funny thing is, all my hunting companions know that I have never sat for more than $2^1/2$ hours at a time. I called my brother and told him the story, and we both laughed about how I was planning to sit all day, and my hunt was over in less than an hour.

I couldn't believe that I had been "dealt" another big 8. My second 8-pointer measured $148^3/8$ inches and had a $22^1/2$-inch inside spread.

This is one season I will never forget.

— *Kevin Muehlenkamp*
Dubuque, Iowa

For Iowa Hunter, Nothing Beats Hunting at Home

Rick White hunts several states each year as part of his job for Hunter's Specialties, the Iowa hunting-products company. The success of the company's *Primetime Bucks* video series depends on its pro staff logging many miles and hours in a constant quest for great buck footage.

Despite all the travel, some of White's most memorable successes have happened right at home. "That time when the rut really starts cranking up at home has been magic for me the past few years," he said. "Leading up to the 2004 season, I'd shot three bucks in three years from the same stand. Those kills were on Nov. 6, Nov. 5 and Nov. 6, and we got them all on film for *Primetime Bucks 6, 7* and *8*."

On Nov. 2, 2004, White headed out to his favorite stand with cameraman Phillip Vanderpool. For three days they watched more than a dozen small bucks moving through the area. As much as he believed in his stand, White didn't want to commit the basic sin of overhunting it. So, early on Nov. 5, he and Vanderpool slipped into a different stand several miles away.

"I couldn't help but think about the date that morning," White said. "With all the bucks we'd been seeing, I just knew this was going to be the day."

About an hour into the hunt, White tried rattling while working a grunt tube. The sound carried well on the clear, calm morning.

"It wasn't five minutes after I'd

Rick White, a Hunter's Specialties pro-staffer, travels all over the country each year to hunt trophy bucks. However, he killed his biggest buck, this 173-inch 10-pointer, on familiar ground near his Iowa home.

stopped rattling that Phillip spotted the buck and pointed him out to me," White said. "It was hard to tell exactly how big he was because of the brush, but I could see a lot of antler. There's no way I could shoot, but since he'd crossed a creek to get to us, I was pretty sure he'd keep on walking to check out my rattling and calling."

Things happened quickly after that. The buck stayed in the brush for a few moments and then worked his way into the open, giving White his first good look at him. He didn't have to look long. When the buck hesitated, standing broadside, White released his arrow. The buck piled up next to the creek.

Although White has tagged thumper bucks all across the United States, measuring the massive 10-pointer told him what he already figured: This was his biggest bow-kill ever, and the fact he had done it on his home turf made the experience even sweeter. He later scored the buck at 173⁶/₈ inches. And yes, Vanderpool caught all the action for *Primetime Bucks 9*.

"I'll try not to think about all of that when Nov. 5 rolls around next year," White said. Then, grinning, he added, "But I think it's a fair bet I'll be hunting at home."

— *Jim Schlender*

Backyard Stand is Pure Magic for Big Bucks

While lying in bed recovering from hip-replacement surgery, I thought what better time to reflect on the last five years of my short hunting career! The last three seasons have been a dream come true for a new bow-hunter. Being a greenhorn and having no clue as to the ways of the whitetail, the first two years were not very successful, although I did harvest two does with a shotgun.

Living in northwest Indiana — some of the best hunting in the state — I've had many chances to harvest a deer. The only thing holding me back seemed to be the know-how to accomplish this. My bow-hunting career started in 2002 when I bought a used compound from a friend. I started to practice with two of my older brothers that spring and summer. Soon, hunting fever had ahold of me.

That first year was a blast. I harvested three does: two in the early season and an old doe during the late season. My oldest brother has had 180-plus acres of property to hunt for some time, and after not hunting for 25 years, he also had good luck, harvesting an 11-point bruiser that fall that tipped the scales at 207 pounds dressed. I also managed a very respectable 10-pointer on opening day of shotgun season by setting up a ground blind on the border of our property overlooking a state-owned refuge. It was my first buck ever!

My family and I had been living in Merrillville, Ind., for 10 years, and with the building boom in northwest Indiana being what it was, I had started looking for some property to build a new home on. Being in the construction business, it was sensible to contract our own home. So that fall, we began to look for property.

We found a 3-acre parcel north of Lowell, Ind., that was a bargain. So the winter of 2002-2003 was spent getting ready to build the following spring. This property had almost a quarter of an acre of swamp on it, and my brothers teased me, "You could hunt out your back door." I laughed at this, but wasn't very enthused about it. But the more information I gathered about deer activity and deer habits, the more interested I became in hunting behind my house the next season. So after I started construction in May, I set one stand in back in an old cottonwood in a good location for prevailing winds and planned on maybe hunting there on weekend mornings before I worked on our house. The way the property is set up, I thought it would only be good during the rut as a staging area or a travel corridor for bucks, and was I right!

As the 2003-2004 season blew in, I didn't have much time to hunt because all my spare time was spent working on the house. I did manage to bag a doe on my brother's property, but as the rut came in, I hadn't had a whole lot of luck seeing bucks. That all changed as the last week of October rolled in.

I started seeing a lot of deer traffic around the new house, so I said to myself, "This weekend I will sit Saturday and Sunday mornings before work and maybe I'll get lucky." Well, as luck would have it, that first morning was all I needed.

There was a full moon that Friday evening, so as I went to my stand, I pocketed my flashlight. The wind was perfect as I made the four-minute trek to my stand. A little after 7 a.m., I began to stiffen and get cold, so I thought I would stand and stretch to work some warmth back into my limbs. Standing, I spied a doe jump across the road to the south and head straight for the swamp. I grabbed my bow and watched as she came in and bedded right under my stand. Because my freezer was full, I sat down to wait her out until my help showed up for work.

After five minutes of watching, I heard a low grunt behind me. I quietly waited to see what the buck would do. Softly grunting, he slowly moved around my left side and approached the doe from her rear. As the buck concentrated on the receptive doe, I quickly grabbed my bow and stood. As the buck browsed in a circle, he finally stepped into a big enough lane for me to draw and get off an 18-yard shot! He jumped straight in the air and took off like a shot. He headed south across the road into a swampy island in the field next door. Shaking, I waited 20 minutes before climbing down and giving my brother a call on his cell phone to announce I may need some manpower later in the morning. After getting permission from the landowner to search his property, we finally found the big 8-pointer about three hours later! What a buck! He scored in the 120s and field dressed at 185 pounds. My first bow buck was a dandy.

We moved into our new home the following Valentine's Day. I was already planning the year's hunt in

Bob Watson lives on a 3-acre lot in Crown Point, Ind. Although the property is small, the bucks he's killed on it are anything but! While hunting on this property, Watson arrowed a 120-class 8-pointer in 2003, and a 130-class 10-pointer in 2004.

my stand behind the house.

In May I was diagnosed with a circulatory disease that affected both of my hips. After my operation, recuperation was slow, and walking was almost impossible. I was unable to get to most of our stands on my brother's property, so I decided to put a few stands on my boss' overgrown apple orchard. That property had been bulldozed so surveyors could access it, making it easy for me to sneak in and out.

During the first three weeks of early bow season I saw more bucks on this property than I had seen in two years anywhere else. I didn't hunt too much during that time, but I did manage to harvest two does to fill my meat quota.

By the end of October I hadn't had

any luck with bucks, but I became hopeful that my luck would change as the rut heated up.

The first weekend of November I had a Saturday evening hunt with my brothers, with venison sausage making planned afterwards at my brother's house. We were going to hunt the next morning, but after getting home that evening well after midnight, the thought of getting up early enough to return to my brother's place wasn't that appealing. With a fuzzy head the next morning, I decided to take it easy and just crawl into my backyard bungalow for a couple of hours and hunt with the boys that evening.

Watson made it two-for-two when he arrowed this 130-class 10-pointer in 2004, during his second season hunting behind his house.

By the time I got my gear together and headed for my stand it was already getting light. As I rounded the corner of our house, I spied two deer in the field behind the swamp, and with all the racket I made, I spooked them. I deposited doe estrus scent around the base of the old cottonwood and climbed into my stand with intentions of getting the remainder of my clothes on and getting set for an uneventful morning. I didn't get the chance!

As I hung my bow, I saw the biggest buck I had ever seen heading straight for me at a trot. My mind raced as I tried to decide what to do. My heart sank as I told myself the big boy was going to keep trucking right past me and never look back. As he headed around my right side, he slowed and began to pick his way through the swamp at my rear, giving me just enough time to stand, grab my bow, and get in position. He gave me a quartering-away shot that I couldn't pass on.

After the release, I saw the arrow penetrate his right hindquarter, and as he took off, I mentally started to kick myself because I knew he was gone and wouldn't be back. The buck made it 25 yards into the open field behind the stand, took two stagger steps and piled up! He lay there for almost 30 minutes before I could find enough strength to get down and check out my trophy. The buck sported 10 points and scored $139^{4}/_{8}$ inches. It was one of the most unbelievable mornings of my life!

It seems I severed the femoral artery. I'll never know if the shot was deflected, but there definitely was good luck riding with me on this day.

Hopefully by this season I'll be fully recuperated so I can spend more days afield. One thing's for certain, come rutting time you'll find me in my stand behind the house!

— *Bob Watson*
Crown Point, Ind.

Hunter Captures Breeding Sequence on Film

Ken Dolota may not have tagged a buck during Wisconsin's 2004 gun season, but that doesn't mean he went home empty-handed. On Monday, the third day of the nine-day season, Dolota was driving at about 2:30 p.m., when he noticed two deer in a field. Seeing it was a buck and a doe, he pulled over. Judging by the deer's body postures, it was apparent Dolota was about to witness something he'd never seen before.

The doe hunched up her body and backed into the buck. Dolota grabbed his digital camera and began snapping photos. The deer were only about 25 yards off the road. Because it was an overcast day, the camera's flash went off, but the deer merely looked at Dolota, then continued breeding. Dolota captured the whole breeding cycle, which lasted from 7 to 10 minutes. When the deer were finished, they merely walked away, only 10 yards from Dolota's truck. Dolota has been a deer hunter for more than 20 years, but has never seen anything like this before!

— *Joe Shead*

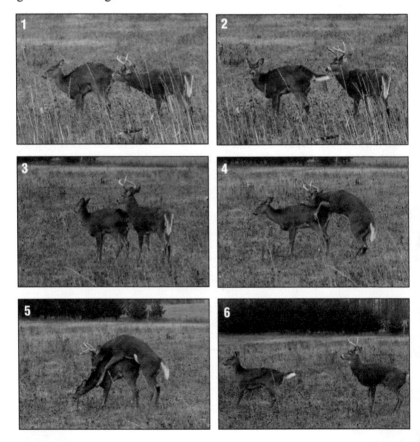

BIG-BUCK
HUNTING SECTION
Pages 165-207

Daniel E. Schmidt

Pat Reeve

Hunters can sometimes access urban areas with high deer populations if the community views hunters as a "service" to control high deer numbers. Not only do urban areas sometimes have a lot of deer, they often harbor huge bucks.

Getting a Key to the City

How to Get Urban Landowners to Demand Your Bow-Hunting Services

Archers are often the best solution for controlling the booming whitetail herds of suburbia, but accessing a metro area's private woodlots can befuddle most bowhunters. Not Rob Lucas. At his day job, Lucas is a physician's assistant in New York City; in his free time he's a crusader for bowhunting near his home in Norwalk, Conn. — a community besieged by deer. Intelligent and passionate, Lucas has the green light to hunt more property than he can handle. Here's his five-step plan for landing hunting permission in the 'burbs.

Fight the Good Fight

Anti-hunting folk are alive, well and highly vocal in Norwalk. Members of at least three major organizations weigh in on whitetail management issues in local media. But Lucas won't let their lies go unchallenged.

"Whenever an (anti-hunting) individual writes to a newspaper and doesn't have his/her facts straight, I write my own letter," he said. "I answer with a calm, well-reasoned defense of hunting that may include data from the CDC (Centers for Disease Control) to quotations from Gandhi. And then I sign my name and include my address and telephone number."

Lucas' step-to-the-plate approach infuriates the Bambi crowd, but it's endeared him to many local homeowners who've tired of deer damaging their gardens, automobiles and loved ones (Lyme disease is common in the area). "I've had people call and ask me to hunt their property," he mused. "And at many of the homes I visit, the owner has already heard of me. Being a vocal, but reasonable, proponent of hunting has helped open the door for me."

Act the Ambassador

When Lucas visits landowners for the first time, he hands them a packet of information about himself. "It includes a business card, an introductory cover letter summarizing my background, my experience as a hunter, a copy of my hunting license and hunter's safety certificate (Lucas is an instructor), even photos of myself and my vehicle," he said. "Providing such contact information makes it clear I'm a responsible person who'll be accountable for his actions."

Lucas' approach extends to his behavior in the field. He respects property lines, doesn't flaunt dead deer during transport and observes each landowner's wishes for checking in and out. "Some people grant permission, then

Bow-Hunters as Community Servants

The seven-county area surrounding Minneapolis and St. Paul, Minn., isn't the only metropolis struggling to control its whitetail herd. It is, however, home to one of the most innovative programs for managing metro deer. The Metro Bowhunter's Resource Base (MBRB), an umbrella organization representing several state bow-hunting groups, was formed in 1995 to help communities run special archery-only hunts.

MBRB maintains a database of bow-hunters willing to participate in hunts. To make the list, archers have to pass a bow-hunter education course, complete an MBRB application, sign an ethics pledge and pass a proficiency test. Typically, communities with deer complaints are directed to MBRB by their local Department of Natural Resources (DNR) wildlife manager. Then MBRB members attend community meetings and explain how they can safely, humanely and effectively reduce a deer herd.

MBRB has plenty of evidence of the latter; just last fall the group was asked to cull a herd at the Minneapolis Water Works, where whitetails had overpopulated the 80-acre facility. Bow-hunters killed 35 deer in a one-day hunt. Currently, MBRB claims 2,500 members and estimates those members have removed 1,200 deer in special hunts held in the last eight years.

— Scott Bestul

want you to disappear," he said. "Others want to know every time you're there. It's important to learn how each landowner wants things to work and respect their wishes."

Carry the Load

Killing enough does is Deer Management 101 anywhere; doing so in suburbia gets you invited back, Lucas says.

"If I were hunting farm country, I'd help the landowner by baling hay or doing field work. In the suburbs, the way you help landowners is to shoot deer, especially does. The people who let you hunt have deer damage problems and they want solutions. Passing up countless does to wait for a buck is the ultimate form of 'taking' and does the landowner — and hunting — a disservice."

Lucas likes antlers as well as anyone; he shot three fine bucks last fall. He also shot 23 does. What does he do with all the venison?

"I helped set up a program where a local processor hauls a meat cooler to a central location each fall. Any bow-hunter who shoots a deer can take it to the cooler, which the butcher checks every day. If the hunter doesn't want all or part of the meat, he can donate it to local food shelves through our Hunters for the Hungry program. Many landowners volunteer to pay processing costs."

Get an Agent

Lucas is as good as anyone at cold-calling landowners, but he knows word of mouth is the best advertising.

"After I've hunted a place for awhile, I ask the property owner to recommend me to other landowners experiencing deer problems in the neighborhood," Lucas said. "It's one thing for me to show up and announce to a property owner that I'm an ethical, respectful, person; when the guy he talks to across the fence tells him, it just carries more weight."

Inform and Educate

At the end of each season, Lucas prints and distributes a newsletter to each cooperating landowner. "It's my year-end summary," he said. "I tell them how many deer we (Lucas occasionally hunts with friends, if the landowner consents) harvested, compare it to last year's total and examine goals for next year. I also discuss the big picture; two years ago I lobbied for a one-month season extension here. Many residents helped me by supporting that measure. And this year, our management area moved into second place for total deer harvest among Connecticut's suburban units. We've increased our deer kill five-fold in only three seasons. Bow-hunters know we can help in situations like this, we just need to prove it, then not be shy about pointing to our success."

Suburbs Hold Big Bucks

As Scott Bestul mentioned in this article, when invited to hunt on a landowner's property to control deer numbers in an urban or suburban setting, killing deer — any deer — should be your primary goal.

However, with that said, it's a well-known fact that these areas often hold some gigantic bucks. Urban and suburban areas shield deer from hunting pressure, allowing them to grow to maturity — a vital component to antler growth. They often have ready access to abundant forage — much to many a gardener's chagrin — and forest preserves, parks and vacant lots provide plenty of shelter. For urban bucks, traffic — not hunters or other predators — is the primary hindrance to survival. If they can survive cars, they can survive anything.

If you gain access to bow-hunt urban areas, and if you can justifiably hunt for mature bucks, keep these tips in mind.

Just like rural deer, urban deer need food and cover. Identify bedding and feeding areas, and plan an ambush somewhere in between. Even if you cannot hunt the lot where the buck beds or feeds, you may be able to set up in a travel corridor.

Although suburban deer are used to people and may be more tolerant of human odor, don't get sloppy with scent control. Remember, whitetails are wary creatures no matter where they live.

— Joe Shead

Shooting a wall-hanger whitetail is no easy task. Few hunters have the desire and the know-how to consistently shoot mature bucks.

Big-Buck Hunting Tips

Downing a Mature Buck Takes Hard Work, Determination and a Commitment to Your Goal

If your goal is to shoot a big buck, you might have to go to extreme measures. You will almost certainly expend a great deal of time and energy researching big-buck behavior and scouting the best hunting areas. You might have to hunt far from home, and you might have to book an outfitter. You also might have to rethink your hunting strategy. Following these tips might help you put a brute buck in your sights.

• **Check the record books.** A thorough review of record books, such as those produced by the Boone and Crockett and Pope and Young clubs will not only show you which states and provinces are producing the most record-class bucks, but also, which individual counties or parishes are best. Plus, the year the animals were taken will be listed, which shows you which areas are hot now, not 10 years ago.

• **Choose your hunting area carefully.** After reviewing the record books, check with area wildlife managers to learn more about the local deer herd. Ideally, the area should have a low number of deer. Too many deer in a given area forces them to compete for limited food. However, few deer on the range gives deer an abundant food supply, which helps them grow larger.

• **Prepare for the hunt.** You may invest thousands of dollars and countless hours preparing for your hunt. When your buck of a lifetime steps in your sights, don't blow your chance. Practicing often with your bow or gun in real hunting situations is cheap insurance when the moment of truth finally arrives.

• **Gear up.** Make sure your equipment, including clothing, footwear, bow, gun, ammunition, arrows, binoculars and other accessories, are up to the challenge. When you're sitting on stand during a downpour thousands of miles from home during the peak of the rut is not the time to find out your binoculars are fogging up and your rainwear isn't as good as you thought it was. Test your gear before your hunt, and buy the best equipment you can afford.

• **Don't shoot a buck you're not happy with.** First off, in some states you are only allowed to shoot one buck each season. If you fill your tag with a buck that doesn't quite meet your standards, your season is over, and so is your quest for a big buck. If you pass on a small buck, if nothing else, you give it a chance to become a larger buck. Plus, you never know when Mr. Big could be skulking right behind the little guy. If you're serious about shooting a big deer, convince yourself that you're shooting a wall-hanger or nothing.

• **Learn to field-judge bucks.**

Deb Salzer

Spend time in the off-season thoroughly learning your hunting area. Intensively scouting in spring shows you features such as rubs and scrapes from last fall, without disturbing deer during the open season.

When a buck walks in front of you, you'll probably only have a few seconds to decide whether to shoot or pass. Practice judging deer every chance you get, whether it's in magazines, videos, deer shows or in the field. This will help you make an accurate snap-decision when it really counts.

• **Hunt closer to bedding areas in the evening.** The first deer you'll see coming out to feed on an evening hunt are usually does and fawns. Young bucks may show up soon after. However, big bucks routinely wait until after the cover of darkness to feed. They often leave their bedding areas during the last few minutes of daylight, than wait in staging areas within heavy cover until they're sure it's safe to walk out into the open. If you set up your stand in these staging areas, you might see bucks you'd never otherwise see hunting along a field edge.

• **Hunt the rut.** This certainly isn't news to anyone, but during the rut is probably the best time to tag a wall-hanger buck. Bucks not only let down their guard in their relentless search for estrous does, they also are roaming the woods at all hours of the day. You're likely to see bucks this time of the year you never knew existed in your area.

• **Get away from the crowds.** You're not likely to find a bragging-sized buck on heavily hunted land, public or private. However, that's not to say you can't find a bruiser buck in such a place. The key is to get away from the crowds. Get a mile from the road or more, and you're likely to have the spot to yourself. Or, perhaps, find a place that other hunters ignore. Old, smart bucks will frequent some pretty unusual places to duck the crowds; you should too.

• **Get to know the area.**

Topographic maps and aerial photos can give you a quick indication of the terrain features in a given area, but it also pays to get out into the woods and spend time during the off-season getting to know your hunting area. Late winter and early spring are good times to learn the lay of the land without disturbing deer during the hunting season. Signs from last fall, like rubs and scrapes, will still be visible. Plus, you may be able to find sheds, proving that a large buck has survived the hunting season. This information will help you plan your fall hunt without disturbing a buck during hunting season.

• **Do a background check.** If you're booking a hunt with an outfitter, make sure you're getting what you pay for. Ask the outfitter for a list of past clients, and ask the clients about the quality of their hunts. Ask whether there were too many hunters in camp, if the area was overhunted, whether the outfitter made an honest effort to get them a deer and whether the caliber of bucks met the clients' expectations.

• **Keep at it.** Shooting a trophy buck takes dedication and a commitment to sticking to your goals. Don't be afraid to sit in your stand another hour, or to hunt all day, even in the worst weather. You never know when your buck of a lifetime will be on the move. Keep a positive attitude and in the end, things may pay off.

One for the Books ...

If you're looking to give your trophy buck the respect and recognition it deserves, there are a number of antler-scoring organizations that may be able to help fulfill this recognition. Some clubs are weapon-specific (bow-only, muzzleloader-only, etc.) while others limit entries to specific geographic regions. Also, your state or province might have its own scoring club.

As a general rule, the more primitive the hunting method used, the lower the minimum entry score. Also, state record books usually have a lower minimum entry score than national or international record-keeping organizations.

Here is a list of scoring organizations to help you properly recognize your trophy buck.

Boone and Crockett Club
The Old Milwaukee Depot
250 Station Drive
Missoula, MT 59801
(406) 542-1888
www.boone-crockett.org

Pope and Young Club
15 E. Second St., Box 548
Chatfield, MN 55923
(507) 867-4144
www.pope-young.org

Longhunter Muzzleloading Big Game Records Book
P.O. Box 67
Friendship, IN 47021
(812) 667-5131
www.nmlra.org

Safari Club International
4800 West Gates Pass Road
Tucson, AZ 85745-9490
(520) 620-1220
www.safariclub.org

Northeast Big Buck Club
390 Marshall St.,
Paxton, MA 01612
(508) 752-8762
www.bigbuckclub.com

Feeling left out? If you can't access private hunting grounds, don't give up hope. Despite their reputation of having more hunters than deer, public hunting areas produce some wall-hanger bucks each year.

Making Public Land Work

I didn't start deer hunting on public land, but that's where I received my education. I cut my whitetailer's teeth on my great-grandpa's homestead in central Wisconsin; 600-some private acres hunted only by relatives and a handful of friends. Deer were abundant, stand locations respected and camaraderie was the word of the day. I killed a nice buck in each of my first two seasons, when my Remington 1100 was only slightly shorter than my scrawny frame. My pre-teen buddies thought I was some kind of deer-hunting god, and I said nothing to stop their idolatry.

Then we moved far away, where relatives were absent and landowners were reluctant to grant permission, even to a polite kid who offered to help with farm chores. I was from the big city, and that was enough. So my alternatives were two; quit deer hunting or go public.

I never considered the first, but I might have if I'd known more about the Princeton Marsh.

It certainly had game; whitetails and mallards, cottontails and ringnecks. And there was habitat everywhere, from sprawling grain fields to cattail marshes to lovely river-bottom hardwoods. But the parking lots spoiled it. From October through January, they were chock-full of vehicles, which their owners parked between broken beer bottles and empty shell casings. Like everyone else, I just gritted my teeth and went hunting.

I'd never seen so much deer sign and so few deer, and when I finally killed a nice 8-point one November day in high school, I didn't know whether to pat myself on the back or play my luck and ask out this girl I'd been eyeing up. Princeton Marsh whitetails had Navy Seal survival skills, and I was a cadet playing catch-up.

I moved away before I got good at hunting that place, and I have this itch to go back. Part of that is because I'm a better deer hunter now, and I'd like another shot at those high-pressure, schizophrenic, river-bottom bucks. But there's something more at work. I've got a fondness for public land, probably because that's all I had at a time when I needed hunting so much. Challenge — which I always savor — is certainly another element. And a final part is my love of an underdog. Sure, public lands can be tough; they're often hunted hard and managed little. But whenever I hear about a monster whitetail killed on one, I celebrate somewhere deep inside, just like I do when an underrated football team knocks off a Goliath.

In the years since, I've been fortunate to hunt some sprawling private grounds that grow big bucks, some of which I've killed. I treasure each experience and every deer. But I sometimes feel like I've cheated. Not in the hunting,

Steer clear of public lands open to ATV traffic. Instead, pick out hard-to-reach areas that require some legwork and leave other hunters behind.

but the access. Those years at Princeton made me a blue-collar hunter to the core: I had no money, no contacts, no leg up. When I drove in that parking lot, I was just another Joe Lunchbucket who loved deer hunting, and no place is more blue-collar than a public-hunting area. Not all of them can produce whopper whitetails, but some do. For the guy willing to put in the time and effort, killing a big buck on ground he paid for with his tax dollars is entirely possible. In my mind, there's an all-American beauty in that. Here are six ways to change your mind-set and get 'er done.

Think Analytically

Finding big whitetails is no different than finding trophy-class elk, mule deer or pronghorns; you read the record books, talk to hunters and look at trends. Then you begin looking at public areas within the state or region that could help you meet your goals. Big deer can pop up anywhere, but the places that pump them out consistently do so for a reason — season structure, management schemes, awesome habitat, superior food sources, reduced hunting pressure or any combination of the above.

It's no secret that the Midwest is a big-buck hot spot. States like Ohio, Wisconsin, Iowa, Kansas and Illinois have dominated the record books of late. But there are others. Kentucky is coming on like gangbusters, and Alabama is a consistent producer. But don't overlook sleeper states, especially those that feature prairie, mountain foothills or other habitat that most whitetail hunters ignore. Naturally, not all public areas in these general regions will hold mature whitetails in significant numbers. But in most cases, at least some public ground in a top state will offer quality hunting.

Think Big (and/or Nasty)

Just because hunters can go anywhere on a public tract doesn't mean they will. And because one key to finding and killing a big buck is simply getting away from competition, locating a property that contains pockets of lightly- (or non-) hunted ground is critical. This is easiest to accomplish on large tracts, or those with difficult access. We've all read those studies about how few hunters venture further than a quarter-mile from a road, and they're still accurate. I hunted a large state wildlife area in Iowa last fall, and I never spotted another hunter once I left the parking lot for the 1/2-mile walk to my stands.

This is true wherever foot travel is the only access to bigger country. I recognize ATVs for the useful tools they are and use them on some private lands I hunt, but I'd ignore any public tract with motorized-vehicle trails that penetrate every corner. Check out wilderness areas or those with walk-in-only access. And the bigger (and rougher) they are, the better.

A couple years ago, three hunters scouted a huge national forest in Minnesota's North Woods. When these backcountry brush-busters emerged from the woods after opening weekend, they'd filled their tags with bruiser bucks, two of which qualified for Boone and Crockett. They aren't talking much, but I'd bet they didn't encounter any competition.

Think Limited Entry

You don't need wilderness to find monster bucks ... or lose other hunters. Many state or federal properties offer controlled hunts where hunter numbers are limited either for safety reasons or to meet specific harvest goals. Although drawing a tag might take a year or two, the wait can be worth it. In my home state of Minnesota, Camp Ripley — a military base — hosts an annual archery hunt that produces some giant whitetails. Two one-weekend hunts are held, and hunter numbers are tightly regulated. For most guys, Ripley is an every-other-year hunt, but they keep coming back.

Booming whitetail numbers have made limited-entry hunts more popular in state parks and other preserves typically closed to hunters. One of the true growth areas in drawing hunts is in suburban parks and natural areas. Often these hunts require special orientation or training for participants, and some even demand that hunters tag a doe before shooting a buck. But if, like me, you've noted the hawg whitetails being shot near population centers, these requirements seem like minor hurdles. Even better, metro hunts close to home eliminate the expense and time of lengthy travel.

Think Non-Peak

Another fundamental of avoiding pressure is simply to focus your efforts on time periods shunned by other hunters. I learned early at the Princeton Marsh that weekdays beat weekends by a long shot; more than 70 percent of my buck sightings came Monday through Friday. Holidays marked another spike in hunter effort. Thanksgiving's long weekend was a fracas, and the days on either side of Christmas were equally nutty. By devoting my visits to weekdays and off-peak windows, I managed to enjoy some nice hunts.

You can take this a step further. The most popular time for firearms hunters is the opening weekend of the general gun season. Although the increased pressure of the opener can certainly plop a trophy buck in your lap, it's a gamble with long odds. But hunt during an early- or late-season black-powder hunt, and the reduced (often nonexistent) pressure allows you to pattern more-relaxed bucks near food sources. In large part, maximizing opportunity on public ground is a matter of analyzing what most hunters do, then going out of your way to do the opposite!

Think Oddballs

One of Minnesota's best whitetails in recent years — a 23-point nontypical that green-scored 224 inches — was shot in a Waterfowl Production Area. For those unfamiliar with WPAs, they are tracts purchased by federal agencies for growing ducks and geese. The marshes, river bottoms and Conservation Reserve Program fields comprise ideal habitat for growing big deer, and WPAs are rarely visited by whitetail hunters. This is important because 1. you want to hunt public ground when others are not, and 2. you want to get to places others never go.

WPAs are but one example of non-classic deer cover; I'm sure you can think of others. Never forget that whitetails are ever-adaptable. Give a buck safe bedding, adequate feed and some does to harass come November, and he doesn't care if he lives in a cattail slough or on an oak ridge. One of my buddies almost killed a whopper Kansas buck on a state wildlife area managed for pheasants. Another floats a little river flowing through a big public hunting area, shooting bucks without ever leaving his canoe, while most deer hunters climb the surrounding timbered ridges. College professors and business people call this "thinking outside the box." I just call it smart deer hunting.

Think Positive

It's almost cliché that people with a positive mental attitude make things happen while others waste time calculating the likelihood of failure. Sometimes clichés are true. Case in point: my friend Bob Borowiak. He was helping some buddies with some work at their local sportsman's club one October Saturday a while back.

Sometimes less-traditional deer hunting areas, such as open grasslands, produce big bucks. Most deer hunters overlook these areas, and bucks can grow to a ripe old age in the grassy cover.

During a break, Bob took a stroll in the woods behind the lodge. Ten minutes later he called his buddies to show them a scrape line containing the largest whitetail track he had ever seen.

Bob's friends were impressed, but they quickly reminded him that they were standing on public land. "That buck is either nocturnal, or just made those scrapes as he was passing through," they harrumphed before walking away. Bob conceded the point, but he is a big-buck killer with ceaseless drive and endless optimism. After the work session, he returned to the scrapes and hung a stand. Three days later he had the wind direction he needed, hunted the spot and arrowed 160-class buck that field dressed at more than 250 pounds.

Naturally, a hard-core skeptic would dismiss Bob's buck as a stroke of luck of the highest order. But I've got files full of such stories; tales of men and women who got over the mental hurdle of hunting public land, did their homework, hunted right, and tagged a trophy. Maybe they're all lucky. Or maybe public land isn't the bastard child everyone makes it out to be.

How to Remove a Jaw Bone for Deer Aging

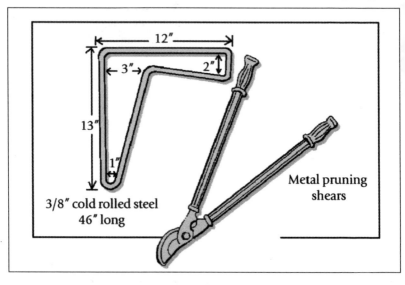

The success or failure of any deer management program is often measured by the number of deer harvested, or more frequently, by the size of bucks harvested. One of the most reliable and accurate indicators of management success is deer health.

Complete and accurate data collection is essential to monitoring deer health. This article will describe the technique for removing and labeling deer mandibles (jaw bones). A labeled lower jaw bone from each harvested deer is an essential part of data collection.

Wildlife managers determine the age of deer by jaw tooth replacement and progressive wear. The jaw teeth of white-tailed deer are replaced in a predictable age-related sequence. As an adult, a deer has three premolars and three molars on each side. The loss and replacement of baby teeth follows

a predictable schedule. By 17 months of age, the deer's premolars become loose. Three permanent premolars are fully exposed by 19 months of age. At the same time, the last molars are being cut. After all of the permanent jaw teeth have come in, age determination is made by examining the amount of wear on the molars.

Once the age of the animal is determined by examining the lower jaw bone, the corresponding weight for bucks and does is used to determine deer health. Years of research throughout the country have determined expected or potential weights for each age-class of deer. Data collection allows wildlife managers to determine the ideal weight and condition of a yearling buck in good condition. Without a corresponding age, weight and antler-development information is practically

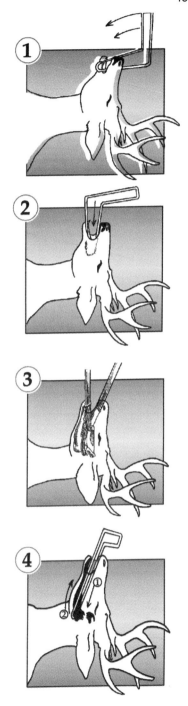

useless. A 6-point buck weighing 130 pounds could be an excellent yearling or a poor $3\frac{1}{2}$-year-old. Over time, data comparisons allow managers to determine harvest recommendations in response to changes in herd health.

For proper jaw bone extraction, you must have two essential tools. The first is a jaw opener-extractor made from a 46-inch length of $\frac{3}{8}$-inch cold-rolled steel. In addition, the hunter should have pruning shears.

1. Place the back of the deer's head on a flat surface and open the deer's mouth by inserting the small end of the jaw opener from the side of the deer's mouth between the front teeth (incisors) and the first jaw teeth (premolars). Rotate the tool 90 degrees to open the mouth.

2. Insert the jaw opener between the cheek and jaw bone. Push the

182

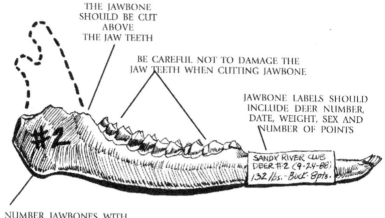

THE JAWBONE SHOULD BE CUT ABOVE THE JAW TEETH

BE CAREFUL NOT TO DAMAGE THE JAW TEETH WHEN CUTTING JAWBONE

JAWBONE LABELS SHOULD INCLUDE DEER NUMBER, DATE, WEIGHT, SEX AND NUMBER OF POINTS

SANDY RIVER CLUB DEER #2 (9-24-88) 132 lbs. - Buck - 8pts.

NUMBER JAWBONES WITH A PERMANENT MARKING PEN

ILLUSTRATIONS BY RON CHAPIESKY

jaw opener downward toward the base of the jaw to free the skin and muscle attached to the lower jaw along the gumline.

3. Insert the closed pruning shears into the deer's mouth with the curve of the blade facing inward. Open the shears and place the cutter bar behind the last jaw teeth (molars) on the outside of the jaw bone. Place the handles of the shears parallel to the roof of the animal's mouth and cut the bone and muscles. Be careful not to break the jaw teeth.

4. Remove the shears and push the small end of the jaw opener-extractor through the cut made in Step 3. Place one foot on the deer's neck, antlers or ear and pull the tool out of the deer's mouth, causing the tool to slide along the underside of the jaw bone, removing the muscles. The jaw bone will separate between the incisors and can be lifted out. If the crests of the jaw teeth are malformed or broken, age determination may be impossible. If the jaw teeth are malformed or broken, carefully remove the other jaw bone to determine age. Careful jaw removal will not damage the head for mounting.

Jaw bones can be cleaned by simply dropping them on the ground and vigorously rubbing each side with your foot, followed by wiping with a cloth. Number each jaw bone with a permanent marker. Some managers prefer to attach a label to each jaw bone with the deer number, date, weight, sex and number of points. Jaw bones should be stored away from scavengers and allowed to air dry. A wire cage, fish basket or ventilated wooden crate works well when used in an outbuilding or garage. A few mothballs will prevent insect problems. Freezing, refrigerating or storing jaw bones in plastic bags will cause offensive odors and labels may become illegible.

— *South Carolina Department of Natural Resources*

Typical B&C Entries: Crunching the Numbers

The odds of a buck reaching Boone and Crockett-class proportions are astronomical. Out of the millions of bucks killed each year, only a few hundred reach the B&C minimum standards.

Simply making the record book is accomplishment enough, but how hard is it to place *high* in the record book? We crunched the numbers for typical whitetail entries to find out.

According to *Records of North American Whitetail Deer, 4th edition*, there are 3,300 typical whitetails that make the all-time awards minimum of 170 inches. When you increase the threshold to 180 inches, there is a sharp decline in the number of entries. Only 702 bucks, or 21.3 percent of the total all-time record book entries, score 180 inches or higher. That means nearly four out of every five bucks in the record book fall in the 170- to 180-inch range.

The 190-inch barrier raises the bar even higher. Just 112 bucks (3.4 percent of the total entries) have been entered in the book at 190 inches or higher so far, and when you hit the magical 200-inch mark, only 12 deer (0.4 percent of the total) have qualified.

More than two-thirds of the total record-book entries (2,240 entries) come from the top 10 states and provinces. These same states and provinces also account for 71.2 percent of the 180-inch entries (500); 75 percent of the 190-inch entries (84); and 91.7 percent of the 200-inch entries (11).

Most of these states and provinces are in the Midwestern United States or western Canada, where fertile soils and agricultural crops help provide excellent nutrition. This, combined with good genetics, helps deer grow to record-book proportions.

Just making the Boone and Crockett minimum score of 170 inches for a typical whitetail is a feat few hunters will ever accomplish. But scoring in the upper echelon of the record book is even more difficult. And the fact that only a dozen 200-inch bucks have ever been entered into the record book, just shows how rare truly world-class deer are.

Top 10 States/Provinces for Typical B&C Whitetail Entries

State	170+	180+	190+	200+
Iowa	363	83	20	1
Minn.	305	76	11	2
Ill.	289	62	13	2
Wis.	282	51	4	1
Sask.	257	57	12	3
Texas	174	30	5	0
Alberta	152	42	6	1
Mo.	149	38	5	1
Kan.	140	35	7	0
Ohio	129	26	1	0

Scores of Typical Whitetails as a Percentage of All-Time Book Entries

Score	170+	180+	190+	200+
Entries	3,300	702	112	12
Total %	100 %	21.3 %	3.4 %	0.4 %

How to Age a White-Tailed Deer

Biologists and deer researchers agree that analysis of tooth replacement and wear — though not perfect — is the most handy and reliable field method for aging whitetails. That's because, regardless of where they live, whitetails lose their baby "milk" teeth and wear out their permanent teeth on a fairly predictable schedule.

At birth, white-tailed fawns have four teeth. Adult deer have 32 teeth — 12 premolars, 12 molars, six incisors and two canines.

Aging analysis often is based on the wear of the molars, which lose about 1 millimeter of height per year. It takes a deer about $10^1/_2$ years to wear its teeth down to the gum line. Therefore, it's difficult to determine the age of a deer that's older than $10^1/_2$ years.

Most importantly, the ability to estimate a deer's age based on the wear of its teeth is something most hunters can learn with a little study and practice.

To order a full-color poster of our complete guide to tooth aging, call (888) 457-2873.

Instructions: Cut one side of a deer's jaw all the way to its socket. Prop open the jaws and compare the lower jaw to these photos to estimate age.

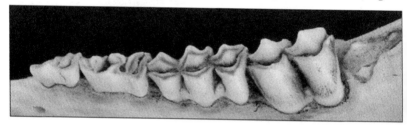

Fawn

Few hunters have difficulty aging a white-tailed fawn, whose short snout and small body are usually obvious when viewed up close. If there is doubt, simply count the teeth in the deer's lower jaw. If the jaw has less than six teeth, the deer is a fawn.

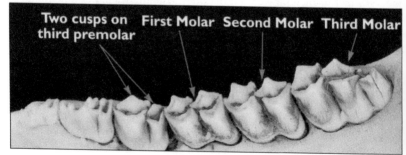

Two cusps on third premolar   First Molar   Second Molar   Third Molar

Yearling: At Least 19 Months

At about 1 year, 7 months, most deer have all three permanent premolars. The new teeth are white in contrast to pigmentation on older teeth. They have a smooth, chalk-white appearance and show no wear. The third molar is partially erupted.

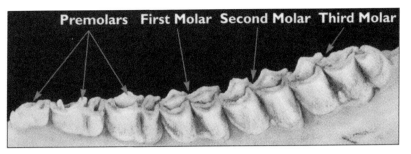

2¹/₂ Years

The lingual crests of the first molar are sharp, with the enamel rising well above the narrow dentine (the dark layer below the enamel) of the crest. Crests on the first molar are as sharp as those on the second and third molar. Wear on the posterior cusp of the third molar is slight, and the gum line is often not retracted enough to expose the full height of this cusp.

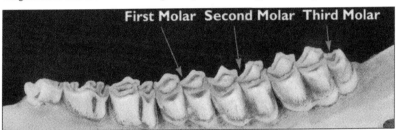

3¹/₂ Years

The lingual crests (inside, next to tongue) of the first molar are blunted, and the dentine of the crests on this tooth is as wide or wider than the enamel. Compare it to the second molar. The dentine on the second molar is not wider than the enamel, which means this deer is probably 3¹/₂ years old. Also, the posterior cusp of the third molar is flattened by wear, forming a definite concavity on the biting surface of the teeth.

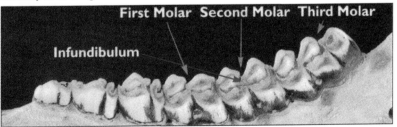

4¹/₂ to 5¹/₂ Years

At this point, it's often hard to distinguish between the two age classes. The lingual crests of the first molar are almost worn away. The posterior cusp of the third molar is worn at the cusp's edge so the biting surface slopes downward. Wear has spread to the second molar, making the dentine wider than the enamel on first and second molars. By age 5¹/₂, wear has usually spread to all six teeth, making the dentine wider than the enamel on all teeth. Because the first molar is the oldest, it wears out first. Also, by 5¹/₂, there might be no lingual crests on the first and second molars, although rounded edges might appear like crests. A line drawn from lingual to outside edges of first and second molars generally touches the enamel on both sides of the infundibulum.

Daniel E. Schmidt

The average hunter can be a successful buck hunter. All that's required are a few realistic goals and the dedication to stick to them.

Blue-Collar Hunting Tips

One of the best whitetail hunters I know is someone you've never heard of. He has not appeared on any hunting videos. He is not an elite member of a pro-staff. He has never had his mug featured on an ad campaign or on a glossy cover. In a world chock-full of whitetail celebrities, my buddy is a nobody.

But I would pit his hunting skills against any deer hunter I know, and I know some very, very good ones; names you would recognize, folks whose faces have graced magazine or video covers, guys who've established themselves as death on big whitetails. I've hunted with the experts and I've hunted with my friend ... and he's as good as anyone I've met.

Robert works for the city in a rural Midwestern hamlet. He does not own, lease or have exclusive hunting rights to any property, nor can he afford to hire a guide. He would not be insulted if I referred to him as a classic Joe Lunchbucket; a regular guy working a regular job who manufactures hunting time while the rest of his life — which includes work, family and community obligations — keeps chugging along.

Robert has tagged 10 trophy-class whitetails in the last 10 years near his home and added a couple more from other states during that time. And he's done it without losing his job, getting divorced, going broke or getting full of himself. Robert's passion is hunting big whitetail bucks, and he's found a way to kill them consistently. Naturally, some folks are tempted to think Robert has some shortcut to success: a secret hot spot, a special gift or maybe even a willingness to bend the game laws a little. Not so on every count, as anyone from his wife to the local game warden will testify.

So how does he find and shoot big deer every year? Robert would be the first to insist that there is no blueprint. But I do think he'd agree there are some concrete things that hunters like him — I call them "blue collar trophy hunters" — can do to increase their odds. Let's take a look at some specific steps that others like him can do to consistently score on big deer.

Set Reasonable Goals

It wasn't long ago that anyone who shot a mature whitetail had bagged his or her "buck of a lifetime." After the lucky hunter nailed that big one, his life settled back to normal and he continued shooting deer the same way he had in the past. But the last decade or so, we've heard more about the exploits of such folks as Myles Keller, Don Kisky, Stan Potts and the Drury brothers, and we've come to realize that what was once a buck-of-a-lifetime for most hunters is now an annual event for others. Simply put, our expectations have been raised to the point that, once some hunters kill one big deer, they expect to immediately kill another, just like our heroes do.

Resist getting caught in this trap. First of all, whitetail hunting is not a competitive sport, and trying to kill as many (or even the same caliber) bucks as a pro-staff hunter is like expecting to outshoot Tiger Woods on the driving range. Full-time whitetailers have more and better ground to hunt than most of us, and some of the really blessed ones have nothing — NOTHING! — on their schedules but hunting from September until January. Obviously, folks like us do not have that luxury.

Because the playing field isn't level, hunters who set attainable goals will be less likely to experience frustration and be more satisfied with the results when they do tag a buck. Trophy hunting is a time- and labor-intensive sport and, for most of us, the challenge of fooling any mature buck is a tall one. Think hard about a reasonable expectation for this fall and be happy when and if you attain it.

What's a reasonable goal? Only you can determine that, but try to match your expectations to your hunting experience, your available hunting time and the quality of the ground you access. Remember, success is a relative entity. I know blue-collar folks who routinely pass shots at 140-inch bucks, waiting for a true Goliath. Now, in the vast majority of whitetail range, a 140-class deer is about as good as it gets. But these guys live in primo country, have killed big deer before and want a monster or nothing. For a budding trophy hunter to set a similar goal would be ludicrous and result in nothing but frustration.

When I think of goal-setting, I'm reminded of another skilled whitetailer: my cousin Scott. He is a fine hunter and an excellent shot who has the skills to kill a big buck every year. But Scott is a self-employed carpenter whose job doesn't stop come fall. Consequently, he's set a goal to take a nice buck every three to five years, and he's succeeded. Although less-skilled hunters with more time shoot more bucks than Scott does, he is content with his pace. He's set a reasonable goal.

Hunt the Good Spots

Deer hunting has very few absolutes, but this much is certain: you can't kill a buck that doesn't exist. So the first step in shooting big deer is simply finding where they live. If there are no mature bucks in your hunting areas, don't frustrate yourself waiting for them. Instead, find another region or state where they do live and make the commitment to hunt there. This requires time, research and possibly travel, but it's a necessary process.

If you're not plugged into where big bucks live, consult the Boone and Crockett and Pope and Young record books. Poring over these record books will get you homed in on the hot spots in a hurry. There are even maps now that have the number of trophy entries for both clubs, with the number of trophy entries, per county, for every state.

Once you've identified the Golden Zones, you're faced with a new question: Can a guy without a big wallet actually hunt such places? The answer is a cloudy "maybe." If you're thinking Texas, for example, forget it. But Iowa, a primo trophy state, can be a different story. There are still places in the Hawkeye State where you can access private land and some public areas that are nothing short of outstanding. My buddy, Robert, for example, killed a monster 10-point a few years ago on a state-owned wildlife-management area. The problem with any Iowa hunt, of course, is simply drawing a tag. One of the reasons that state has so many big deer is it severely restricts nonresident opportunity.

Thankfully, there are other options. They come in the form of "sleeper areas" that, due to less publicity, nastier terrain, and/or lower hunter numbers, produce big deer but are frequently overlooked. How to find such spots? Research and ingenuity. I won't draw any maps, but I will provide a couple concrete hints. Much of northern Minnesota, for example, consists of huge tracts of timber where most sportsmen fear to tread. It also contains huge deer. Similarly, prairie states like Nebraska and South Dakota have all the elements needed to grow huge bucks, but many hunters ignore such terrain because they don't know how to hunt open country — which is why the bucks continue to grow old!

Hunt When It's Hot!

If all blue-collar hunters share a common woe, it's limited hunting time. This makes nailing down the prime windows of opportunity that elevate the chances for success. Since we don't have unlimited vacation days, scheduling the few we do enjoy should coincide with peak movement times for mature deer. If you need to secure your time off long in advance of deer season, consider three peak periods.

Naturally, the best time to kill a trophy buck is in the weeks just prior to the rut. Mature bucks are the most active during the breeding season, and hunting the rut simply maximizes your effort. For example, when I first hunted the prairies of western Kansas, I made several calls before my trip to determine when the best breeding activity occurred. Two hours on the phone helped me nail down the two best weeks, so I scheduled my five-day hunt for the middle of that period. I saw more mature bucks in that short hunt than I would in two seasons back home!

If you can't make the rut, hunt early or late. Two of the most overlooked months for tagging a monster are September and December. Early fall finds bucks still in summer feeding patterns, often with other members of a bachelor group. By December, most bucks become serious about groceries again, making them vulnerable to harvest at prime food sources. And because these time frames are often neglected by hunters, access to prime private ground is better than during the rut, when everyone wants to be out there. If you're hunting public ground, count on less competition as well.

Learn the Land

One of the most-talked-about-and-least-done aspects of shooting big deer is scouting ... at least among frustrated trophy hunters. The guys who kill big deer consistently are scouting all the time. Robert, for example, could probably ignore most of the farms he hunts for a year or two and still shoot big bucks; he's simply dialed in to how deer bed, feed and travel on those properties. But every spare minute Robert has is spent walking his land, hunting for sheds and glassing bachelor groups. As he'll tell anyone who'll listen, "You can never know too much about how deer, especially big ones, use a property. I'm always looking for more pieces to the puzzle."

Naturally, frequent scouting trips are easier to pull off if you're hunting close to home. For out-of-state safaris, extra effort and ingenuity are necessary. If I know I'm going to hunt an area the next fall, I'll schedule a late-winter or early spring weekend and drive there for a two-day scouting/shed hunting blitz. Arranging a spring turkey hunt to the area is another way to do some pre-season recon (and hopefully kill a gobbler, too). While such short forays won't tell you everything you need to know, you'll at least get a strong glimpse of the land and be far better off than walking in cold come fall.

Minus a scouting trip, get your hands on aerial photos or topo maps of your hunting ground long before your hunt and learn to read them. If you don't know what terrain features equate to good stand setups, an excellent resource is the book *Mapping Trophy Bucks* by Brad Herndon. This well-written, beautifully photographed guide will tell you exactly what to look for when reading maps and photos. If you're looking for a source of good topo maps and aerial photos, visit the Mapcard Web site (www.mapcard.com.) For a reasonable subscription fee, you can download, customize and create maps of any area in the country. Short of visiting an area, I can think of no better way to scout ground than studying topos and aerials.

Become Your Weapon

All the scouting and hunting effort you devote becomes meaningless if you can't shoot the buck you find. Of course, misses are a part of hunting and even the experts muff a gimme now and then. But it's amazing how few hunters devote the time necessary to become proficient with their guns and bows. You don't have to be an ace marksman, just be able to deliver the goods in that tension-packed, high-adrenaline moment when a big buck appears.

Summer is the perfect time to start shooting. Make a short shooting session part of your schedule several times a week if you're a bow-hunter, once a week if you'll hunt with a firearm. Start

One of the easiest things you can do to ensure you don't choke at the moment of truth is to practice. It makes no sense to waste months of planning and scouting, only to blow a shot when a big buck finally passes your stand.

simple, with backyard, close-range shooting that just gets you intimate with your weapon. As the summer progresses, try to simulate hunting situations by shooting at 3-D courses (archery) or at ranges that allow for longer shots (firearms). With a couple months of practice under your belt, putting that broadhead or bullet should be a reflex action, which is just as it should be when that wide-racked

monster finally appears!

Will following these steps ensure a dandy trophy for a hopeful blue-collar hunter? Of course not. Chasing big deer is a process full of hard work, endless commitment and plenty of uncertainty. But as Robert has proven, success is still within reach of men for whom whitetail hunting is just a hobby, not a job!

Ryan Gilligan

Embarking on an out-of-state deer hunt is exciting, but plan carefully so the only memories from your trip are good ones.

The Traveling Deer Hunter

Things You Should Know Before
Booking a Deer Hunting Trip to Canada

It's no big secret that Canada offers some of the best deer hunting in North America. From British Columbia to Quebec, hunters not only find huge whitetails, they hunt pristine wilderness areas with little pressure from other hunters.

What's more, most Canadian deer hunts are relatively inexpensive, considering many outfitters offer fantastic accommodations and top-notch guide services. However, it's unwise to book any hunt without doing a lot of homework. Although most outfitters offer hunting packages, many details are left to the hunter.

The following items are just a few you should investigate before booking a Canadian hunt. For more information, contact the bureaus and information centers listed within this article.

Tax-Refund Policy

Before writing a check for what seems like an affordable hunt package, double-check to see what taxes you owe. In many cases, package hunts are quoted on price, but they do not include federal and provincial taxes.

Nonresidents are eligible for a reimbursement of 50 percent of the taxes paid on a package. An outfitter who sells a package directly to nonresidents can request this reimbursement on their behalf and deduct it from the price of the package.

For more information, contact your outfitter or call Revenue Canada at (613) 991-3346.

Canada's Updated Gun Law

Canada requires visitors to register their firearms. The registration form can be completed in about 10 minutes. However, because it is a declaration, visitors should not sign the form until they are before a customs officer. The fee is $37 ($50 Canadian) per gun.

Trip Cancellation

Whether you are dealing with an outfitter or an intermediary, inquire about cancellation policies. Conditions should appear in the agency's guidelines or the outfitter's brochure.

Agency/Outfitter Responsibility

Canadian hunting agencies serve as intermediaries between travelers and travel service organizations. Because they do not exercise any control over suppliers, agencies cannot be held responsible if the suppliers fail to provide services.

Neither intermediaries nor outfitters can be held responsible for any damage, loss, delay, illness, injury or inconvenience arising from:

✓errors, negligence or omissions on the part of other suppliers, such as carriers, hotels, etc.

✓strikes, mechanical failures, a quarantine or other restrictive government action, meteorological conditions or other factors beyond human control such as forest fires.

✓failure on the part of the customer to carry necessary travel

Canada offers some of the best whitetail hunting on the planet. However, your dream hunt could become a nightmare if you don't make the proper preparations before your trip.

documents.

✓ any airport delays on the customer's day of departure, for whatever reason.

✓ material damage, loss of property or theft.

✓ illness, injury and/or death.

Insurance

Most agencies offer trip cancellation, medical and baggage insurance. For information on such policies, contact the fishing and hunting agency of your choice.

Terms of Payment

If the trip has not been completely paid for before your departure and you do not intend to settle the bill with cash, you should verify whether the outfitter accepts personal checks, traveler's checks and/or credit cards.

Baggage

Before departure, check if the airline has weight limits and baggage allowances. Most airlines tightly monitor baggage regulations.

Climatic Conditions

While every effort is made to comply with published timetables, irregularities in flight operations can occur in some regions, due to poor weather. Such conditions can also affect the schedule of activities at an outfitter's camp. There is no refund for adjustments to activities resulting from such irregularities.

Permits and Quotas

Hunters must purchase provincial hunting licenses, generally available at sporting goods stores in most cities and towns, and from many outfitters.

Nonresidents are not obliged to produce a hunter's safety certificate to purchase a hunting license.

Deer Hunting

Nonresidents are limited to purchasing particular hunting licenses and frequenting specific hunting zones or areas, according to

Where to Write

Alberta
Department of Forestry,
Lands and Wildlife
Main Floor North Tower
Petroleum Plaza
9045 108th St.
Edmonton, Alberta CAN T5K 2G6

British Columbia
Ministry of Environment,
Fish and Wildlife
780 Blanchard St.
Victoria, British Columbia
CAN V8V 1X5

Manitoba
Dept. of Natural Resources
Wildlife Branch
200 Saulteaux Crescent
Winnipeg, Manitoba,CAN
R3J 3W3

New Brunswick
Bureau of Natural Resources
Fish and Wildlife Branch
Box 6000
Fredricton, N.B. CAN E3B 4X5

Newfoundland
Inland Fish & Wildlife Division
Wildlife Building, Trans-Canada Highway
Pasadena, N.F. CAN A0L 1K0

Nova Scotia
Dept. of Lands and Forests
136 Exhibition St.
Kentville, N.S. CAN B4N 4E5

Ontario
Ministry of Natural Resources
Room 1-73, MacDonald Block
900 Bay St.
Toronto, Ontario CAN M7A 2C3

Quebec
Dept. of Recreation, Hunting
Box 2200, 150 E. St. Cyrille
Quebec City, Quebec, CAN G1R 4Y1

Saskatchewan
Parks and Renewable Resources
3211 Albert St.
Regina, Saskatchewan
CAN S4S 5W6

the species hunted.

Nonresidents pursuing whitetails can hunt in all zones where hunting is allowed. However, nonresidents cannot participate in computer drawings to obtain a hunting license for antlerless deer during gun season.

Deer Registration

When returning to the United States from Canada, U.S. hunters must register their kill when going through the U.S. Customs.

Transporting Game

All successful deer hunters must immediately detach the appropriate transportation tag from his or her license and affix it to the deer. The tag must remain affixed throughout the registration process and until the animal has been dressed and stored.

Safety Regulations

All hunters must wear at least 400 square inches of blaze-orange material — covering their back, shoulders and chest — while gun-hunting for deer. The clothing must be visible from all angles at all times.

In addition, a life jacket must be provided for each person using any kind of boat. All boats must be equipped with a bailer, a sound-signaling device and a pair of oars.

Money

It's wise to change your currency into Canadian dollars before leaving the United States. Traveler's checks and major credit cards are accepted in most establishments, but it's advisable to check with your outfitter in advance.

— Daniel E. Schmidt

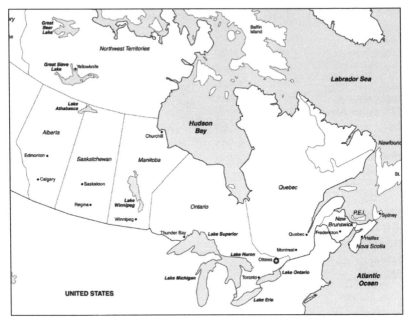

Miscellaneous Tips and Notes

✓When deer hunting in Manitoba, nonresidents must be accompanied by a licensed Manitoba guide. No more than three hunters can use the services of the same guide at the same time. In addition, nonresident deer hunters must book their hunts through a registered lodge or outfitter.

✓Planning a hunt in Saskatchewan? Topographic maps and aerial photographs can be purchased for all areas of the province from Saskatchewan Environment and Resource Management district offices (except the Regina office). Hunters can also order maps from: Sask Geomatics, 2151 Scarth St., Regina, SK, CANADA S4P 3V7, or call (306) 787-2799.

✓For current weather conditions and extended forecasts in any province, visit Canada's most popular weather Web site: www.weatheroffice.com.

✓Alberta whitetail hunters enjoy tremendous success. Nearly 80,000 hunters pursue whitetails in the province each year, and they harvest about 32,000 deer, a success rate of 40 percent.

Nonresident Fees for Deer Hunting

Province	License*
British Columbia	$75
Alberta	$183
Saskatchewan	$280
Manitoba	$185
Ontario	$123
Quebec	$260

*Nonresident fees as of February 2001. Other fees might apply. For example, Ontario charges a $30 export fee for taking deer out of the province, while Alberta requires hunters to purchase a Wildlife Identification Number for $8. If you plan to hunt deer in Canada, contact the respective province's department of wildlife for complete cost information. Contact information is on Page 195.

Traveling With Heightened Airport Security

The Sept. 11, 2001, terrorist attacks probably affected air travel forever, especially for those traveling with firearms and ammunition. If you're planning an out-of-state hunt and are depending on air travel to get to your big-buck destination, follow these precautions to ensure your trip goes smoothly.

First, when traveling with a firearm, declare the weapon immediately when you check in at the ticket counter. Also, store the firearm in a locked, airline-approved gun case.

Whenever possible, purchase ammunition when you reach your destination instead of buying it at home and bringing it with you on the plane. However, when flying to remote areas, this might be impossible. In such instances, pack ammunition separately from your firearm in the manufacturer's original package, or locked in a fiber, wood or metal box.

Also, call your airline for information on current policies regarding transporting guns and ammunition. These regulations often change without notice.

When you declare your firearm at the check-in counter, you must show the gun is unloaded and sign a "Firearms Unloaded" declaration.

Keep entry permits in your possession for the country or countries of destination or transit.

Ammunition Restrictions

The amount of ammunition you can check varies by airline. For example, Delta permits passengers to check 11 pounds of ammunition — 10 pounds on its SkyWest flights.

Ammunition weighing more than 11 pounds or containing incendiary projectiles is prohibited.

If necessary, you may purchase a hard-sided, 12-by-52-by-4½-inch gun case with suitcase-type locks for $75 plus tax at most Delta ticket counters.

Airlines generally permit passengers to check one item of shooting equipment as part of their free checked-baggage allowance. One item of shooting equipment is defined as one or a combination of the following:

One firearms case containing:

✓ two or fewer firearms — rifles, pistols or shotguns. Cases containing more than two firearms will be assessed an excess baggage charge.

✓ one shooting mat
✓ one small pistol tool kit
✓ noise suppressors
✓ pistol telescopes
✓ noise suppressors

Finally, remember that each airline might have different firearms restrictions and regulations change, especially in the wake of terrorist activity. Therefore, always call ahead or check your airline's Web site for its latest regulations before packing for your hunting trip.

— *National Wild Turkey Federation*

State Wildlife Agency Contact Info

Alabama Dept. of Wildlife and Freshwater Fisheries
64 N. Union St.
Montgomery, AL 36130
(334) 242-3469   www.dcnr.state.al.us

Arizona Game & Fish Department
2221 W. Greenway Road
Phoenix, AZ 85023
(602) 942-3000   www.gf.state.az.us

Arkansas Game & Fish Commission
#2 Natural Resources Drive
Little Rock, AR 72205
(800) 364-4263   www.agfc.state.ar.us

Colorado Division of Wildlife
6060 Broadway
Denver, CO 80216
(303) 297-1192   www.dnr.state.co.us

Connecticut Dept. of Environmental Protection
391 Route 32
N. Franklin, CT 06254
(860) 424-3105   www.dep.state.ct.us

Delaware Dept. of Natural Resources
89 Kings Hwy., Box 1401
Dover, DE 19903
(302) 739-5295   www.dnrec.state.de.us

Florida Fish & Game Commission
620 S. Meridian Farris Bryant Blvd.
Tallahassee, FL 32399
(850) 488-3641   www.state.fl.us/gfc

Georgia Wildlife Resources
2070 U.S. Hwy. 278 SE
Social Circle, GA 30025
(770) 414-3333   www.dnr.state.ga.us

Idaho Fish & Game Department
Box 25
Boise, ID 83707
(208) 334-3717
www.state.id.us/fishgame/fishgame.html

Illinois Dept. of Conservation
524 S. Second St.
Springfield, IL 62701
(217) 782-7305   www.dnr.state.il.us

Indiana Division of Wildlife
553 E. Miller Drive
Bloomington, IN 47401
(317) 232-4080   www.state.in.us/dnr

Iowa Dept. of Natural Resources
Wallace State Office Bldg.
Des Moines, IA 50319-0034
(515) 281-4687 www.state.ia.us/wildlife/

Kansas Dept. of Wildlife
Box 1525
Emporia, KS 66801
(620) 672-5911   www.kdwp.state.ks.us

Kentucky Dept. of Wildlife
#1 Game Farm Road
Frankfort, KY 40601
(800) 858-1549   www.state.ky.us

Louisiana Dept. of Wildlife
Box 98000
Baton Rouge, LA 70898
(225) 765-2887   www.wlf.state.la.us

Maine Dept. of Inland Fisheries and Wildlife
284 State St., State House Station 41
Augusta, ME 04333
(207) 287-2571   www.state.me.us/ifw

Maryland Division of Wildlife
4220 Steele Neck Road
Vienna, MD 21869
(410) 260-8200   www.dnr.state.md.us

Massachusetts Wildlife
Westborough, MA 01581
(617) 727-1614   www.state.ma.us/dfwele

Michigan Dept. of Natural Resources
Box 30028
Lansing, MI 48909
www.dnr.state.mi.us

Minnesota Dept. of Natural Resources
Box 7, 500 Lafayette Road
St. Paul, MN 55155
(651) 296-4506   www.dnr.state.mn.us

Mississippi Dept. of Conservation
Southport Mall, Box 451
Jackson, MS 39205
(800) 546-4868   www.mdwfp.com

Missouri Dept. of Conservation
Box 180
Jefferson City, MO 65102-0180
(573) 751-4115
www.conservation.state.mo.us

Montana Dept. of Fish and Wildlife
1420 E. Sixth Ave.
Helena, MT 59620
(900) 225-5397   www.fwp.state.mt.us

Nebraska Game and Parks
Box 508
Bassett, NE 68714-0508
(402) 471-0641   www.ngpc.state.ne.us

New Hampshire Fish & Game
Region 1, Rt. 2, Box 241
Lancaster, NH 03584
(603) 271-3422
www.wildlife.state.nh.us

New Jersey Division of Fish & Wildlife
Box 418
Port Republic, NJ 08241
(609) 748-2044   www.state.nj.us/dep/fgw

New York Dept. of Conservation
50 Wolf Road
Albany, NY 12233
(518) 402-8985
www.dec.state.ny.us/website/outdoors

North Carolina Wildlife
512 N. Salisburg St.
Raleigh, NC 27604-1188
(919) 733-3393
www.state.nc.us/wildlife

North Dakota Game Department
100 N. Bismarck Expy.
Bismarck, ND 58501
(701) 328-6300   www.state.nd.us/gnf

Ohio Division of Wildlife
1840 Belcher Drive
Columbus, OH 43224
(614) 265-6300   www.dnr.state.oh.us

Oklahoma Department of Wildlife
1801 N. Lincoln, Box 53465
Oklahoma City, OK 73105
(405) 521-3851   www.state.ok.us

Oregon Dept. of Fish and Wildlife
400 Public Service Bldg.
Salem, OR 97310
(503) 872-5268   www.dfw.state.or.us

Pennsylvania Game Commission
2001 Elmerton Ave.
Harrisburg, PA 17110
(717) 787-4250
www.pgc.state.pa.us

**Rhode Island Dept. of
Environmental Management**
83 Park St.
Providence, RI 02903
(401) 222-6822   www.state.ri.us/dem

**South Carolina Dept. of
Natural Resources**
Box 167
Columbia, SC 29202
(803) 734-3888
www.dnr.state.sc.us

South Dakota Division of Wildlife
Bldg. 445 E. Capital
Pierre, SD 57501
(605) 773-3485
www.state.sd.us/gfp/index.htm

Tennessee Wildlife Resources
Box 407
Nashville, TN 37204
(888) 814-8972
www.state.tn.us/twra

Texas Parks & Wildlife
4200 Smith School Road
Austin, TX 78744
(800) 895-4248   www.tpwd.state.tx.us

Vermont Dept. of Fish and Wildlife
103 S. Main St.
Waterbury, VT 05671
(802) 241-3701   www.anr.state.vt.us

Virginia Dept. of Game and Fisheries
Box 11104
Richmond, VA 23230
(804) 367-1000   www.dgif.state.va.us

Washington Dept. of Fish and Wildlife
600 Capitol Way N.
Olympia, WA 98501
(360) 902-2200   www.wa.gov/wdfw

West Virginia Wildlife Resources
State Capital, Bldg. 3
Charleston, WV 25305
(304) 367-2720   www.wvwildlife.com

Wisconsin Dept. of Natural Resources
101 S. Webster St.
Madison, WI 53707
(608) 266-2621   www.dnr.state.wi.us

Wyoming Game and Fish
5400 Bishop Blvd.
Cheyenne, WY 82002
(900) 884-4263   http://gf.state.wy.us

State and Provincial Blaze-Orange Requirements

The following are general guidelines to each state and province's hunter orange requirements for deer hunters. They are not complete regulations and are subject to change. Waterfowl, turkey and other hunters may be exempt in some cases. The word "orange" herein refers to fluorescent hunter orange, which must be worn as the outermost layer. Check with individual states before planning a hunt. Some states have more restrictions, such as the brightness of the orange or other special regulations.

Alabama All hunters during gun-deer season must wear a vest or cap with at least 144 square inches of solid orange, visible from all sides. Deer hunters in tree stands more than 12 feet off the ground need not wear orange, except when traveling to and from stands.

Alaska Wearing orange is strongly recommended for big-game hunters.

Alberta There are no garment color requirements.

Arizona Orange is strongly recommended for big-game hunters.

Arkansas Deer hunters and anyone assisting them during gun or muzzleloading season must wear at least 400 square inches of orange above the waist, and an orange or chartreuse hat.

British Columbia There are no garment color requirements.

California Orange is strongly recommended for big-game hunters.

Colorado Deer hunters must wear at least 500 square inches of solid orange above the waist, part of which must be a hat visible from all directions during muzzleloader and rifle seasons.

Connecticut Gun-deer hunters must wear at least 400 square inches of orange above the waist, visible from all sides. Landowners hunting on their own property are exempt.

Delaware All hunters must wear at least 400 square inches of orange when firearms deer seasons are open.

Florida Gun-deer hunters and those accompanying them while hunting on public lands must wear at least 500 square inches of orange above the waist.

Hawaii All persons in any hunting area where firearms are permitted must wear an orange outer garment above the waist, or a piece of orange material of at least 144 square inches on both their front and back, above the waist. A solid orange hat is recommended.

Georgia Deer hunters and those accompanying them during firearm deer seasons must wear at least 500 square inches of orange on outer garments above the waist.

Idaho Orange is strongly recommended for big-game hunters.

Illinois It is unlawful to hunt during the gun-deer season in counties open to gun-deer hunting when not wearing 400 square inches of solid blaze orange and a hat.

Indiana Bow- and gun-hunters must wear at least one of the following solid-orange garments: vest, coat, jacket, coveralls, hat or cap when gun-deer season is open.

Iowa All gun-deer hunters must wear at least one of the following articles of external apparel in solid orange: vest, coat, jacket, sweatshirt, sweater, shirt or coveralls.

Kansas Deer hunters and individuals assisting them must wear orange clothing, consisting of a hat with an exterior at least 50 percent orange, an equal portion of which is visible from all directions. They must also wear at least 100 square inches of orange on both the front and back of their torso.

Kentucky All deer hunters must wear solid orange when any gun-deer season is open on at least the head, chest and back. Mesh weave openings must not exceed $1/4$ inch. Camouflage orange garments are not allowed.

Louisiana All deer hunters must wear at least 400 square inches of orange during the gun-deer season. People hunting on privately owned, legally posted land may wear an orange hat instead of the 400 square inches of orange. People hunting from elevated stands on property that is privately owned and legally posted, or bow-hunters hunting on legally posted land where firearm hunting is not permitted by agreement of the owner or lessee are exempt.

Maine Anyone who hunts with a firearm during any firearms deer season is required to wear two articles of solid-orange clothing that is in good condition and visible from all sides. One article must be a hat. The other must cover a major portion of the torso.

Manitoba A solid blaze orange hat and an additional 2580 square centimeters of blaze orange above the waist and visible from all sides must be worn by big-game hunters. Bow-hunters are exempt during bow-hunting seasons or in bow hunting areas only. At least 50 percent of camouflage orange clothing must be orange.

Maryland All hunters and those accompanying them must wear either a solid-orange cap, or a vest or jacket containing back and front panels of at least 250 square inches of solid orange or an outer garment of camouflage orange worn above the waist that contains at least 50 percent orange. Bow-hunters during archery-only season are exempt.

Massachusetts All hunters during shotgun and primitive-firearm deer seasons must wear at least 500 square inches of orange on their chest, back and head.

Michigan All firearm hunters (and archers during firearms season) must wear an orange hat, jacket or other outer garment, visible from all sides. Camouflage orange is legal, provided 50 percent is solid orange.

Minnesota A person may not hunt during firearms deer season unless the visible portion of the person's cap and outer clothing above the waist, excluding sleeves and gloves, is blaze orange. Orange includes a camouflage pattern of at least 50 percent orange within each square foot.

Mississippi All deer hunters during any gun-deer season must wear in full view at least 500 square inches of solid, unbroken orange visible from all sides.

Missouri During firearm deer season, all hunters must wear an orange hat and a shirt, vest or coat. Orange must be plainly visible from all sides while being worn. Camouflage orange is not allowed. Bow-hunters in Department of Conservation areas where deer hunting is restricted to archery hunting are exempt.

Montana All big-game hunters and those accompanying them must wear at least 400 square inches of orange above the waist. A hat alone is not sufficient. Bow-hunters during special archery season are exempt.

Nebraska Firearms deer hunters must wear at least 400 square inches of orange on the head, back and chest.

Nevada Orange is strongly recommended for big-game hunters.

New Brunswick Every hunter or guide accompanying any person engaged in hunting shall wear a hat and upon his or her back, chest and shoulders, an exterior garment of not less than 2580 square centimeters (400 square inches) of orange, plainly visible from all directions.

Newfoundland Big-game hunters are strongly recommended to wear a minimum of 2580 square centimeters (400 square inches) of orange.

New Hampshire Orange is strongly recommended for big-game hunters.

New Jersey Firearms deer hunters must wear a cap of solid orange or another outer garment with at least 200 square inches of orange visible from all sides.

New Mexico Orange is strongly recommended for big-game hunters.

New York Orange is strongly recommended for big-game hunters.

North Carolina Firearms deer hunters must wear an orange hat or an orange outer garment, visible from all sides. Landowners hunting on their own land are exempt.

North Dakota Big-game hunters must wear an orange head covering and an orange outer garment above the waist, totaling at least 400 square inches and worn conspicuously. This does not apply to any person hunting big game with bow and arrow during

special bow-hunting seasons. Additionally, while the muzzleloader and the gun-deer seasons are in progress in an area, all big-game hunters, including bow-hunters, are required to wear a head covering and an outer garment above the waist of solid orange totaling at least 400 square inches.

Northwest Territory Orange is strongly recommended for big-game hunters.

Nova Scotia All hunters and those accompanying them must wear a cap and a vest, coat, or shirt of solid orange visible from all sides. Camouflage orange is not legal during firearms deer season.

Ohio All deer hunters during gun-deer seasons must wear a visible orange hat, cap, vest or coat.

Oklahoma All firearm deer, elk or antelope hunters must wear a head covering and outer garment above the waist with at least 400 square inches of orange. Camouflage orange patterns are legal as long as there is at least 400 square inches of orange.

Ontario Big-game hunters are required to wear a minimum of 2580 square centimeters (400 square inches) of orange.

Oregon Orange is strongly recommended for big-game hunters.

Pennsylvania All hunters during the regular firearms deer season, and special archery deer season hunters during any portion of the archery season that coincides with the general small game or turkey seasons, must wear at least 250 square inches of orange on the head, chest and back, visible in a 360-degree arc. Flintlock season deer hunters are exempt.

Prince Edward Island Orange is strongly recommended for big-game hunters.

Quebec Hunters, guides and companions must wear 2580 square centimeters (400 square inches) of orange on their back, shoulders and chest, visible from any angle.

Rhode Island From Oct. 17 to Feb. 28, hunters must wear an outer garment consisting of a minimum of 200 square inches of solid orange material worn above the waist, and visible in all directions. This may be a hat and/or vest. Statewide, during shotgun season for deer, all hunters must wear an outer garment containing a minimum of 500 square inches of orange, worn above the waist, visible from all directions and must include a head covering. (Exceptions: during muzzleloading season all hunters must wear 200 square inches as stated above.)

Saskatchewan All big-game hunters must wear a complete outer suit of scarlet, bright yellow, orange or white, and a head covering of any of these colors except white. Bow-hunters and black-powder hunters during special seasons are exempt.

South Carolina On all WMA lands and lands within the Central Piedmont, Western Piedmont and Mountain Hunt Units during the gun-deer season, all hunters must wear a hat, coat or vest of solid orange.

South Dakota Big-game firearms hunters must wear one or more orange garments above the waist.

Tennessee All big-game firearms hunters must wear at least 500 square inches of orange on a head covering and an outer garment above the waist, visible front and back. Those hunting on their own property are exempt.

Texas All hunters and persons accompanying a hunter on national forests and grasslands must wear a minimum of 144 square inches of orange visible on both the chest and back, plus an orange hat.

Utah Four hundred square inches of orange is required while hunting big game. Orange must be worn on the head, chest and back. Camouflage orange is not legal. A person is not required to wear orange during an archery or muzzleloader hunt unless a centerfire rifle hunt is in progress in the same area.

Vermont Orange is strongly recommended for big-game hunters.

Virginia Hunters during firearm deer season and those accompanying them must wear orange on the upper body, visible from all sides, or an orange hat, or display 100 square inches of orange within body reach, at shoulder level or higher, visible from all sides.

Washington All hunters must wear at least 400 square inches of orange exterior, worn above the waist and visible from all sides. Bow-hunters are exempt.

West Virginia All deer hunters during gun-deer season must wear at least 400 square inches of orange on an outer garment.

Wisconsin All hunters during gun-deer season must have 50 percent of their outer garments above the waist, including any head covering, colored orange. Camouflage orange is permitted, but not recommended.

Wyoming All big-game hunters must wear one of the following in orange: hat, shirt, jacket, coat, vest, or sweater. Bow-hunters during special archery season are exempt.

Yukon There are no garment color requirements.

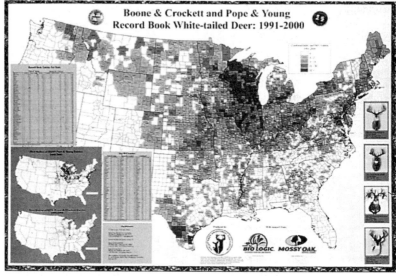

Quality Deer Management Association Offers Map of Record-Class Whitetail Kill Densities

Have you ever wondered which areas produce the most Boone and Crockett and Pope and Young bucks? Well, today, answering that question is easier than ever, thanks to detailed maps compiled by the Quality Deer Management Association.

The maps, created by QDMA intern Joel Helmer, reflect how many record-class bucks each county in the Unites States produced from 1991 to 2000. To illustrate concentrations of record-class buck kills registered with B&C and P&Y during the 10-year period, each county is color-coded in shades of red, with the darkest shade indicating the most big-buck kills.

The map reveals some fascinating aspects of how geography, climate and soil conditions affect deer size. For example, some of the highest concentrations of record-class bucks have been killed along the Ohio and Upper Mississippi rivers, where mineral-rich soils enhance antler growth.

The map also illustrates the fantastic hunting and big-buck potential of states like Wisconsin and Illinois, where almost every county produces high numbers of B&C and P&Y bucks.

In addition, the map lists the top 50 counties for record-class buck kills, and shows how many P&Y and B&C bucks each of those counties produced from 1991 to 2000.

To obtain a copy of the poster, contact the QDMA at Box 227, Watkinsville, GA 30677.

Boone and Crockett Score Sheet

OFFICIAL SCORING SYSTEM FOR NORTH AMERICAN BIG GAME TROPHIES

ecords of North American
g Game

BOONE AND CROCKETT CLUB®

250 Station Drive
Missoula, MT 59801
(406) 542-1888

nimum Score:	Awards	All-time
whitetail	160	170
Coues'	100	110

TYPICAL
WHITETAIL AND COUES' DEER

Kind of Deer: _____

Detail of Point Measurement

	Abnormal Points	
	Right Antler	Left Antler
Subtotals		
Total to E		

SEE OTHER SIDE FOR INSTRUCTIONS				Column 1	Column 2	Column 3	Column 4
A. No. Points on Right Antler		No. Points on Left Antler		Spread Credit	Right Antler	Left Antler	Difference
B. Tip to Tip Spread		C. Greatest Spread					
D. Inside Spread of Main Beams		(Credit May Equal But Not Exceed Longer Antler)					
E. Total of Lengths of Abnormal Points							
F. Length of Main Beam							
G-1. Length of First Point							
G-2. Length of Second Point							
G-3. Length of Third Point							
G-4. Length of Fourth Point, If Present							
G-5. Length of Fifth Point, If Present							
G-6. Length of Sixth Point, If Present							
G-7. Length of Seventh Point, If Present							
H-1. Circumference at Smallest Place Between Burr and First Point							
H-2. Circumference at Smallest Place Between First and Second Points							
H-3. Circumference at Smallest Place Between Second and Third Points							
H-4. Circumference at Smallest Place Between Third and Fourth Points							
			TOTALS				

ADD	Column 1		Exact Locality Where Killed:	
	Column 2		Date Killed: Hunter:	
	Column 3		Owner: Telephone #:	
	Subtotal		Owner's Address:	
SUBTRACT Column 4			Guide's Name and Address:	
			Remarks: (Mention Any Abnormalities or Unique Qualities)	
	FINAL SCORE			

(Sample — Not for Official Use)

Deer Harvest Records

Year _____ Name of Camp _____

Month & Day	Time of Day	Hunter Name	Buck (points)	Doe	Dressed Weight	Bow or Gun	Shot Distance	Tracking Distance

Blood-Trailing Log

Hunter: _____

Location: _____

Deer/Age: _____   Shot Distance: _____

Bow/Gun: _____   Broadhead/Bullet: _____

Pass-Through? _____   Time Allowed: _____

Trail Distance: _____   Recovery? _____

Indicate Shot Placement:

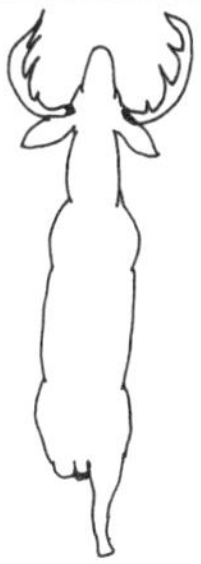

Trail details:

_____

_____

_____

_____

_____

_____

_____

_____

__ One Lung   __ Both Lungs
__ Liver   __ Heart
__ Paunch   __ Ham
__ Shoulder Blade

_____

_____

_____

_____

_____

_____

_____

_____

_____

Show Us Your Best Buck!

Have you recently tagged your best buck?
Send us your notes and photos, and we might
publish them in the next edition of
The Little Book of Big Bucks!

Size does not matter — any buck can be a trophy,
especially if it has an interesting story behind it.

Send your contributions to:

Deer & Deer Hunting Magazine
Attn: Big Bucks Book
700 E. State Street
Iola, WI 54990-0001

If we publish your contribution, you will receive
a free copy of the book. Sorry, due to the
large number of submissions received,
photos cannot be returned.